BISON
BOOKS

Left Handed, Son of Old Man Hat

A NAVAJO AUTOBIOGRAPHY

Recorded by Walter Dyk

Foreword by Edward Sapir

University of Nebraska Press
Lincoln and London

☉ The paper in this book meets the minimum requirements of
American National Standard for Information Sciences—Permanence
of Paper for Printed Library Materials, ANSI Z39.48-1984.

First Bison Books printing of this edition: 1995
Most recent printing of this edition indicated by the last digit below:
10   9   8   7   6   5   4

Library of Congress Cataloging-in-Publication Data
Left Handed, 1868–
[Son of Old Man Hat]
Left Handed, son of Old Man Hat: a Navajo autobiography / recorded
by Walter Dyk; foreword by Edward Sapir.
p.   cm.
Originally published: Son of Old Man Hat. New York: Harcourt, Brace,
c1938.
ISBN 0-8032-7958-2 (pbk.: alk. paper)
1. Left Handed, 1868–   . 2. Navajo Indians—Biography.
3. Navajo Indians—Social life and customs. I. Dyk, Walter. II. Title.
E99.N3L545   1996
973'.04972'0092—dc20
[B]
95-37149   CIP

Originally published in 1938 as *Son of Old Man Hat: A Navaho Autobiography* by Harcourt, Brace & World. First Bison Books edition 1967. The title has been changed for this new Bison Books edition.

FOREWORD

IT is one of the consequences of the gradually deepening consciousness of modern man that curiosity arises about the daily life of communities which are of utterly different race and culture from our own. The systematic ethnologist has done a great deal to map for us the essential cultural outlines of primitive societies and has given us more than a hint of the astounding variability of the forms which man creates and conserves in the course of his struggles with nature and fellowman. There is no dearth of information about primitive houses, artifacts, cooking methods, kinship systems, rituals, and folk-tales. The reader who is not something of an anthropologist, however, comes away from most of this material a little fatigued and confused. He is not schooled to analyze the details of cultural patterning into their tiniest elements, nor to trace out historic lines of development and ethnic interchange of custom running through these patterns and sub-patterns of socialized behavior. He finds it hard to think of custom as a severely objectified network of historically determined patterns, for custom to the average man is merely what you and I do and think because of the unplumbed necessities of our common human nature, and such variations from custom as are not immediately accepted as immaterial embroideries on understood themes are anxiously questioned as to their reasonableness. The ethnologist proudly withholds all value judgments, leaving his more naive—or shall we say, his less completely revised?—reader in the grip of conflicts of judgment. "If only," cries this man in the street, "I could really and truly understand why these rather interesting people have to avoid all commerce, however innocent, with their mothers-in-law! or why these other, possibly even more appealing, folk make such an ado about obviously unnecessary problems of ritual cleanliness and pacification of spirits!"

In the long run the tight-lipped scientist of custom cannot hold us off with smiles and shakings of the head. There is something valid, at any rate something not wholly to be frowned off the stage of intelligent interest, in these untutored questions about values and meanings. Customs are not merely eccentricities of history. They must all have meaning, however obscurely and indirectly, in terms of what you and I find intelligible in our own lives and in our own experiences with other people. The truth of the matter is that in their efforts to be precise, detailed, objective, and impersonal, the ethnologists have inevitably been drawn away from the recognition of universal modes of behavior, of universal feelings, of inescapable human necessities. Their triumph can only be transitory, however, for psychology, which is their natural critic and which has, for the most part, been beguiled into charitable absent-mindedness because of an even more intensive preoccupation with what is derivative of man yet not truly man, is now, in its less legitimate and more interesting off-hours, asking the very questions, though in a more commendable vocabulary, that have always been asked by the man in the street.

And so there arises, partly under cover of orthodox ethnology, partly in unconcern of it, the primitive case history—biography or autobiography. One discovers that a "primitive" can talk, often prefers to talk, about his personal memories even where they do not seem to give the ethnologist chapter and verse for some important rubric in his filing cabinet. His certainty, at any rate his interest, concerning what actually happened to him at various points in his experience obviously equals his assurance about "what we people do." Now it is clear that such a case history can serve various ends, and its form and content are likely to be molded in no small degree by these ends, which may in turn be dictated by temperament, by fashion, by what the questioner is looking for. Before we undertake to estimate the meaning and value of this truly remarkable document, let us be clear as to what it is not and does not pretend to be.

In the first place, it is not a cultural museum. There are historical novels and primitive romances, also a few primitive records of individuals (notably Paul Radin's fascinating Winnebago autobiography, "Crashing Thunder"), which aim to show a given culture in operation, as it were. Such works are dramatizations of cultural patterns, of the mechanics of custom, rather than human documents in the simple sense. They aim to give us the glamor of exotic custom as a background for more or less interesting events affecting people in other times and other places than our own. It seems to be generally agreed that this vivification of custom itself is a ticklish business, for the individuals who are requisitioned for this somewhat technical process—medicine men and Carthaginian priests and outlaws of the Scottish border—have a disappointing way of dying in the meshes of the tapestry which they are commanded to enliven. There seems, indeed, to be something inhuman about the conscious articulation of custom, just as there is something in us all which rebels at the analysis of words. There is no doubt—at least, I presume there is none—that the Son Of Old Man Hat is as completely in the grip of his own culture as any other Navaho. No doubt the detailed picturesqueness of sand-painted gods and goddesses, perhaps even the secrets of divining and witchcraft, are as present to his cultural consciousness as to that of any Navaho who is urged, or paid, to talk about such matters. But there is no declaration of them in this book, merely a quiet, subtle assumption of their reality in the minds of men. It is as though the intricacies of our economic system had to be pieced together out of such episodic hints as that "she sent Sally to the five-and-ten-cent store to buy herself a pink ribbon" or that "when the crash came the Joneses sold their summer cottage." Navaho culture, so clearly patterned as an ethnological artifact, is here in the mind of the narrator an electrically charged solution of meanings, and Dr. Dyk has been skillful in the transcript, leaving out little that was essential, injecting nothing out of the spirit of romance or scientific curiosity.

Nor is this book a heavily documented contribution to individual psychology. It is in no sense the study of a personality. It is a sequence of memories that need an extraordinarily well-defined personality to hold them together, yet nowhere is this unique consciousness obtruded upon us. We are in constant rapport with an intelligence in which all experiences, remote and proximate, "trivial" and "important," are held like waving reeds in the sensitive transparency of a brook. Such concepts as "ego" or "frustration" seem heated and out of place when we try to feel with this intelligence. Our science tells us that the record is actually as instinct with personality as it is essentially complete in its cultural assumptions, but the stream of memory is too close to the actuality of events to be analyzed in simple psychological terms. We who dramatize life into the eager self and its resisting medium, the physical and cultural environment, will find it difficult, yet soothing, to surrender ourselves to a consciousness in which neither cultural nor personal values are raised, both resting unassembled at its periphery.

What this singularly untroubled narrative does for us is to destroy all turbulent dichotomies of self and not-self. It is as far removed as possible from the romantic spirit, the self-exploitive phase of which is the sign manual of contemporary American feeling. And so the Son Of Old Man Hat, not by hinting at human likeness or difference but through the sheer clarity of his daily experiences, resolves all cultural and personal conflicts and reminds us that human life is priceless, not because of the glories of the past nor the hopes of the future, but because of the irrevocable trivialities of a present that is always slipping away from us. And for this reason the book is actually closer to us in its universality than the most accurate portrayal of modern conflict could ever be.

I should like to quote two passages, one near the beginning, the other near the end, of the narrative. "About this time I began to herd around the hogan, in the morning and evening when the sheep came home. But I was so small. I went out with the sheep like a dog. I just walked along with them and stayed right in the middle of the herd. I was afraid to go around them, but while I was in the middle of the sheep I wasn't afraid of anything." What psychologist or ethnologist could have anticipated this delicate interplay of the cultural implications of sheep-herding in the lonely Navaho country and the child's timid acceptance of his companionship? Is he the boss or is it the flock? And was ever security more accurately defined?

"He was lying still, just breathing a little all that night, and just as morning came, just as you saw a little white and blue sky coming over the mountain, he passed away. He died that morning and all his relatives and friends began to cry. As soon as he died they told me to go and round up the horses,

and while his relatives and friends were holding him and crying I started out, and while I was running I was crying too."
Those who wish to know something of Navaho culture
should consult the priceless ethnological records of Washing-
ton Matthews and the Franciscan Fathers, but in all their
pages it is not told what a boy who happens to be about is
expected to do when an old man dies.

EDWARD SAPIR

PREFACE

IN 1934, as fellow of the National Research Council, I went
to the Navaho reservation to collect material for a study of
clan and kinship functions in Navaho society. Throughout
that year several men, in and around Lukachukai, acted as my
informants, some discussing ideals and theories, others relating
illustrative anecdotal material. Valuable as anecdotes are, they
tend naturally to cluster around such highly dramatic events
as birth, death, murder, suicide, incest, witchery. . . . They
tell nothing of the commonplace, the homespun stuff from
day to day with which life everywhere is so largely con-
cerned. To get this, some more pedestrian tale was needed,
some long slow narrative that recalled the ordinary, the petty,
the humdrum insignificant affairs as well. With a view to ob-
taining such material, not alone for the light it might throw
on the functions of clan and kin but on Navaho life in general,
I asked one of my informants, an old man, Left Handed by
name, to relate what he could remember of his life, insisting
that he leave out nothing, no matter how trivial.

Left Handed, who belongs to the Bitahni Clan, his father
was a Many Goats (Old Man Hat was his father's older clan
brother), began his narrative with the story of his birth, in
the spring of 1868, while the Navaho were journeying home-
ward after their four years' stay at Fort Sumner. In this present
volume it ends with his marriage about twenty years after.
Like most Navaho of his age, Left Handed did not know
English, and therefore the story had first to be told bit by bit

to an interpreter who then translated each fragment in turn. As it is set down here it differs in no essentials from that first telling. I have tried to add nothing and have left out only some few minor experiences and repetitious episodes, besides recurring passages, such as the details of moving from day to day, when it seemed to me these would only burden the reader and add neither to his knowledge nor his pleasure. Likewise it seemed advisable to rearrange the episodes of early childhood into what would appear to be a more exact chronological order from that in which they were originally given. Not until he began to speak of things that happened in what was about his fourteenth year, the year in which they moved to the San Juan River and Navaho Mountain (Cf. page 104) was he able to adhere to that strict temporal sequence which is so striking a feature of the material thereafter.

A word about the kinship terminology is, perhaps, necessary for the reader who comes to these pages without some previous knowledge of Navaho culture. No kinship term in Navaho corresponds in usage exactly to any term in English. Thus "mother" refers to a great many other women besides one's real mother. In fact, wishing to distinguish his mother from among all these other women, who stand in different relationships to him and are also called mother, a Navaho must state explicitly, "my real mother," or use some such circumlocutory phrase as, "she who gave me birth." All Navaho kinship terms invariably refer in this manner to men and women other than one's real parents, grandparents, brothers and sisters, uncles and aunts; and moreover often emphasize distinctions and differences in relationship, age, and sex that we tend to neglect, while they disregard others we insist upon. Thus the terms translated "my uncle" and "my nephew" refer to men who are, respectively, older or younger than the speaker, regardless of whether they belong to the generation above or below him; while the term translated as "my cousin" refers only to cross-cousins, children of a mother's brother or a father's sister.

So as to avoid all chance of error and misunderstanding, kinship terms and names, as of people, places, clans, and ceremonies, were left untranslated by Philip Davis, the interpreter, who instead repeated each one in Navaho. Later many of these were translated for me by Father Berard Haile. In the case of a few places which have well-known English names, these were used instead (for example: Fort Defiance, Ganado). In several instances where no satisfactory translations were forthcoming, anglicized forms of the Navaho names have been used (for example: Bitahni, a clan name; sometimes found as the personal name of a member of that clan. Abaa, his mother's name; acquired, so they say, by some ancestor for exploits in war. Nda, the popular Navaho term for Enemy Rite, one of the many healing ceremonies; often referred to in English as the Squaw Dance).

I wish to express my sincere gratitude to the National Research Council who so generously made possible the collection of this and other material; and to Yale University with which I was affiliated over this period. My obligations are very great to Professor Edward Sapir of Yale, under whose auspices I began my research, and to Dr. Henry A. Murray, of the Harvard Psychological Clinic, for their continued interest and many helpful criticisms. Father Berard Haile was of great assistance in contributing translations out of his long and intimate knowledge of Navaho life. He and the Franciscan Fathers of Lukachukai often received me with cordial hospitality, and of them, as well as many other friends on the reservation, both Navaho and traders, I cherish affectionate and pleasant memories. To Philip Davis of Lukachukai are due not only my thanks but my praise also, for through his patient and skillful interpreting this material was made available, and indeed to it owes much of its present style. To my wife, Ruth Belcher Dyk, who has been my companion and fellow-worker throughout our days in the field and during the preparation of this book, I am most deeply indebted.

In conclusion I wish to pay tribute to my informant and my friend, the author of these memoirs, Left Handed, the son of Old Man Hat. May this narrative of his life help allay once and for all that strange and monstrous apparition, the "Primitive Mind."

W. D.

SON OF OLD MAN HAT

1. *He is born before his time and is taken by his mother's older sister to live with Old Man Hat . . . Trials and tribulations . . . He has lots of fun playing with Paiute children . . . Jealousies and quarrels.*

I WAS born when the cottonwood leaves were about the size of my thumb nail, but the date was not due yet for my birth. It should have been another month. Something had happened to my mother, she'd hurt herself, that was why I was born before my time. I was just a tiny little baby, and my feet and fingers weren't strong, they were like water. My mother thought I wasn't going to live.

She was very sick when I was born and had no milk, so her older sister picked me up and started to take care of me. She didn't have any milk either, but she went among the women who had babies and begged them for some. She had many necklaces of different-colored beads, and when she brought the women and their babies home with her she'd divide a necklace and give each one a string. Then she'd pick me up and hand me over to one of them. That's where I got my milk. After a while she didn't have to go around among the women anymore, because four of them lived right close by. All four had babies, and every day they came to our place. Whenever they wanted to nurse me one of them would come and give me my feed. They helped me out until I was able to eat. All four were still feeding me while we were moving back to the reservation from Fort Sumner, as far as Chinlee. There they quit, and I was able to eat anything from

3

there on. My mother * and her husband were the only ones who took care of me.

When we returned from Fort Sumner we settled at Chinlee. My mother's husband had another wife in a hogan close by, and he left to visit her. While he was gone my mother's former husband came. She had been married to him before the Indians went to Fort Sumner, but he'd stayed behind on the reservation by himself for four years. When he heard we were back he started to hunt for my mother, and at Chinlee he found her. From then on he lived with his wife again. His clan was Many Goats, his name was Old Man Hat.

My mother decided to go with him to Black Mountain where some of his relatives were living. She took me to a hogan where an older clan sister of mine lived and said, "I'm going away, and I'm leaving my baby here with you. Please be sure and take good care of my baby, your younger brother, just as though he were your own child." My sister said, "You can go. Don't worry, I'll surely take good care of him."

This was a year after we returned from Fort Sumner. There were no sheep, and we had nothing to live on. My mother had gone to Black Mountain, but when she got there it was the same. At that time her husband had a slave, a Paiute woman. He took his slave to a man who owned many sheep and traded her. He got seven head and brought them back to where he lived.

A year after she left me my mother came back. She looked all around, outside and inside the hogan, but she couldn't find me. She looked all over and asked, "Where's the baby?" but no one said anything. She asked again, "Where's the baby?" Someone said, "The baby was around outside; he must be

* Mother's older sister.

4

outside somewhere." I'd been outside, playing where the ashes were piled, and while playing in the ashes I fell asleep. There she found me, lying in the ashes, fast asleep. She grabbed me and picked me up and began to weep and cry as she held me to her breast. She had a broken heart. She took me to where her horse was standing, and as I stood under the horse she reached down and lifted me up. She didn't say a word. We just started off for Black Mountain and got home where my father, Old Man Hat, was living.

All at once, quite a few days later, I took sick. My bowels became loose, and I got worse and worse every day. Soon I was hardly able to walk or play or do anything. I was so weak I just lay in bed. My mother and her husband wondered what had happened. My father said, "He must be hungry for mutton." My mother said, "That must be it." So he saddled his horse and rode to where the sheep were and killed one of the seven he got for his slave. When he brought the meat home I was lying in bed and saw the horse stop in front of the hogan, right at the doorway, with the mutton tied on the saddle. I said to my mother, "I saw meat outside on the horse. I'd like to have some meat." Then they both hurried and built a fire, and when the meat was done they gave it to me, and I ate some mutton and broth. Sure enough, I'd been hungry for meat, and I got well.

In winter we lived on Black Mountain, but in the summer we moved down to the foot of the mountain, to a place called Another Canyon. In this canyon, where there were many lakes, my father, Old Man Hat, and my uncle, Bitahni, planted corn. One day, in a summer when we planted there, it started to rain. It rained hard, I remember that. Outside our hogan stood two cedar trees, right close together, and the one closest to the door the lightning struck. Three times, one after another, it struck the same tree. When it struck the third time my father ran out with his pouch. As soon as he got under it the lightning struck again; my mother and I could see it twisting all around him. She thought, "The old man is gone. He's struck by lightning." She told me not to look at him, so I turned and looked the other way. But he came in; nothing had happened to him. He said he had mixed beads and corn pollen out there with him to give to the thunder. As soon as he placed the beads and pollen there it never struck any more, not on the ground anywhere close. Lightning flashed, but it was in the air, and the sound of thunder was way off and low. From there on it just rained heavy and slow.

I had a little puppy, and I played with him in the sunshine every day when it was nice and warm. I used to talk and play with him as though I were with another boy. One day we were playing on the top of a little rocky hill. I ran around a rock, and he ran after me, but he wasn't running fast enough, and I ran down the hill. All at once I saw a coyote running towards me. As soon as I saw him I screamed and ran towards home. My mother came out of the hogan, and at that moment the coyote caught the puppy and carried him off. Then I cried more than ever, and my mother was going after the coyote as hard as she could, screaming and hollering and running. She was gone quite a while. When she came back she said, "I couldn't find the puppy anywhere. The coyote has carried him away." I was about to quiet down, but when I saw her coming without my puppy I started again, crying as hard as I could, and I remember I was dancing as I cried. She said, "It's your own fault. I told you not to go far from the hogan. You've given the coyote your puppy. If you'd minded me you'd have your little dog with you right now. If it hadn't been for the puppy the coyote would have gotten you and carried you away. You mustn't go far away; you must stay close to the hogan all the time, because you know coyotes are around here. If you go far from the hogan he'll get you and carry you away."

At lambing time they always separated the lambs from their mothers every morning when they took out the herd, and as soon as the herd left I went among the lambs and played. One day I was chasing the lambs and running after them when, all at once, I fell flat on my belly. It was a sloping place, and I slid to the foot of the corral into the mud. I had on a new muslin shirt, and it was full of sheep manure. When I looked at my shirt I began to cry. I didn't know what to do. I was afraid to go back in the hogan. However, I gave myself up and went over. As soon as I got inside my mother looked up, and as soon as she saw me she scolded me for that. "You dirty little thing. Look at yourself," she said to me. "Now you can just go like that. You don't want your shirt to be clean." She picked up a stick and cleaned a little off my shirt and let me go. She said, "I told you not to go in the sheep corral. You mustn't play with the lambs. You'll kill them. You might run over one, or fall on one. So you stay around here." And my clean white shirt was all black with manure.

In the evening my father returned with the sheep. "Well," he said, "what's happened to you?" As soon as he said this I began weeping again. My mother said, "He was out chasing the lambs and fell in the sheep manure. I've told him many times not to go in the corral and chase the lambs, but he doesn't mind me at all." My father said, "That's all right. You mustn't stop him. Let him play all he wants to. While he's out there chasing the lambs he's making all kinds of noise. In that way the coyotes won't get them. If it's quiet the coyotes will surely get them. So let him play."

About this time I began to herd around the hogan in the morning and evening when the sheep came home. But I was so small. I went out with the sheep like a dog. I just walked along with them and stayed right in the middle of the herd. I was afraid to go around them, but while I was in the middle of the sheep I wasn't afraid of anything.

They used to tell me to race early in the morning, and so every morning while it was still dark they woke me, and I'd start to run. I'd run for a little way, and then I'd start to walk. I'd walk a little way from the hogan, and there I'd stop and sit. I'd sit for a long time, until I could see a long way. I was afraid of something—I don't know what—I was afraid to go away from the hogan. That was why I hid myself. Then, when I could see things way off, I'd get up and start running as hard as I could back to my home. And I'd be standing, or lying, or sitting around, making believe I'd run a long way, making believe I was almost out of breath. I'd been doing this for a long time, but in that I was mistaken; they grew suspicious of me and found me out. They said, "You don't run, you walk from here and sit and hide yourself, and when it's almost daylight you come out and start running back."

But soon I ran a little way, and soon I was getting not to be afraid in the morning while it was still dark. They always told me to run every morning. "If you do that you'll be lively all the time, even when you get to be old you'll be lively. That's what running a race early in the morning is for. It's good exercise for you and your lungs."

In the winter, when they both went out, my mother used to tell me to grind up corn. So while I stayed at home, watching the place, I used to grind corn for our food, but I never ground enough. Once she told me to grind some, but it was a little too hard for me; I wasn't strong enough to break up all the kernels. All at once, as I was grinding, a man came in. His name was Red Wife Beater. He said, "Are you grinding corn?" I said, "Yes, I'm grinding some corn." "Do you have to grind corn?" he asked. I said, "Yes." "Why do you have to grind up corn?" "Because we want to eat it," and I said, "My mother told me to grind it." "Why doesn't she grind it? You can't grind all that corn. You're not strong enough." I had a dishful of corn sitting beside me. He said, "Get up." I got up, and he began to grind the corn. While he was grinding he said, "Look, and watch how I'm holding this rock. Watch how I'm working it." I did, and I learned how to hold the grinding-stone and how to work it. My mother never did show me how to hold the rock, and how to use it. She'd just say, "Go ahead and grind up the corn," that was all, and then she'd go out with the herd. After he'd ground it all up he said, "Now I've made it easier for you. Go ahead now, and grind it a little finer." Then he went away.

One summer, just as the corn was getting ripe, a woman and her daughter came to our place to help us. She was a relative of my mother's. A lot of crows were getting after our corn, and I used to go to the cornfield and watch and scare the crows away. The girl's mother said, "Go with the boy, so that he won't hurry home. You can stay with him until you get hungry, and then you can both come back." The girl and I were the same size. She was half Navaho and half Mexican.

So we stayed where the crows always went, way in the end of the cornfield. We made a little brush hogan, and she made a knife out of a tin can and got some corn and cut it up and started grinding it. But we had no fire with us, so she ground the corn for nothing. She said she was going to make corn bread, but we didn't have a fire, we weren't allowed to carry fire around. When she sat in this little brush hogan I'd be lying right close beside her, "because," I thought, "she's my wife, and I'm her husband." I remembered what my mother had said when I asked her about men and women. She'd said, "The man who goes around with a woman is husband to the woman, and she's wife to the man." So I thought, "I'm a husband to this girl, and she's a wife to me."

Mostly Paiutes lived along the foot of Black Mountain, and in the summer at Another Canyon we lived with them. These Paiutes were poor. They had only an old rag around their hips and camped under the trees in brush hogans. But they used to help us a great deal; they were always willing to do something in order to get clothing or food. We were not much better off, but we had enough to eat and enough clothing.

There were many Paiute girls, and once I went among them and began to play. They said to me, "We'll be goats, all of us girls will be goats, and you be the billy-goat." That's how we started, and they said, "Do to us as the billy-goat does to the goats. Get on top of us." I did that. Just like a billy-goat I jumped on the girls and laid over them. Some had on only one dress, and when I'd get on them they'd scream, and I'd bend over and throw myself back, just like a billy-goat. They sure did like it. After we became acquainted we liked each other, and so we played that way every day.

A Paiute girl came to our place, and my mother told her to herd for us. "Go out with my boy, so that later on he'll know how to herd." She was a big girl. While we were out herding she'd lie down in the shade and go to sleep and tell me to watch the sheep. One day, as she lay all stretched out and sound asleep, I went up to her and lifted her dress. There I saw something. I thought it was a black sheep pelt, and I wondered why she had a pelt on her like that. I tried to see something besides, but all I could see was a great, big thing that looked like something between her legs. Twice I did that to her. I always thought she might have a c—k.

One day we were out of salt. The Paiute Indians got a kind of salt out of the rocks, and this girl, with whom I used to herd, knew just where it was. They said to her, "Go and get some salt, because we haven't any." My mother told me to go with her. We went a long way up in the canyon, and then we started climbing. It was way up, half way to the top of the canyon, where they got the rock salt. In places where the rocks were high she picked me up and lifted me on to them. About half way she said, "Stay here and wait for me." She climbed on, and there I was, sitting all alone for a long time, and I began to cry. I thought, "She's left me here. She's gone away, back to her place." I got up and stood around and walked a little back and forth, and then sat down again, crying as hard as I could. And in the canyon all the wall around me helped me cry. I thought it was some kind of people making fun of me. She must have heard me and came down. When she got up to me she grabbed me and held me to her breast and started crying too. She told me not to cry. I thought she was awfully kind. She had a little salt, and we started back. She carried me all the way down to the foot of the canyon.

Once I was out herding with four Paiute children, three girls and a boy, and we took the herd up in the canyon. There were lots of lakes up in this canyon, and around them were all different kinds of brushes and weeds and lots of flag. Something sweet grows on the end of this flag, and we got into the brush for these sweet things. We took them off and ate them. After a while the girls went away, and the boy too, and I was all alone there in the brush at the edge of the lake. When I started to go, there was a snake lying in front of me. I started back, I went back a little way trying to get out of the brush, and there was another. Then I called the Paiute children. The boy came, and I said, "There's a snake." There was nothing around, no sticks or stones, and when we'd try to get out one way a snake would be lying there. Soon they were all around us. We called for the girls, but they were away, and we started crying. We were afraid of the snakes.

We were standing there, crying, and at last the girls came. The boy spoke to them—I don't know what he said, but I guess he called for some rocks and sticks—and they began throwing them to us. But the rocks didn't reach us; they dropped into the water, and so did the sticks. They couldn't throw them far enough. He must have wanted them to come for us, but they shook their heads and said, "No." One of us would start crying and then the other, and soon we were out of voice. We'd been standing in the water all afternoon until the sun was pretty well down, when, as we started toward one place, nothing was there. We kept on moving along, holding each other, until at last we were out of the brush and water. We were so hungry, and we were voiceless too, from crying.

One morning I went out with the herd again in the canyon. I was wishing for more of those sweet things up by the lakes, but I was afraid to get in the brush. Finally I got three of them. While I was there looking for more I peeked all around in the brush to see if there were any snakes, and I saw what I thought was a sheep pelt. I went close and looked at this thing, and it was tied with a rope. I took it out of the brush and thought, "What a nice soft kid's skin it is." But in the middle there was something on it. Then I broke off a willow and put it between my legs for my horse with the skin for a saddle and started to run.

When I got home with the sheep my mother was walking around outside. I ran up to her and said, "I found a nice, soft kid's skin." As soon as she saw it she was afraid of it. She said, "Throw it down! Throw it on the ground! That's a dangerous thing to have. It'll kill you. It'll break you all in pieces. That thing will set on all your joints; it will get on every joint of yours. That's what's called menstrual." It was what the women used at that time for their monthlies, and there was blood on it.

She picked it up with a stick and took it away and told me not to leave. "Stay there and stand there." She ran up to the cliff, half-way to the top of the canyon, and from there she brought weeds and roots and leaves of various things and different brushes. She mashed it up with rocks and put it in a big pan of water and mixed it and told me to drink some.

13

And she took off my clothes and washed me all over with it. Then she put my clothes in it and washed them. That was a medicine for this thing.

Then she told me to go inside. I went in and put a robe around me, and after she'd washed my clothes and spread them out to dry she came into the hogan and talked to me again. "Those things, they use them when they're passing blood. All women, every month, pass blood. That's a dangerous thing to handle." I asked her again, "What will it do to you?" She said, "I told you before. If you handle those things it'll break your foot, or your legs. It'll get on any of your joints, around your fingers and your back, around your ribs. It'll get on every joint and twist your feet and fingers to all directions. It'll break you, break all your joints, and at last it'll kill you, if you don't get medicine for it." She scared me again. From there on I used to be afraid to touch anything that lay in the brush.

One day, while I was herding quite a way from home, a Paiute girl came to me. I had chewing gum in my mouth, a gum that I got from piñon trees, and she wanted me to give her the gum. I said, "No." She was after me for it, and pretty soon she grabbed me and tried to take it out of my mouth. She jerked me around and said, "Give me the gum." I started fighting her, but I was so small, and I wasn't strong enough. I thought, "I'll get hold of her legs and throw her down." As soon as I grabbed her around the knees she stretched her legs so that my hands slipped, and I got hold of her c—. That made her madder than ever, and she began to beat me. At last I fell on the ground. She got on me and said, "Give me the gum. If you give it to me I'll let you go." She was beating me, and I began to cry. At last I gave up and let her have it. Then she let me go and walked away, chewing the gum. I was almost killed for it. They were cruel, those Paiutes.

One morning when I went out with the herd I picked up my buckskin rope and took it with me after the sheep. We had a little goat that we'd raised, giving her milk when she was small, and she was awfully tame. While I was out with the herd I roped this little goat. After a time I began to play with something else and let the rope and the goat go. I must have gone quite a distance with the sheep when I heard the goat crying. I ran back, and there she was in the willows, almost choked to death. The rope was around a willow, and she was caught. I tried to drag her, but she was too heavy for me. I did my best to loosen her, but I didn't move her at all. In a few minutes the goat was dead. Then I untangled the rope; I had a hard time getting it off the willow, but finally I got it loose and took it off the little goat. I thought she'd get up. I tried to make her get up, but she wouldn't. Then I knew she was dead, and I started to cry and went over to the herd and drove them back to the hogan.

When I got home I told my mother about the goat. I said, "My little goat,"—Gray-goat, I used to call her,—I said, "Gray-goat is dead. One of the goats ran against this little goat and knocked her down, and my little goat fell over and never moved again. I tried to make her get up, but I found that she was dead, and I started to cry. It's one of the goats that killed her." But they didn't believe me. They began asking me questions, and I must have missed telling something; they must have got me in a corner, and I must have said something about the rope. There they caught me. "You roped the goat, and you choked it to death, that's what you did, didn't you?" they said to me. I didn't go another way; I said, "Yes, I roped the goat, and I let her go with the rope, and she got caught in the willows. She must have gone around the willows, and that's how she choked herself." They said, "What have you been doing?" I forget what I said, but they didn't give me a scolding, they just let it go.

Bitahni's Sister went over and brought it back, and they butchered it. It was good and fat. My mother said, "We shouldn't let him go out with the herd alone. That was a young goat; perhaps after it began getting little ones there'd soon have been ten or twenty goats, or maybe we could have got more than that out of it. And now he's killed it." She said to me, "You think you killed just one. You've killed a lot." From there on I could herd only close around the hogan, where they could see me, and I wasn't allowed to take the rope. "If he carries a rope after the herd pretty soon he'll kill them all by choking them to death."

At that time my father was also married to Bitahni's Sister. She was a clan mother of mine and my mother's clan sister. We were all living together in one hogan. I don't know how he came to be married to her. Maybe my mother told him to marry her, or it may be my father asked my mother, saying he wanted to marry her. Anyway my father had two wives, but it wasn't long before my mother and her sister quarreled.

One afternoon my father and mother began fighting. I was sitting outside watching them. Finally my father threw my mother down and sat on her. Then my uncle's sister dragged Old Man Hat off my mother, and my mother got up and went after my father again. My uncle's sister let them go; she was standing there, watching them too. My mother was just like a man; she was a strong woman. They were fighting for a long time, and then the old man was thrown, and my mother was on top of him. He got up with her, and they wrestled around, fighting and cussing. They fought and fought for a long time. At last they stopped, they must have tired, and just cussed each other. My mother sure did swear and cuss my father and her sister. It was all due to jealousy.

It was evening by the time they quit. My father went inside the hogan and packed his stuff and started to go away. He was going to leave my mother. As he tried to go she cried out and grabbed him and began begging him not to leave her. My father said, "I can't stand this trouble any longer, so I must go and leave you and the whole place." He was standing in the middle of the hogan with a big pack on his back, and she was crying and begging him not to go. They talked for a long time. Then he put down his pack, and for a long time after that they talked. At last they all apologized to one another, and my uncle's sister built a fire.

Sometime after this my mother and father got into a quarrel again over her sister. They quarreled and swore and cussed each other for a long time, and my mother was crying. Then she went out and separated her sheep and goats from my father's herd and saddled her horse and put all her stuff on it. She had only one horse. She got on it and told me to come. I went up to her, and she reached down and lifted me up and sat me behind her. Then we started off and left my father. We went on, driving the herd, and soon we got to Flowing From Rocks. We passed there and went on and got to Anything Falls In that evening where we camped that night.

The next morning she packed all the stuff on the horse again and said, "We'll go back, my son, to your father. We left your poor father yesterday, and he's all alone now. We'd better go back to him." So we turned around and drove back the sheep. When we got home my father was sitting in the hogan smoking. As soon as we got inside she walked up to him and put her arms around his neck and held him against her breast. She was crying and talking, saying, "I'll be with you all the time. I'm not going to treat you like this any more. Forgive me, my husband. I'm sorry for what I've said and done to you. I'm very sorry. Forgive me, right now." And she said again, "I'm not going to treat you like this any more in my life. I'll be with you always." She talked for a long time while she cried and held him. When we returned they all apologized to one another again, and we lived with Bitahni and his sister all that year. I remember we planted corn at Another Canyon that summer, while they were still with us. In the fall they left.

Friend Of Who Has Children came to our house one day while my father was away. He was a Red Clay. My mother and I were just starting to eat, and she told him to eat with us. There was only one spoon, and we all used it. Once, as the man was using the spoon, my mother asked for it. He handed it to her, and she reached over and took it. After we'd eaten my mother went out with the herd, and he went away.

When my father came home he asked me, "Was anyone here today?" I said, "Yes." "How many people came today?" I said, "Only one." He asked me who it was. I knew the man very well, and I said, "Friend Of Who Has Children. He came, and we ate with him." "Where'd he sit while you were eating?" my father asked. I said, "On the north side." "Where'd your mother sit?" "On the west side, close to this man." "Where'd you sit?" "I was sitting on the south side." And I added, "We ate with the spoon. The man had the spoon, and my mother took it away from him." My father got up, picked up the spoon and handed it to me. "Now you hand it to me just as the man handed it to your mother." I handed it to him. "Just like this," I said. He took the spoon,

"Now," he said, "I'm the man, and you're your mother. How'd she take hold of the spoon?" "This way," I said, and I did just as my mother had done. After I told him all this he got on his horse and rode away. While my mother was herding he got after her and whipped her. That was for my story.

As they were bringing back the herd they were talking to each other. Then they came inside and started fighting in the hogan. My mother was crying and talking. She said to me, "Now, you little liar, you, you lied to your father about me, and he believes it, and for that I am suffering. You told him some kind of story, and he's whipped me, and now he's going to leave us." My father said, "It's true. I believe the boy, so I'm not going to stay with you any more. I'm going to leave right now and go back to my relatives." My mother was crying and hanging onto him, begging him not to go, "because," she said, "the boy doesn't know what he's talking about. He told you something, and you believe it. I didn't think you'd believe all the little things you hear." For a long time she begged him not to go. After a while my father looked at me and laughed. "Well," he said, "that's what my boy told me. I didn't like that." And there I was, sitting, hanging my head. I never said a word.

There was a boy of my clan,—today we call him Cripple, he's my younger brother,—and I used to treat him cruelly. Whenever he came around I always made him cry. He had a little blanket, and I used to take it away from him. Once I took it away to where a dead tree was lying on the ground close to the hogan. I spread it out on the tree and then went over and got the ax. I wanted to chop it to pieces, but I hit it once, and there was a great, big hole through the blanket. Then I changed my mind, I thought, "If I hit it once more they'll give me a good scolding, or I may get whipped for it." I took the ax back home, nobody had seen me carrying it, and let the blanket lie there.

The boy hadn't seen me, and when he found his blanket he must not have noticed the hole. But then his folks found it, and they asked him about it. He said that I always took the blanket away from him, so they claimed I cut a hole through the blanket with a knife, and they got after me for it. But I said, "No, I never had a knife." That was true too. My mother said, "No, I don't think he did that, because he never carries a knife around with him. I don't let him, and I don't allow him to have a knife, because he hasn't enough sense to carry one." I said, "No, I didn't cut that blanket with a knife." I told the truth, but they didn't find out what I meant. I said, "I didn't cut that blanket with a knife," but if they'd asked, "What did you cut it with?" I'd have said, "I cut it with the ax."

His mother said, "Your boy hasn't any sense at all. He always destroys things. That's what he did to my boy's blanket. I know he cut through it with a knife. I know it's cut. I can tell it's cut. It's been cut with a knife." I said again, and I thought I told the truth, "No, I didn't cut the blanket with a knife." My mother said, "You think your boy has sense. Your boy's worse than mine. When he comes around and plays with my boy, my boy learns a lot of bad things from him. It's your boy who hasn't any sense at all, because you haven't any sense either. You don't talk to your boy, and I, I talk to my boy all the time." The woman didn't say another word. If she had my mother would have jumped on her, but she didn't, she just walked away.

One summer they gave an Nda for Ruin's mother. The day they decorated the stick my mother said, "Go and stay inside, because you'll be treated also." While I was inside they brought in the stick and started decorating it. My father came in and sat by the fire, waiting; he was the one who was going to take the decorated-stick away. When they were through putting the various things on it they said, "It's ready now, you can take it." Before he got up he pulled out one of his teeth and looked at it and then threw it into a corner of the hogan and spat out some blood. Then he took the stick and went out, and everybody went after him.

Red Wife Beater's wife told my mother about it. She said, "My uncle, my son, pulled out one of his teeth. He looked at his tooth and threw it to a corner of the hogan and spat out some blood. Then he walked over and took the decorated-stick with him. I think he shouldn't have taken the decorated-stick. He ought to have let someone else carry it. I don't think it's right for him to do that. He took the decorated-stick with him after he pulled out his tooth. I think it's a bad thing to do."

2. *They move to Lukachukai Mountain for the summer where his mother talks to two black bears . . . Landi lands in trouble . . . . . . He learns about the Yeibichai and what singers will do to disobedient children . . . They are always happy when visitors arrive.*

ONE winter we lived on Black Mountain at Willows Coming Out. In the spring, all at once, I discovered we were moving. We moved down from the mountain to the flat, to a place called Bush Sitting Up. There we located late that spring. From there we moved across the valley to Lukachukai Mountain, to a place called Green Valleys Coming Together. Not far from there, right on top of the point, we stopped and located. We took all our stuff off the horses, and they said, "We won't move any further. This is a good place to locate."

Then Quiver's sister, Moving On, and her husband, Landi, who was of the Walk Around You Clan, came to where we camped. They were driving some sheep and goats which they put in with our bunch. After that Slim Man and his wife arrived, and not long after Slim Man's mother. He'd been raised by this woman; she was his mother's sister. She and her husband and her daughter and her son and her son-in-law came with a herd also. They felled two pine trees right close together and used that for a sheep corral. They made a partition between them, and one corral belonged to us, and the other belonged to Slim Man's outfit.

Early one morning before the sun was up,—the sun was up, I guess, because the light was on top of the mountain, but down in that hollow there was no sunlight yet,—I was outside and saw two bucks running across the trail. I said, "Mother, there are two bucks, two black bucks, running down across the trail." She came out and started hollering and talking to those two black things. I thought, "She must be crazy, talking to the animals," and I was looking at her and listening. She said to them, "What are you around here close to us for? You mustn't come around close to us. You two get away and hurry back into the mountain. Get back into the canyons and gulches. Don't be out here again in the open. We don't want to see you two out here again, because we're living here." They'd run away, and my mother said to me, "You don't want to bother with those things. That's what you call 'bear.' " So they were bears, and I'd thought they were two black bucks.

While she'd talked to them they'd stopped and almost lay down. They were sitting up and turned their heads and looked towards us, as though they were bashful. They sat for a while and then started running again, down in the wash and across. As soon as they got in the woods they beat it away. My mother was still talking, telling them not to come out again, telling them to watch over us and take care of us and help us along, "so that no danger will come to pass, so that we'll live long and be safe all the time. Be sure and be on our side, and watch and take care of us, grandparents." I was looking at her and thought, "She doesn't know what she's saying. She's just talking to herself." It was kind of funny to me, the way she'd talked to these animals.

My father and mother wanted to visit their relatives. They were people from the other side of the mountain. They said,

"They're up on the mountain now; while they're there we'll go and visit them." They went and were gone all day and all that night. I thought they'd come back the next day, but they didn't, and I was all alone again, though the people who lived with us were there, and I was with them. The next day I was so lonesome I just couldn't stand being without my mother and father any longer, so I went after them. I thought they'd gone only a little way from the hogan.

I went down and crossed the wash and on to a point. I could see this point from the hogan, and they'd gone around it. I went on around the point, thinking they were behind it, but there was no one. Then I got into the forest, a thick wood, where weeds and bushes and dead trees were lying about, and suddenly I was lost. I was in the mountain, in the forest, not knowing where to go, nor how to get out again. As I was going along I heard somebody tearing up a log. It sounded like someone breaking up a dead tree. I stopped and listened; it was right in front of me. I said, "Mother." There was no sound. I thought she'd say, "What?" to me. I went to where the sound had come from, and there a dead tree was lying, rotten and all torn up. I saw a track, and then I knew for certain it was my mother, that she'd walked around in her bare feet, and I began to cry. I looked at the track closely and tried to follow it, but I couldn't follow it for more than a little way. I went back to that same place and called my mother and cried and tried tracking her again, but I always lost it.

I'd been out in the thick wood all day when, all at once, I heard someone hollering. I started for that sound, and every once in a while I stopped and listened, and soon I could hear him saying, "Come on! Come back!" I went right straight through the woods. It was kind of dark in the forest. At last, when I got out, I saw the sun was down. The fellow was still calling me. I went around the point and on down into the wash and across and got to where we lived. It was dark then. When I got close to the hogan they saw me and said, "There he is, coming back." Mexican's mother grabbed me; "You poor boy," she said. "Where've you been? I thought you were lost. A good thing you turned around and came back. If you'd gone into the thick woods you'd have been lost tonight. It's a good thing you didn't get into the thick woods. Your father and mother went to a long way from here, to Bay In The Mountain and to Red Willows Coming Out."

They were all worried about me and said, "It's a good thing he didn't get in the thick woods. If he'd gone in the thick woods he'd have been lost." They kept saying to me, "You'd have been lost if you'd gotten in the thick woods tonight." I said, "I saw my mother's tracks in the woods. She walked around there a while ago." They said, "He must mean the bear. That was a bear track," they said to me. "You must have tracked the bear. That's a dangerous animal to go near. A good thing he didn't get you. If he'd gotten you he'd have taken you way off some place." They laughed at me, because I'd been tracking the bear and thought it was my mother.

My father and mother were gone for a long time. When at last they came back they brought with them many different kinds of cloth and buckskins and lots of other stuff which they'd gotten from their relatives.

A few days after their return my mother said, "We'd better move down. We've been here a long time, and the sheep are hungry for salt-weed. We ought to take them down. And the corn and other stuff must be getting ripe too." My father said, "I'll go out first and collect different medicines, medicine for sheep, horses and for men. I'll gather up these weeds, leaves and roots." The next day he was out all day. When he came back in the evening he had four bundles of medicine.

The day after all those who lived around us gathered at our place and began to talk of moving. My father said, "We'll move back to our place. We'll go with my little one." He meant my sister, Moving On; he wanted to take her along back to our country. "What do you think about it?" he asked her. "Do you want to go back with us, my little one?" She said, "Yes, I'm willing to go." Then Mexican's mother's outfit and Slim Man and his mother's outfit all said, "We want to move and go to where our relatives are living at Bay In The Mountain. We'll be living over there with them." So they all decided where they'd move to, and the next day they got the horses and started packing. Slim Man said, "We'll all move together, for if some of us stay on here we'll be lonesome." When everything had been put on the horses we started moving. We went along, following the wash; the others went up the wash and over the mountain.

I don't recall the places we moved to, until we were living at Vine Coming Up Over. From there my brother-in-law, Landi, went to Canyon de Chelly. When he came back he brought some peaches with him. They were still hard, but we ate them anyway.

One day, while we were living there, my older sister, Moving On, told me to do something, but I didn't want to. She said, "Do what I told you to do." I said, "What are you talking about? You must be having an erection." That's what I said to my sister, but I didn't know the meaning of it. That's what they used to say. I used to hear them saying it, but I didn't know what it meant. She said, "Don't you say that to me again. You mustn't say that to me," and she told my mother and father what I'd said. My mother scolded me for that. "You mustn't say that to your sister. You're an evil spirit, an evil-spirited boy," she said to me. "If you say that to your sister you'll get into the fire. You'll be burned."

There are many things like that, and many a thing I learned that way. I said all kinds of things that I shouldn't have said and did a lot that I shouldn't have done, but I always learned a lesson from them. Every time I said something that I shouldn't have said they'd tell me I shouldn't say it. From there on I wouldn't say it any more. And when I did something I shouldn't have done it was the same, they'd tell me I shouldn't do it. Many things are like that, and I got to know them all. That's the way to be when you are young, and that's the way I was.

After a time we moved across the valley and lived at Sloping White Rock Wall, close by a lake. One day while we were living there a man came to our place. He stayed awhile, then left and rode to where my sister lived. There he got off his horse and went into the hogan. Quite a while after my sister and her husband came out and went to the lake where the sheep were. She caught one and gave it to this man, and he started butchering it. About then my father handed me something and said, "Take this back to that old man. He gave me this and said it was a white horse, but that's not a white horse. That's just a white stone; that's a rock. So you take it back to him and tell him it's not a white horse." I took it back and gave it to him and said, "My father wants me to give this back to you. He said it's not a white horse, it's just an old rock." The man opened his pouch and put it in and said, "Well, he doesn't know anything about it." I went back and told my father, "The man said you don't know what that is." My father said, "Evil spirit, evil-spirited coyote! Poor cheater, he cheats the people, and that's the way he gets something to eat." The old man had given one of the rocks to my sister, and that's what she'd given him the sheep for.

One day they wanted to move again, down to Coyote Water. They said, "They're going to have a Night Chant at Chinlee. It's coming up soon, so we'll move closer." We started for that place, and Ruins and Tunes To His Voice and three women who didn't have any husbands moved with us. These women belonged to the Bitter Water Clan. They were full sisters, and when we got to Coyote Water they settled down close by us.

There one of the women got after my sister's husband, or he went after her; anyway my sister saw him with this woman. She came to our place, and she was awfully mad. When her husband came after her she said, "Don't bother with me any more; I don't want you to touch me again. And I don't want to bother with you, or touch you again. Go back to your wife, Big Comanche Woman. Go back to her. You think she's a beautiful woman, but she's not, she hasn't any nose. So you just go back to your beautiful wife, that old, big, fat thing. You think she's pretty, so go back to her and lie over there."

My mother was away at the time, but when she came home my sister told her about it. They were talking to each other,— I didn't know what they were talking about, I wasn't paying any attention,—when all at once my mother got up, and she was mad. She said, "Let's go to that woman's place. You don't want to let her treat you like that. She's just making fun of you. She thinks she is, that's what she's thinking now, but she won't be thinking that way when we get there, when we get her. So let's go to that old evil spirit, evil-spirited woman. Evil spirit, evil spirit, woman of an evil spirit, treating you like that. We'll go over there right now. We won't let her go. I'll hold her for you, and you can tear up her c—. Pull off all the hair and scratch it up and fill it with dirt. You mustn't be afraid to do this, because that's what she wants. After that we'll chase the man over to her, and from there on he can have that woman, if he wants her."

They started over, it wasn't far to where they lived, but they must have seen them coming, for the two oldest got on their horses and rode away. My mother and sister stopped and stood, and there where they were standing they cussed and swore. My mother said, "What ever time that they come back we'll surely lick her. We'll beat her to death." But they were gone and didn't show up again.

When they returned my sister went over to her place and told her husband to go. "Go after your wife. Leave right now and go on foot. The horse is mine, and the sheep are mine. So you go after your wife without these things. They don't belong to you now." But he just hung his head and smiled. She didn't beat him, she didn't do anything to him, she only gave him a talking to.

That evening, when my father came home, my sister came and told him about it. My father was lying there, it seemed as though he didn't pay any attention to it, he didn't say a word. She was telling about all that her husband had done, and all that she'd done, and he just lay there. Every once in a while he gave a snore; maybe he was asleep, maybe he wasn't, maybe he was only making believe. She said, "I told him just now to go after his wife. I mean it. I don't want him any more, because he has a better wife than I am."

Then my mother started in and told him exactly the same. "We were going over to her place and beat her to death, but before we got there they saw us, she and her sister, and rode away. We don't want her to make fun of us, but we'll make fun of her." But my father just lay there, he never said a word. Then, when they were through talking, he got up. He sat for a long time saying nothing. Then he said to my sister, "Leave your husband alone. If he wishes to leave you, let him go, don't bother him. It's up to him. If he likes that woman he can go with her. Perhaps he likes her better than he does you. So when he wants to go just let him go. And you, well, you are exactly the same. When you like and want a man you'll get him, even though your husband is around. So don't bother him. Let him stay with you until he leaves, and when he leaves don't try to hold him." He said to my mother, "What do you want to get into this trouble for? You have no business butting into it. That man isn't your husband. Why do you want to get after that woman?" She said, "Even though you talk to me like that I won't listen. I mean it, whenever I see that woman again I'll beat her to death, because she got after my daughter's husband. She's making fun of my daughter, but she won't make fun of us."

After that my father said to me, "Go and tell your brother-in-law I'd like to talk to him. Tell him to come over." I went to where he was and said, "My father wants you over there." "What does he want me for? What shall I do over there?" he asked me. I said, "I don't know. He wants you to come over." When we got inside the hogan my father told him to sit beside him. Then he got up and started talking. "Well, my son-in-law," he said, "you must have wished for that woman for a long time, and now, today, you received it, you've tasted it, you've felt it, and you've found out everything about it. You know just how it is now. So it's up to you. If you want to go with that woman you can go. It's all right with me. And if you want to quit bothering her and stay with my daughter, it's all right too. But if you

30

wish to stay with my daughter you must promise me that you won't bother with that woman any more. That was why my wife and your wife were going to beat her up. It wouldn't have been nice for them to have done that. It wouldn't have been nice for you. I'm glad they didn't do anything to her. If they had, if they'd beaten her, they'd have started trouble, and we'd have trouble now. They might have killed that woman, for all we know. So, now, you think about it, which way you want to turn, whichever way you want to go."

Then he said, "You think that woman took the c— of this man with her. Well, she went without it; he still has it, so I don't see why you've been after her. You can't get anything out of her." My mother said, "Yes, even though she hasn't taken that man's c— away from us she received it, and she knows just how it is. That's why it's as though she had it." My father said, "Why do you want to talk about it? It doesn't belong to you or to my daughter. We have no business discussing it, for a man's c— belongs to himself. He has his own c—, and it belongs to him and to none of us. So why do we talk about it?"

To my sister he said, "Now, you ought to go away from here. I don't want you to stay with your mother, because she'll make trouble for you. Tomorrow you'd better go to where your sisters live. They have a big cornfield. They have watermelon and muskmelon, and other things are ripe by now. So you must go over there tomorrow and have good and sweet things to eat. What we're talking about now, we can't get anything out of it. So you'd better go and find yourselves something to eat. You'd better both go tomorrow. Patch it up between yourselves. It's up to you, my son-in-law, you can do whatever you want to. If you want to leave my daughter it's all right with me. If you want to stay with her it's all right too. Only I don't want to hear that you've done

31

one thing, I don't want you two to have a quarrel, I don't want you two to have a fight over this little trouble. I don't want you to beat my daughter, my son-in-law; if you do that you might make me think, you might make me talk, you might make me do something to you. And you, my daughter, I don't want you to take anything away from him. You said you wanted to take away his horse. Don't take his horse, let him have it, because he wants to go around. But the sheep and goats, if you wish to leave my daughter, my son-in-law, I don't want you to take them with you; leave them with my daughter, and then you can go wherever you want to."

In the morning my sister came into our hogan and said, "We're going to the cornfield today." She asked my father, "Shall I take the sheep and goats with me, or shall I leave them here?" "Where's the man?" he asked. "He went after the horses." "What did he say?" "He said he wanted to go to the cornfield." "Well, then," he said, "you can go, and take the sheep and goats with you. Take good care of them; you'll need them, for when you get to the cornfield and start eating corn, watermelon and other sweet stuff you'll soon get hungry for meat. So you'll have meat whenever you want it, and you'll have milk. The sheep and goats are like your father and mother, and it'll be as though I were with you. So you must take good care of them. And don't bother with your man. Let him go wherever he wants to. Don't pay any attention to him. Just pay attention to your food, and to your sheep and goats."

My sister said, "There's another thing I want to say to you, my father." "What is it?" he asked. She said, "I'd like to have some medicine, medicine that one uses for sheep and horses, so that I can raise them. I haven't any medicine for them. I haven't anything, so I'm not strong." My father said, "All right. Whenever any of my children ask me for something I'll do it, I won't refuse them, for they're my children. I'm glad you asked me." He got his sack and took out his medicine-bundle, and she spread a cloth for him to put it on. He said, "Now, remember, this is for the horses, and this other one is for the sheep. They look exactly alike, but you must remember which is which. However, I have something for you to remember them by." He opened his pouch, took out his corn pollen, opened that and from it took a red-bead-horse. He gave it to my sister, and she put it in the medicine for the horses. She said, "Thank you very much, my father, my mother, thank you very much," and again she said to him, "Thank you, my father, my mother."

While the others were out separating the sheep and goats she asked him, "What shall I use besides this medicine?" He said, "The rest, you know it all. I've told you all about it, so you know it all. And remember all, too, that you want to use for your sheep and horses. It all turns into property. When you acquire horses it'll give and make you property, and if you raise sheep and goats it'll give you and get you property. So you must take good care of them. About the songs, your older brother knows all the songs about the horses and sheep and about the various properties. So you want to go to your brother and ask him about the horse song, the sheep song and the song you use for property."

That was all. They separated their sheep and goats, they had about thirty, and moved away. My mother and sister were holding each other, crying because my sister was leaving. My mother started cussing that woman again. "That old, big, fat evil spirit, evil spirit. She looks just like an evil spirit. She made trouble for us, and you have to leave. If she hadn't made trouble you'd live with us all the time. But that old, big, evil spirit, evil-spirited woman, she looks like an evil spirit, made trouble, and so you have to leave."

I was up on a hill with our sheep as they were going along way out in the valley. Every once in a while my sister turned and looked back. I was on the hill, watching them go, and when I saw her turn around I started crying. I was so acquainted with her, and she treated me awfully kind. She was so kind to me. I thought of all those things, and that made me cry, until they went over the hill.

After some days we moved again across a little valley towards the south, to Sand Lake. When we got there they said, "Now we're close to the chant. We can go there from here, for it's close at hand." My father and mother and three others got on their horses and rode over. The next day they all came back bringing corn, watermelons, cantaloupes and peaches. They said, "Everything is good and ripe now. Over at the chant they have all kinds of things to eat. And today the Yeibichai will be going around to different hogans, and they'll begin dancing tonight."

That's what they said when they came back, to make me scared of the Yeibichai, I guess. My father said, "These Yeibichai are going around to different hogans today, looking for children. They have a sack into which they put the children who have disobeyed their fathers and mothers. They may come here today. So you must do what you're told. When they come you must get water and wood, so that they won't bother you. They'll know, then, that you are a good boy. Those children who are bad they whip first, after that they put them in their sacks and take them home. There they dig a hole and build a fire. That's where they bury the children and cook them, in order to eat them. So you must do what you're told to do."

I asked my mother, "Where do these Yeibichai live?" "They live in the rocks, in walls of rock. That's where they're from, and that's where they take the children. They cook them there. Children, who do not behave, who disobey their fathers and mothers, they whip those children." I said, "With what?" "With a soap-weed stalk. They make a whip out of that. They have a long whip made out of soap-weed. So, now, you want to behave and obey. You must herd the sheep all the time." And she asked me, "Will you obey?" I said, "Yes." "Will you do what you're told to do?" I said, "Yes." "And will you herd the sheep all the time?" I said, "I will. I'll herd the sheep all the time." "Well, then," she said, "I won't tell the Yeibichai about you."

At that time singers used to go about on foot carrying their medicine-outfits on their backs. I used to wonder what they had in those sacks. "They must be carrying their grub around with them," I thought. But then, seeing hair come out of the sack, I'd think, "What kind of hair is that the man has in his sack?" One singer, Grinder by name, often came to our place. When he came he would hang his medicine-outfit, the whole sack, on a tree, and I used to go around and look at it. I always thought, "Sure that's the hair of something, of somebody." I asked my mother, "What's Grinder carrying around? Why does he carry hair? What does he do with it?" She said, "That's the hair of boys who disobeyed their fathers and mothers. If a boy doesn't do what he's told to do his father and mother will tell this man. Then he'll go after the boys and cut their heads off. That's why he has lots of hair and is carrying it around." But later I found out they were only the tails of rattles.

I used to believe her when she'd tell me this. Once she told me that again, and I asked her, "What do they do to the boys? What do they do to them after they cut off their hair?" She said, "They kill them. They kill them, and after

35

they've killed them they go after the brains and eat the brains. That's what they're after. That's why they always go around all over, because they like to eat the brains of boys." I believed her. But all those things were not true, although I always thought they were at that time. That was what they told the boys. "If you don't behave, if you disobey, the man will take you and cut your head off." That was to make them do the things they were told to do, and so I always did all my mother told me. I obeyed my mother, because I was afraid I'd have my hair cut off, and because I didn't want to be killed by that man. Whenever I saw him passing our place I wondered what boy it was he was carrying along with him again. I used to be afraid of him. I didn't want him to get me and kill me and eat my brains. I didn't ask about the body, but I thought, "I wonder what he does with the body? I wonder if he eats the body too?"

One winter we lived on Black Mountain at Willows Coming Out. There my mother put up a hogan while my father went out herding. She put one up in two days. A few days later she wanted to go to Keams Canyon to visit my mother, my real mother. She said, "I want to visit my sister. I'd like to see my sister again, so I want to go and visit her." She left, she went by herself, and was gone seven days. At the end of seven days she came back and brought some things with her. She handed me a little pouch, decorated with white beads around the edges and the middle, and said, "Your younger brother gave it to you. There are some matches in it." That was the first time I saw a match. She showed me how to strike it and told me to get some cedar bark and make it fine. I got the bark and made it fine by rubbing it together. I rubbed it together and made it fine and struck one match, and there the blaze was, out from that little stick. I was so surprised to see a little stick with fire on the end.

In the pouch was another kind of thing with which to start a fire. That was a piece of rock and iron. But we had one, my father had one, and I knew about that. When you got a spark out of it, onto cedar bark or anything soft, you had to blow a long time before the fire started. But this little thing starts the fire pretty quickly. As soon as you strike it the fire's a-going.

When my mother handed me the pouch she said, "Those matches are from the white people. That's what they use to make fire with. They have a lot of them at Keams Canyon. The Indians around there can get them any time. A white man who came and is living there now said he was going to put up a store. He has all kinds of things, different kinds of grub, flour, coffee, sugar, all different kinds of calico and colored blankets and dishes, and these matches. He has a great many matches. He wants to buy wool, skins and blankets from us. He said his name was Billy; that's what he said, 'My name is Billy.' And it seems he's a kind man. So now there's going to be a store at Keams Canyon, and we can buy anything we want."

Well, so that was the first time I saw a match. There were about fifteen in this little pouch my brother gave me. I was sure pleased to have them and the other thing with which to start a fire and the pouch. The pouch I carried hanging down over my shoulder. I had it with me all the time, looking at it every once in a while and at the matches and other thing that starts a fire.

In the spring they said, "We'll move down to the valley." We took the trail going out to Water In Bitter Weeds. There we stopped and camped, right at the end of the narrow plain hill by Water In Bitter Weeds Lake. Stutterer and his wife and her sister, Bitahni's Sister, and a fellow named Suffering Hip were living there. We located close by them.

The morning after we arrived Stutterer's Wife came with a son of hers, Cripple, or his younger brother. She said to my father, "I came to get a nice, good fat mutton from you. You've been with my older sister for a long time"—she meant my mother—"and have done all you've wished to do with her. So, now, you've got to pay me for that. I'd like a nice, fat mutton from you." That's the way she was joshing my father, and they were all laughing about it. He said, "You ought to go to Suffering Hip and ask him for mutton. I'm not Suffering Hip. Go and ask him." She said, "Yes, he's the best man in the world. Whenever I ask him for something he always helps me. And he's helping you right now, he's taking care of your wife for you." Bitahni's Sister used to be my father's wife. "Suffering Hip is all right," she said, "he's taking care of your wife, and he always does me a favor. So I want you to help me out, just as he does." My father said to my mother, "Go get her a wether." My mother went out and caught a great big one. They tied it up under a tree and cut the throat and butchered it. The meat was all white, for it was good and fat. They packed it up, and she carried it to her home. The little boy took only the head. She hurt herself, carrying all that meat. It was too heavy for her. We heard she was lying down, that she'd hurt herself carrying a big pack on her back.

One day a man and his wife stopped at our hogan. His name was Slave Of The Texan; he was an Along The Stream. His wife was Bitahni. They were going to Cheek to visit a man called Bunch Of Whiskers who was a relative of Slave Of The Texan. They stayed at our place that day and all night. In the morning my mother killed a sheep for them. They were so thankful for the meat. "This meat tastes a whole lot different than ours," said the woman.

My father said to my mother, "You say you had a husband before me, and you always say, 'He was better than you. He did a great deal for me.' Had he this many sheep at that time? I don't think so. You always talk about that husband of yours, and you never talk about me. You know I'm treating you well. I believe I'm better than that husband of yours." He said this as a joke, and they were all laughing. They were always happy when anyone came, they always joshed each other.

My father said, "That's the way she talks about her husband. That husband of hers used to bring her a badger or a wild cat, or he might find a jack-rabbit or a cotton-tail. He probably had a hard time getting a squirrel. That's what her husband did. He used to kill coyotes for her. And she says, 'That man was the best man and did a lot for me.'" My mother said, "Yes, that man was all right. When things were scarce, when there was nothing to eat at all, he used to go out hunting. He never came back without something. In that way he saved me from starving to death. He was good and kind. He was kind saving me for you. If he hadn't done that what woman would you have? I know he was kind, because he saved me for you, and now you're staying with me, and you had a big butt saved for you." The woman was laughing away, and Slave Of The Texan was laughing too, they were all laughing about it.

3. *Speculations on man and nature . . . He makes a trip to the Oraibi and a journey to Fort Defiance.*

EARLY one morning while it was still dark it began to snow. When daybreak came it stopped. Soon it cleared up, and the sun came out and was shining. In a little while there was no snow left. The earth was drying, and there was steam on the ground all over. After it dried I walked around upon the hill, looking out over the valley to different places, and everything was getting green. It was so pretty after the snow; it made me so happy. That's the way I used to be, as soon as spring came, as soon as things got green, it always made me happy. When I came back inside the hogan I said, "Everything's beginning to get green. Soon we'll have lots to eat for our stocks."

At that time I didn't know anything about winter and summer, or spring and fall. All suddenly I would notice the heat or the cold. In the spring when it got warm and the brush and weeds and grasses that were dry got green I used to wonder why it all went dry and started getting green again. And I wondered why and where the snow fell from, and about the cold, and what sprinkled the rain on us. In the summer everything was green, but when summer was gone it all dried up, all the green stuff turned yellow and some turned white. I used to think, "Everything ought to be green all the time."

In the fall when it got cold, or around when the first snow fell, my mother would say, "It's a hard time for us. I hate to see things coming on that way." She meant the cold and winter, but I always thought, "Somebody must be going to kill her." Then when summer came she'd say, "We'll go back to our summer camp. We'll live there and have a good time all summer." When she'd say this I'd think, "She was going to be killed by someone, but they must have let her go, the fellow who was going to kill her must have let her go. Maybe that's why she's happy again."

In the winter we'd be living at a certain place, and there'd be snow on the ground, and it would be cold. It would be that way for a long time until spring, and then, from there on, it would start to get warmer. When it got a little warmer we'd move and go to another place and live there all summer. When it got real hot in the summertime I used to think about the place from where we'd moved. "We ought to go back to our other place. Over there it's nice and cold. Here, where we are now, it's too hot to live." But when it was winter, and it was cold and snow was on the ground, then I used to think about the place where we'd been living in the summer. "We ought to move back to that place; we ought to live over there. That's a good warm place with no snow on the ground. Right here we have snow, and it's cold." In the summer it would be nice and warm, but when it got too hot I always thought about winter, about the snow. So every summer I wished for winter, and in the wintertime I wished for summer. I was that way for a long time. But it was the same all over, and I found out that everything was changing all the time.

In the winter when it was cold and there was snow I used to wonder why the sun didn't give enough heat. It was just the same as in summer and gave exactly the same light, yet in summer the sun was hot. In summer the sun passed over us, and it looked to me as though it was far away, but it gave

41

more heat, while in winter it was close to us and didn't give enough.

Whenever daylight came the sun would be up, and I'd see it going along and passing over and going down, and every evening it disappeared. The next day another sun came up and went down in just the same direction, and I'd see it going down in the same place again. It was that way every day. I used to think, "There must be a whole pile there where it goes down. Or it must have melted away." And I thought, "There must be a whole lot there too, where they come from."

And I thought about the moon. Every first quarter my folks would see it, and I'd try to look for it, but I couldn't find it. Perhaps the next day when I looked again I'd see it, and it would be a small thing up there. It would keep on getting larger and larger every evening, and pretty soon it would be a circle. Sometimes when it got to be all good and round, when the moon was full, there'd be an eclipse; then the folks would say, "The moon is dead." From there on I'd see it getting smaller every evening. It would be that way every night, until early in the morning it would be gone and couldn't be seen again. I could see it only up to the last quarter. Then I used to think about what my folks had said, that the moon was dead. So every time of the last quarter I thought the moon was dead, and when the first quarter came up again I thought, "The moon is coming back to life."

When I was small I used to go out in the evening and see fires around all over. My folks would tell me, "Around those fires is where the people live." And so when I looked up to the sky and saw a great many stars scattered about all over I thought the stars were fires, and that a great many people must be living up there above us. Some that I saw were little tiny ones, and I thought, "Those fires are almost going out." Others were large fires, and I thought, "Some people must be sitting around that big fire, and maybe some of them are cooking."

About the year, my folks would say, "This year," or "Next year," but I couldn't discover what they meant. I used to wonder what it meant, when they said, "A year." Sometimes they'd say, "One year," or "Two years," and sometimes, "Many years." I wondered what a year was, and where it was. I used to think, "It must be around here." But I couldn't see it. I always thought that the year must have arms and legs and a head. "It must have a body like an animal." I used to wish that I could see it when it came around again. But I never saw the year.

And they'd talk about the month, they'd say, "Next month," or "Two months." When they'd say that I wouldn't know what they were talking about. I used to wish to see a month. I was wondering what it looked like. When they'd say, "When another month comes," I used to wish, "They ought to tell me when it comes." Then they'd say, "Well, another month has come," but I wouldn't see anything around. I thought it was something that moved or walked about.

The days were all I knew about. When daylight came they said, "Today." I knew the day was on. When the day was gone, around in the evening, they'd say, "Tomorrow." I always thought they meant when the night was over.

That is how I thought of all these things, but at that time I never asked about them. All this while I only saw things; I knew what they looked like, but not what they were for. I was like that until my father, Old Man Hat, was close to his death; even though I was old enough to know things I didn't know about them until he told me.

But about the sun and the moon I never did find out for

a long time, not until I met Chee Dodge the time he put up a store at Round Rock. He told us about the sun, earth and moon, and I believed him. Only one man, Old Man Black Legs, didn't believe what Chee Dodge told us there. Chee Dodge said, "The earth is going around, it's spinning around, and while it's spinning it goes around the sun. The sun is standing still at one place. And the moon is like the earth. But you can't tell about the moon, it moves around to different places; sometimes it goes behind the earth. The moon gives light in the night; the sun gives light to the moon, and the moon gives light to the earth at night. That's the way these three help each other, and help us, giving us light so that we can see at night." But Old Man Black Legs said, "I don't believe you. You don't know what you're talking about. If the earth were going around we ought to be knocked down right now, or the first time the earth moved. Like this store now, and the mountains, they all ought to have been knocked down. So I don't believe the earth is moving."

By the time I was seven and eight years of age, when I began to know things, I used to think about the children, large and small, and boys of different sizes up to a tall man. I used to look at children who were smaller than I was and think they were that small all the time, and I thought that I would be the same size always, and that men too were always that same size. I used to wish I were that tall. It worried me when I looked at myself and thought, "I'm a small boy. I won't grow up to be like these tall men."

At that time the children wore no clothes, and when women came to our place with their babies, some crawling around on the ground, some just beginning to walk, the boys would have a c–k, and the girls would have a c–t. I used to think about the girls and wonder why they had no c–ks. When I looked at myself I had a c—k on me. Still, I thought, "It must be all the same; maybe their fathers or their mothers cut them off." I wondered why and thought, "They ought to have c—ks too." I asked my mother, "Why is it I have a c—k but these other children haven't any?" She said, "Oh, my, you mustn't say that, you mustn't say bad things like that. They're that way because they are girls; they are different from you, because you're a boy. They're girls and are born that way, and you're a boy and born that way."

When I'd be out herding and the girls saw me they'd bring their herds close to mine, and we'd start playing. Sometimes my mother saw me. When I'd get back home she'd ask me if I'd been playing with the girls. I'd say right out, "Yes, mother, I've been playing with the girls." I think I never told a lie to my mother. Whenever she asked me anything I always told the truth. Every time she saw me playing with the girls she'd say, "You shouldn't bother the girls. It's bad for you. The girls will sometime take your c— out and bite it off. It isn't only the girls who'll do that to you, all the other women do just the same." As I was wondering if they'd do that to me with their teeth she said, "All the women have teeth where their c—s are." Then I wondered about the sheep, if the sheep were that way too. But every time a buck got on a sheep he would still have all his c—. I thought, "Perhaps it's only women who have teeth." So I began to be afraid and didn't dare go near them. But she didn't really mean it, she only said this to me because she thought I might lose some sheep while playing with the girls.

I thought about women too, and about babies. I'd look at a woman when she was pregnant and see that her belly was growing all the time. Soon she'd have a great, big belly, and soon I'd hear the woman had had a baby; my folks would say, "The baby has been born." I used to think about these babies and wonder where they got air, and how they breathed, while they were still inside the mother. I thought a whole lot about that. "They're inside their mothers for a long time where there's no air. They must hold their breath for all this while." Sometimes I tried to hold my breath to see how long I could stand it, but I couldn't stand it, except just for a little while. I'd hold my breath until I became almost unconscious. So I thought, "A baby must be strong, because it can hold its breath for a long time while it's inside the mother." But when they were born I'd see they were breathing. That worried me.

I saw many a baby born at my place. When one was born I'd go close and see that the baby's stomach was full. I wondered how they ate and who'd been feeding them inside the mother. When I saw a baby born I'd look at it closely, and it would have legs, arms, feet and toes, hands and fingers and a head just like mine with hair, ears, mouth, nose and eyes, and it would have a body exactly like others. I used to wonder, "What makes them that way? Who in the world makes these babies? It must be someone. Maybe someone makes them that way first, and then, afterwards, they must be put inside their mothers. Or," I thought, "someone must make them that way inside the mother. Or maybe that's the food she eats. When the mother eats the food it must get that way and turn into a baby." When I saw that a baby had everything, just like the rest of us, it worried me a lot.

And about husband and wife. If a man and woman came with some children they'd say, "That man is that woman's husband," and they'd say, "That man's wife." I wondered how they were that way, and what kind of relatives they were to each other. I only knew of father and mother, brothers and sisters, young and old, uncles and nephews. That was all I knew. But when a man and woman came around they'd say, "That man is husband to that woman, and the woman is wife to the man." I wondered how they were related that way. My father and mother never called each other anything.

Once I asked my mother, "What relation is my father to you? What relation do you call him? I call you my mother, and I call my father my father, what do you call my father, and what does he call you? How are you related to each other?" When I said this to her she said, "He's my husband." She said it in a loud voice, and she scared me with what she said. She said, "A man and woman who are around together like that are husband and wife. The man is husband to the woman, and the woman is wife to the man. That's why they call each other my husband and my wife. You'll be that way when you grow up to be a man. You'll have a wife just like these men now." I said, "I don't want to have a woman. I won't go near to a woman. I don't like to go near a woman who's not related to me, because she's not my mother." She said, "You don't know anything about it yet, because you're small. When you grow up to be a man you'll get a woman, and when she wants to leave you, when she tries to leave you, you'll be hanging onto her, even though she's not your mother. You'll be hanging onto her, crying and begging her not to go, just as if she were your mother. That's the way they think about each other, just like father and mother."

When she said this to me I thought she must be crazy. "Why should a man hang onto his wife and cry? In my life I won't get a woman, and I won't cry for one. I won't go near a woman who's not related to me. I can go near a woman who's related to me, but I won't do what you say, I won't hang onto a woman and cry." "When a man talks as you're talking now, he gets that way. As soon as he gets

47

a woman, as soon as they get acquainted, he may start beating his wife, and they'll begin to have a quarrel every once in a while. So you mustn't say you'll be that way when you grow up. It's pretty dangerous to have a wife or a husband. Some men, when they have wives, may kill their wives or may get killed by them, and some commit suicide. So you mustn't talk that way."

I began to think about these things and wonder how they became acquainted when they were not related. When I went out herding and saw a billy-goat or a ram get on a goat or sheep I used to think, "A man must do just the same thing to a woman. They must do just as these billy-goats and bucks are doing." When a man and a woman were around together I used to watch them closely, but I never saw a man get on a woman.

I've thought about men and women, and I always thought a man was bigger and stronger. "A man is sensible, and knows more, and he's smarter than a woman. The man is way ahead, and the woman is way behind, because a man can do anything. A man can do all the hard work. He'll haul big wood, he can carry anything that's big, and work on the farm. Even though it's a big field he'll do all the work on the farm by himself. He'll build a fence around it, and in the fall he'll gather up everything and have it ready for winter. He tends to the horses. He'll pick up a rope and rope a wild horse and break it. The horse may buck, but he tames it. He goes around and travels for long distances. Many things, even though hard to do, he does; he'll work on anything. A woman can do certain work, but all she does is cook and work on blankets and herd sheep and carry water for a short distance and carry just an armful of wood. And she'll do just a little work around the hogan."

I was that way for a long time, until I got gray hair; then

I found out that a man is way behind and a woman is way ahead, because a woman can do all kinds of hard work too. I found out they're in many sufferings, and I found out that they can stand them. Like when they have their monthlies, they'll bleed a lot, but they'll stand it, and when they begin having babies; when they have babies they suffer so much. Even at that they'll stand it and start raising children. Soon they'll have a lot of children, and soon their children will have grown up and be married and start raising children of their own, and soon they'll have a lot of grandchildren. Then they'll all have hogans for themselves and sheep and horses and other things. That's all a woman's sufferings. She suffers a great deal through her generations.

When I found this out I thought, "A woman is stronger than a man. A man will beget children, he makes children all right, but he doesn't suffer, he only makes a woman suffer." So that's why now, today, I think a woman is stronger than a man.

One fall my father said to me, "You'll have to go with me to the Oraibi, because we haven't anything to eat." He and my mother killed some sheep and goats, and we packed our horses. After we'd put on all the mutton he said, "You ride this horse. Get on now, and be careful; watch yourself and your horse; watch everything." We started out, but we didn't get there that day. On our way we stopped and camped at a place all night. The next morning we started again and arrived at the village about noon. A little breeze was coming from that direction, and as we went towards the village a great deal of smoke was coming out. I saw the smoke and smelt something cooking. I wondered what kind of food it was that smelt so good, and I was wondering how it tasted. We were walking our horses along, and I said to my father,

49

"We ought to move a little faster." "Why, my boy?" "I smell something from that direction." "Oh, we'll be there soon," he said to me, "and we'll surely get what we want." So I was glad and happy, but I wanted to get there quickly.

When we arrived we tied our horses beside a stone wall and went in the village. A whole lot of Indians were there, standing and looking at us. When they saw us coming they all started waving their hands. Everywhere we looked they were waving, all wanting us to come to them. We didn't know which way to go, there were so many. We were near a building, sitting apart by itself, so we went for that, and a big, fat woman came out. She was all in black. She had on a woven dress, and her hair was twisted into a bundle on each side of her head. I asked my father, "Have these Indians horns?" He laughed and said, "No, my boy, they haven't any horns. They're just like us." I said, "Sure enough they have horns, my father. Look at that woman; she has horns." "No, my boy," he said, "that's her hair, twisted around and tied with a woven band."

We went back to where we'd tied our horses, and my father said, "Unsaddle your horse." He started to unsaddle his, but I kept turning around and looking where the Indians were standing way on top of the building. Some of the women, standing on the roof, had the same looking things hanging on both sides of their heads again. I let the cinch go, I was just holding the strap and looking to where these women were standing; I didn't know what to make of them. I thought, "Sure they've got horns all right." But I didn't ask my father about it any more.

Two women came down from a ladder and took all our stuff, mutton, saddles, saddle-blankets and everything and climbed way up the ladder. They said to us, "Tie your horses right there." I was afraid to go up; I thought I might fall, but I tried. When my father went up I went right close behind him, and we got up all right and went in the village where the women had taken our stuff. They already had the mutton laid out over the poles that they used for meat. Our stuff was way back in the house, and there was a place for us. They said, "Come in and make yourselves at home. Sit down." We sat down, and they started going around and making some kind of food for us I'd never seen before. They gave us a great many different things to eat. Some I knew, some not. We started eating, and everything tasted different to me, but I liked it all.

They'd all gathered in this hogan, and there was a crowd around us, standing and sitting down. Everything seemed different. They looked different from us and were dressed differently. The same with their language. They were all talking to each other, making all kinds of noise, but I couldn't understand them. They began to talk to us, but my father didn't understand them either, and they couldn't understand us. They started talking to him, just going by motions, and asked when we were going back. My father said, "We want to go now, today." They talked for quite a while with him, asking what we wanted for our mutton. He told them we wanted corn, dried peaches and other foods already cooked. They said, "All right, sure enough, we'll give you some corn and all the other things you ask for."

They spread a blanket on the ground, one that the Navaho women weave, and on it they put the mutton, cut up in pieces. Each Oraibi got a piece. We had a large buckskin sack, and they each gave my father a measure full of corn, pouring it in his sack. Soon the sack was full. There was other food, already prepared, made out of corn. He got almost a half a sack of that, and dried peaches, about a half a sack also. While they were trading I looked around the house. Something was hanging over a pole across the room, and I wondered what it could be. It was some kind of skin, the skin of something. I thought it was coyote hide. I was close to it, and when I thought, "That must be a coyote skin," I got kind of scared and stepped away from it. I asked my father, "What kind of skin is that?" He said, "That's a rabbit's skin, all sewn together. That's what they use for a blanket or quilt. It's called a rabbit-skin blanket."

When my father had our stuff packed and ready they all began to help us take it out. We carried it over to where our horses were and put the saddles on them, tied all the stuff on the saddles and started off. It was late in the afternoon, and we wanted to get back quickly, because my mother was at home alone. Before we left they said, "You must always come here to our place. Whenever you come stop at this one place, because we've become acquainted and are friends now. That's why you should come here. Now you know where to stop. We'll have everything ready for you, so you must come again, my friends." From there on we always went to that one place.

As we were going along on our way I asked my father again about that skin. "Father," I said, "is it really true that that's a rabbit's skin? I think it's a coyote hide. It looked like it to me." He laughed and said, "No, I told you it was a rabbit's skin all sewn together, and they use it for a blanket." Then he said, "Years ago many Oraibi Indians used to live right here. The Navaho came and killed almost all of them. They killed all the older ones and let only the younger go. I was in it. This is the place where we killed the Oraibi. We had a war with them." We went along until dark and then stopped and camped overnight. Early the next morning we started off and rode all day until evening. When we got home we unpacked our horses and carried everything inside. My mother was so thankful for all the food, and she was glad. She opened all the sacks and said, "I surely appreciate all these different kinds of food. Thank you very much," she said to my father. "We'll have something to eat for quite a while."

One spring we moved off the mountain to a place called Tree On Hill. We stopped and camped there and began shearing our sheep. At that time there weren't any shears; we used old cans or any kind of tin for knives. Tin used to be scarce, it was hard to get. When we started shearing we didn't have anything to shear with. A smith lived quite a way from where we'd camped, and my father said, "I'll go to that smith's place. He makes bits, maybe he has some tin or a piece of iron. I know he makes knives too; he may have some made." He went over on horseback. When he came back he brought three iron knives, good and sharp.

A little above us were some hogans. That was Tunes To His Voice's and Ruins's outfits, and Old Man Thankful, who was my clan grandfather, and his wife, who was a Many Goats, and Red Wife Beater, who'd married Tunes To His Voice's wife's sister not long before. They came to our place when we were about to start shearing. The old man said, "I'm glad you people came. I want you all to help us. I'd like to have this shearing done as soon as possible. I've heard a store has been put up at Fort Defiance, and the trader wants skins and wool. I'd like to take my wool there, so you all help me, my nephews, my children," he said to them. "I'd like to get through with the shearing as soon as I can and go to that place with my wool. I think the horses can stand traveling that far."

It took them quite a few days to shear all the sheep. When they were through my mother said, "You can go with your grandfather, Old Man Thankful." He was the one who'd said they could take the wool to the store, so they told him to take it over. While they started packing up the wool I took the sheep to water. I was out all day. When I came back with the herd in the evening there lay the wool, all stacked up in blankets, ready to be carried away.

The next morning they got the horses. They loaned Old Man Thankful one, and he saddled it and put on his wool. They put the saddle on mine and the wool over the saddle. It was a great big pack. On top, between two small sacks, they fixed a place for me. Tunes To His Voice had a load on his horse and a white horse packed with wool besides. He came to our place leading his pack horse.

Before we started off my father said, "Be sure and buy me a good scarf. Buy me one of those to tie around my head. Get me a red one. I'd like something red around my head. And some red flannel and white cloth. That's all I want. From there on it's up to you." My mother said, "Buy me a bucket and a bracelet."

Then we started. They told me to go ahead. My horse was sure a rough trotter. I was holding onto the rope with which the wool was tied, and some places I almost fell. On the other side of Chinlee Wash we went on following the canyon, and got to Trail On The Edge Of The Canyon. It was a narrow place, there where the trail went along. It wasn't very narrow, but it looked that way to me, riding on top of the wool. The wool stuck way out, and it looked as though I was close to the edge. I looked once, and then I turned away. When we passed that place I shivered all over, and my heart was beating. I thought, "What a dangerous place we passed. They ought to put a trail way off somewhere." But that was the only place where one could cross. On the opposite side were sloping rocks, and nobody could cross there. We went on, past Two Gray Hills. A little way from there we stopped for overnight.

The next morning we started and got to Nothing But Rocks when the sun was up a little above the mountain. There we stopped, and the two fellows got off their horses and took out their corn pollen and did something. They must have said their prayers. A little further on were more rocks. They said, "We'll stop there again. On those rocks is a picture of the sun and the tracks of deer and other animals." I looked down when we got on that rock and there was something round and kind of whitish blue, and something else around it. They said, "We'll stop here for a while." They got off their horses, opened their pouches, took out their corn pollen and said some kind of prayers again. Then we went on.

On the mountain, as we crossed the valley towards Mountain Sitting Up, was lots of grass. Tunes To His Voice said, "We'll stop here for a while. We'll let the horses eat some grass, and we'll eat a little lunch too." We stopped and took off all the wool and the saddles and turned the horses loose. Tunes To His Voice said, "Don't hobble them. Let them go that way, and they'll roll and rest up well. If we hobble them they won't have a chance to get rested." We let them go, and they were rolling around in the grass. When they started eating we ate too, but we didn't have anything to drink, so we ate the food dry. When the horses were good and rested we got them and started putting on the saddles. I tried to put the saddle on mine, but I was having a hard time. At last I got it on, and then they saw me. "You got the saddle on the horse, but you didn't put it in the right place. You have your saddle on the horse's neck. You'd better put it on the back of the horse." But I just couldn't, so Old Man Thankful helped me. He put the saddle on for me and the wool and tied it down. Then we started on. We got to Water In Wash when the sun was down.

The next morning we started off and arrived at Fort Defiance before noon. At the store we sold our wool,—I don't know what we got for it,—and then they told us to go to the next store. When we got there the door was open, and that was the store. Lots of things were in that house. On the shelves lay bundles of red flannel and white cloth and dishes, and from the ceiling hung buckets of different sizes and scarfs of all colors. Everything was new to me. I stood and looked, thinking, "What wonderful things they are." While we were in the store a tall white man came in. He had on a pair of pants with a big patch of red buckskin on the seat. He was walking around in the store and whistling, and I was looking at him. I was afraid of the white people.

Old Man Thankful started trading. He bought a roll of black leather, a bundle of white cloth and a bundle of red flannel. At that time they used to pull this flannel apart and make it into yarn to use for designs on blankets. He bought a bucket and bracelet which my mother had asked for, and a scarf and a black hat for my father. Old Man Thankful, my grandfather, said, "Put on that hat." I picked it up and set it on my head. I was standing there with a big black hat, and he was laughing. I was in rags. My clothes were ragged, and my hair was bushy and uncombed. I used to have a whole lot of bugs in my hair; you could see the white eggs plainly. And on top of that I had a brand new hat. I must have looked funny. When I got outside I gazed at my shadow, wondering how I looked. But I couldn't tell. I moved the hat around, I could see the hat on my head, but my hair was sticking out in all directions.

Old Man Thankful knew more about the grub than we did, because he'd been with the Mexicans. He bought some coffee, sugar and flour. He named these things, but I didn't know what he meant. We two didn't buy anything like that.

When we started back in the afternoon they told me to go ahead, and I did, and they were behind me. That black hat was on my head. Every once in a while I heard them talking about me, and every now and then I looked down at my shadow. I was proud of that hat. I thought, "There aren't any boys at my place who have a hat like this. I'm the only one who has a hat." Even though we were on our way I was wishing I was home right then. I wanted the people to see my hat. I was happy with it on me. When the horse trotted I hated to ride, so I'd make him run for quite a way from the two men and then just let him walk. When they'd catch up with me I'd let the horse run again. I kept doing that all the way to Chinlee. They were behind me, talking to each other; I don't know what they were talking about, they'd been talking since we left home.

When we got back, as soon as I got off the horse, the old man grabbed my hat and took it away from me. That was his hat. He said, "Thank you very much," and again he said, "Thank you very much for the hat you've bought me."

4. *Old Man Thankful's wife breaks a leg . . . They hold an Nda for Ruins, in which he is also treated . . . He finds an ancient pot . . . His father tells him what to do and how to live.*

WE lived there all summer. Old Man Thankful moved a little way below us. One day while his wife was taking the horses to water the horse she was riding fell with her. A man came to our place and said, "Old Man Thankful's wife is lying out in the flat. She fell off her horse, I guess, and her leg is broken." They sent word around, and a lot of people gathered where she was lying and carried her home. Close to her home they stopped and put up a little brush hogan for her. Old Man Thankful went after a singer and brought back the man called Black Horse. Her leg was broken right below the knee, slanting. The singer put a lot of medicine on it and washed it and covered it with medicine. They'd prepared some sticks about eighteen inches long and thin, and after he'd set the bone he put them on each side of her leg and tied around them as tightly as he could, so that it couldn't move. He did this while he was singing. He sang for a few days, and then they got another. They said, "There are two singers singing the Knife Chant." Every day while I was herding I could hear them sing a long way off.

At the end of about ten days they said, "Her leg was all swollen, but the swelling is down now. She was suffering very much, but now she's all right. She's quieted down, and the swelling is down too. She's getting along fine." They sang over her for about a month, and all the people who lived around there helped with sheep, taking them over to that place and killing them for the singers and all who helped. My father was there every day. Sometimes he came home, sometimes he stayed there. He helped them with meat too. I was just herding, and I could hear them singing every day while I was out in the flat with the sheep. When they quit singing I went over. The woman was able to walk, but not for very long and only around the hogan. She had two sticks to walk with. In the fall she walked without them, and she'd gotten well.

For a long time there was no rain at all. Then all at once it started. It rained quite a bit out on the flat. They said, "It rained heavily out in the flat at Thumbs Water. Lots of water, lots of little lakes are there." So we moved down towards that place, to where some trees came out from the mountain. A lot of other people moved there too.

Old Man Hat said, "We'll have an Nda for my nephew, Ruins." They began working on the hogan and put up a shade for cooking. There were no wagons at that time; they had to drag the poles and branches in with horses. When they'd finished with everything Old Man Hat went to a man named Always With The Rams. His clan was Standing House; his wife was a Bitter Water. When he came back he said, "In three days we'll take the decorated-stick to that fellow." He lived at Coyote Water.

On the morning of the third day I was herding and saw the crowd go off on horseback. They took away the decorated-stick. They were gone all day and all night. The next day about noon they started coming back. They said, "Tonight is second-night." Everybody went off again to that night's dance, and I stayed around herding sheep. Early the next morning everyone was coming back again. Suddenly I heard a shot, then one shot after another. All at once a great many fellows got on their horses and rode over a hill from where the shots were coming. From there a crowd appeared. They came and rode around the hogan shooting. I thought they were fighting. The sheep were scared and started running, and I was out there, running after them, trying to stop them, and about to run away myself. They kept riding forwards and backwards and around the hogan for I don't know how many times. Then they quit, and everything was quiet, and they just started singing. It was a big crowd.

A lot of meat was cooking at our place, and after they quit shooting my father came over on horseback with some fellows who took all the food away. That was for the people who had come. My father said to me, "You'd better hurry and take a bath. Wash your hair. You'll be treated by the singer too." So I washed myself all over, and I wanted something to eat, but they said, "You shouldn't eat until after you've been treated. You shouldn't eat anything before you're treated." I said, "No, I want to eat something first, because I'm hungry." They said again, "You shouldn't eat anything before you're treated, not until afterwards." So I didn't have anything to eat that morning.

My father got on his horse and said, "Get behind me." I got behind him, and we rode to the Nda. As soon as we went inside the hogan I heard lots of fellows starting to sing outside right by the door. Inside were only a few pieces of calico. Calico was scarce at that time. They used to put up single and double saddle-blankets and buckskins. The buckskins they cut up into pieces big enough for moccasin tops. After they were through cutting it up they tied the pieces into knots and started throwing them out through the smokehole. They told me to throw one out, but when I threw it up

I didn't throw hard enough; I threw it only to the edge of the smoke-hole where I saw it hanging down. A fellow from outside got on the hogan and took that piece away.

Then they began singing in the hogan. I was scared, for they were all making so much noise. One fellow, sitting by the fire, his name was Bilon, was singing louder than all the others. When I looked up they said, "You mustn't look." But every once in a while I looked at this fellow singing. They'd say, "Don't look around. Have your head down," but I just couldn't help it, I had to look up, I was afraid and scared. When they started treating us I was so scared I couldn't get up. They had to raise me and stand me up. They blackened me all over with charcoal dust, and after that they put a white cloth around my hips, and over the white cloth a saddle-blanket and over that they put a belt. The cloth and saddle-blanket were presents for me. The fellow who put these things on me said, "That's your present I've given you. You're my friend now."

When they were through with Ruins and me they said to the crowd, "Bow down. Don't look at these two fellows." We went outside, and everybody was looking down. We passed the crowd and went on to where the skull was lying and dropped the ashes that we were carrying in our fists there on the skull. As soon as we turned around and started back an old man who was standing there with a gun started shooting at it, and when he was through a lot of fellows rode over on horseback and took a shot at it and then came back.

We went back, past the hogan, and over to the place where they were cooking. Ruins's wife came over too, with a crowd of people right behind her. They were her relatives, Mexican People and Two Streams Running To Each Other. They were after her for presents. She had a lot of robes and blanket-skirts, two buckskins, a red belt and a big bundle of red flannel with which they used to weave blankets, and which they put on the decorated-stick. Ruins's wife's mother began giving out these things to her close relatives. She gave the robes and skirts away and tore the red flannel in pieces and gave that out. A skirt and the red belt she put aside for herself. A young man cut the two buckskins in pieces big enough for moccasin tops. The thickest part he laid aside for himself.

There was a white clay mixed in water, and before we started eating they set that in front of us. It looked just like milk. We dipped our hands into it and slapped ourselves all over the body, all over the charcoal dust. We were spotted black and white all over. Then they said, "Now you can go ahead. Start eating the mush first." We started eating the mush and drank some water after it, and when we were through we started eating meat and other food. Some of the people took grub over to the visiting-party.

When we were through eating we went back to the hogan where we'd been treated. In there was a big crowd, all eating too. Everybody must have been eating. I went outside and saw people scattered all over and herds all around them. Out of the herds they were taking one and two heads at a time to where they were cooking. When everyone had eaten they started dancing. They danced a circle-dance all afternoon.

When the sun was pretty well down my father gave me a robe and said, "Give this robe to the man who gave you the presents." I said, "I don't know that man." He said, "You ought to know him. He treated you for the singer." I said, "I don't know him. I didn't recognize him." "Why don't you know him? You ought to know him. Didn't you look at him?" I said, "No, I didn't look at him, because they told me I shouldn't look around, so I was looking down all the time. That's why I don't know him." My father said to Ruins, "You know that man, so take him over." He took me over to where the other party was camping and said, "That's the man." I gave the robe to him; I dropped it on his lap. I don't know who that fellow was. I never saw him again.

Afterwards we went back to the hogan where we stayed for quite a while and had a little lunch. They were still dancing over at the visiting-party's camp. When we were through eating we went out and got into the dance and started dancing too. At that time only men danced the circle-dance. They danced until evening. After they were through we went back to the hogan. In a little while they started singing right by the door again. That was the visiting-party which had come to the hogan where we were staying. They stood close to the door and sang. Then they stopped for a while and stood there. I could hear them talking, and then they sang again, back a little from the hogan. They sang for a long time. About the time they stopped and went back to their camp I fell asleep. The next morning they woke me up, and we went out. It was still dark. They'd been singing for quite a while. That was the last four songs. While it was still dark they quit, and that was the end of it. By sun-up everyone had left. There was nothing around, just smoke.

I can't remember what tribe it was that was bothering me. I wasn't sick, but my mother used to tell me that at night I got up and walked in my sleep. Suddenly I would jump up and holler and scream and begin to cry. She claimed some tribe was bothering me, the same one that was bothering Ruins. That's why they had me in it too. Ruins wasn't so very sick, but he wasn't feeling well.

One day in the fall I went out with the herd towards Thumbs Water. A little below that place were many small lakes and a white wall of rocks going out to the flat. I took my sheep there. I liked to play around where the white rocks were. There were a lot of them out in the flat. As I was playing among the rocks I found a clay pot. I moved it around; it wasn't broken anywhere. Only in the bottom was a little hole about the size of a match. I rolled it around and when I started home with my herd I left it. When I got home I told my mother about it. I said, "I found a clay pot, but I left it, because it had a little hole through the bottom." She said, "Why didn't you bring it with you? You should have brought it home. It must be someone hid it away some time ago. Tomorrow you take the herd over there and bring the pot back with you."

The next morning I took my herd there again and picked up the pot and tied a string around it and carried it after the sheep. Late in the afternoon my father rode a horse to where I was herding. He said, "You go home. Take this horse and ride him back." I got on the horse and went home and gave the pot to my mother. She said, "That's nice. It's a nice pot." She put something in the hole to stop it up and then went out and got some gum of the piñon tree. She put the pot in the fire, and when it was hot she put the gum all over it. She renewed the pot.

I'd come home with the pot when the sun was pretty well down. While she was working on it—I don't know exactly when—I became unconscious. I didn't know anything until late in the evening. All at once I was wide awake. Everything was off me; no clothes were on me, and there was Ruins's mother and my mother holding me. They'd put something all over my body and hair. That was medicine they'd gotten from a tree struck by lightning. I was soaked with that. Ruins's mother, she was my paternal grandmother, was scolding my mother. She said, "There, at that place,

64

where he found that pot, years ago some people were digging wild potatoes. While they were digging the Utes came and killed many of them. A great many things used to lie around there, like clay pots and other things. So that pot that he brought back belongs to the spirits. You ought to know better than that, and you know about it very well. The poor boy is unconscious because he brought that pot back with him. Those people who were killed at that time were after him for it. Why did you want to send your boy after that pot? You were crying, holding your boy when I came here. The blame is all on you."

I got well, but from there on I never touched any more what belonged to the dead. I saw many a thing lie around where the people had died, but I was always afraid to go near the place or near to their things. I went unconscious every once in a while. Whenever I saw anyone coming behind me I thought they were after me, and if I thought a man or woman was grabbing me I went unconscious. Then, when they'd put this medicine over me, I'd be all right again. I did nothing but herd sheep all during the fall. When it got real cold we moved up on Black Mountain.

Every evening after I'd come home with my herd and put them in the corral my father would give me a talk, telling me all about his life and teaching me how to live, how to take care of the sheep and all the other things. He used to tell me I shouldn't sleep too much. I used to go to bed way late at night and early in the morning, while it was still dark, he used to wake me, saying, "Wake up, get up and dress yourself, my boy, it's almost daylight. Your sheep are calling you to come and let them out; they're hungry." As soon as I'd had my breakfast I'd turn them out and start herding. He used to tell me that I mustn't let a coyote get them, and that

I shouldn't take them where there was quicksand, because if I did I'd lose many of them. So I took good care of them, watched them closely and never let them go far away.

In the springtime when they were lambing that's the time I watched them closely. I never lost any of them. He used to say that if I lost just one head it was like losing half a herd. "If you kill one head there are many ways it can be cooked and prepared for food. If you wish to have fried meat, you can fry it; if you wish to cook it on charcoal, that's another way; and if you wish to boil it, you can boil it. If you wish to put it in hot ashes and cook it, that's another way, and they all have different tastes. That's why you shouldn't lose any of them. And you should eat all the meat off the bone. Let only the bones and hoofs and horns go. All the rest is good eating."

After he'd given me a talk he'd say, "Now, my boy, you'll remember my words and keep them." From there on he'd let me go. If he gave me a talk in the fall he'd let me go until spring, when he'd ask me if I still remembered his words. I'd say, "Yes, my father, I still remember them." Then he'd give me another talk and let me go until fall, when he'd ask me the same thing again.

He used to tell me that when I grew up to be a man, if I took his words and remembered all he said, I'd soon have everything, horses, sheep and cattle. Even though I didn't have a farm I could get corn and stuff like that whenever I wanted it, by trading the sheep, horses or cattle for it. And if I wanted clothing for myself, or jewelry, I could do the same. I would be well fixed by taking good care of my stocks. But, if I didn't take his word, later on I'd be a beggar, and everybody who saw me begging would make fun of me and laugh. So I must stick to the work he'd shown me. In that way nobody would make fun of me, because I was well fixed; everyone would know I was a rich man.

When I was ten or twelve years of age we had a great big herd of sheep and many horses. At that time we never took the bucks from the herd. We left them with the herd all the year round and got lambs in the springtime and in the winter. That's how we increased our herd quickly.

Towards the middle of winter, before it got too cold, in the evening while the herd was in the corral, my father used to go out and sing while he walked about in the corral and around outside it. He did this so that if it got too cold the sheep wouldn't freeze, they'd stand the cold, not one of them would be lost through all the winter. This song is called the Owl Song, because the owl can stand anything, it won't freeze at all. After he was through singing he'd say his prayers, saying the sheep will never get any kind of sickness. When he was through with his prayers he'd go back into the hogan and go to bed. Early the next morning, while it was still dark, he'd get up and go out to the sheep again. He'd take out his medicine, mix some in a pan or dish of water, and give that to the sheep and sprinkle it on them and the whole corral, so that the cold wouldn't bother them, nor anything, and they'd be good and strong and fat all the time.

In the winter when it was lambing time we gathered cedar bark and tied it up with soap-weed. We used that for our light. We'd have eight or ten of these bundles ready for use, and whenever a sheep lambed we'd light one, and one of us, either my mother or I, would go out in the corral. If we found a lamb we'd take it into the hogan. We kept dry dirt around the fire, and when we brought the lamb inside we'd lay it by the fire and sprinkle the warm dirt all over it. After the lamb was dry we'd shake off the dirt, and soon it would get up and walk. Then we'd light the bundle again and take the lamb back to its mother. If my mother stayed up until midnight I'd sleep, and around midnight she'd wake me and then go to bed, and I'd stay up the rest of the night until morning. Every few minutes I'd light a bundle and go out into the corral to look for lambs.

We had at times two and three shepherd dogs. They were just like human beings, they knew almost everything. We could talk to them and tell them what to do, and they'd understand. They had a place around the corral, and each knew where to go in the evening. At night if they heard anything, as a coyote hollering, they'd begin to bark. If the coyote was close one or two would stay around the corral barking while the others chased the coyote away. In the daytime, when I was out with the sheep, if they had lambs while I was herding I'd put the lamb in a safe place and tell one of the dogs to stay with the sheep and her lamb, to watch them and not leave them. The dog would stay there, lying by the sheep while I went ahead and herded until another lamb was born. This lamb I'd pick up and take to where the other was and tell the dog I had another lamb for him to watch. It was just like several fellows helping me. By the time lambing was over the dogs would be hungry, because they'd been working hard and hadn't had anything to eat while caring for the lambs for many days. Then we'd kill a goat and give them each a piece of meat and put the rest away for them.

About this time I used to race by myself early in the morning while it was still dark, and in the middle of the day and in the evening. In the middle of the day when it got real hot, when the sun was right in the middle of the sky, I used to run a race under the sun, while the sun was looking down on me. That's the time the sun is having dinner. When he sees me running a race under him he'll try to get me a horse. The sun that we see in the sky is our father, and I'm his son; that's why when I race under him, when he sees me running, he knows I'm after something, he knows I'm after a horse. And soon enough I'll get a horse from my father, the sun, and from there on I won't be on foot any more. It's as when you're working for something, trying your best to get it. Even though it's hard to get you must try and try to get the thing you want. That's the way I used to be; I worked hard for everything.

In the summertime I used to put a lot of sand in my moccasins. I'd squeeze my feet into them even though it hurt. At first I had a hard time running, but after a while I began to get used to it. From there on I hardly knew I had dirt in my moccasins; it seemed to me as though I had nothing in them; I could carry it all as far as I wanted to go. I put the sand in my moccasins to toughen my feet, so as to be able to run anywhere, through sand and through snow and not mind it, so that when I wanted to go through the sand and the desert I could stand it, even though the sand was deep, without getting tired, even though the snow was twelve inches deep or more I could run through it as though there were nothing on the ground. That's how I raced for six miles in order to make my feet and legs strong and my muscles hard. And I used to take a mouthful of water and, holding it in my mouth, run up a great big hill. I did this so as to develop strong wind. I breathed only through my nose while running.

In the winter, when the snow was on the ground, not the first snow that comes but the second,—the second, you know, is colder than the first,—I used to race early in the morning while it was still dark. Even though it was a real cold morning I had to get up without anything on, except my moccasins and G-string, and run for a long distance. While I'd be running on my way I'd go under a young tree and shake the snow on myself. This was a hard thing to do. If you're not strong, every time you shake the snow onto yourself, you'll say, Ah! Before I'd start back for home I'd throw myself in the snow and roll around in it for quite a while. When I'd get home I wouldn't go inside, I'd stop by the doorway, turn around again and run for the water. If there was thick ice on top of the water I'd get a stick or a piece of rock, break the ice, take off my moccasins and jump in. I'd stay in the icy water as long as I could stand it, turning over and over, hollering and screaming so as to develop a good voice. Then I'd get out and put on my moccasins and start for home. While I'd be running on my way my body would be covered with a thin coat of ice, cracking all over me and my c–. My c– would be about frozen. That was the hardest thing; I sometimes couldn't stand it. Before going in the hogan I'd roll in the snow once more. Then I'd go in, but I shouldn't go near the fire, I had to stay away from the fire, until all the ice had melted off my body.

There are only two months in the winter during which one should race and do all these things, from the first of December until the last of January. During that time the bear will have small cubs, and they'll do just the same. She'll have her little ones out in the snow for a long time, even though they're crying. Not until they almost freeze to death will she bring them inside. That's how the bear makes himself tough. The bear can stand anything; he's brave and unafraid. That's the way we must be too. That's why we should do the same.

That's what the old people taught their children. "Every child should race and go into the icy water and the snow, so as to be tough and brave and quick and strong, so that

70

even if something very serious should happen to you you'll be able to stand it, and if anything should try to scare you you won't scare easily, you'll be strong all over. You'll be as brave as a mad dog, able to jump on anything that gets after you, even though it's tough and strong, even though it's big. That's what all the racing and bathing is for. If you don't do these things you'll be killed, even by what's not strong. You'll be weak and lazy and not able to stand anything. You'll be a coward. The people will make fun of you and laugh, because you're a lazy man. They'll know you didn't do these things." That's what my father used to tell me. So, even when I was small, I started doing this in order to make myself tough and get all the things I wanted.

The first spring that they took the herd to the store to shear the sheep I stayed with my father, Slim Man, and his wife. Slim Man and I went out every day, herding the sheep and goats that were left. While we were out herding he used to kill the bugs in my hair. I had a lot of them. He said, "If it wasn't for me these bugs would kill you."

One day I was out with the herd by myself when, all at once, the sheep were scared of something. I looked to see what it was, and there was a jack-rabbit running around in the middle of the sheep. I picked up some rocks and started chasing him, and pretty soon he ran into a badger hole. When I ran up, there he was, lying in the hole. I reached down and got hold of one of his legs and pulled him out. He was sure strong. Jack-rabbit was stronger than I was. He started jumping around and kicking me all over. I tried to get hold of the other leg, but I couldn't, he was so quick. I got hold of one leg with both my hands and tried to throw him on the ground, but I couldn't. Then I thought I'd swing him, but I couldn't swing him, he was too heavy and too strong.

Pretty soon he'd scratched me all over the arms and breast. In places he scratched me deep, and the blood was running down. I tried to drag him to where there were some rocks and sticks, but he was pulling me back and jerking me around so that I couldn't. Then I began kicking him all over the body, and he quieted down. I'd been fighting with him for a long time, and he was tired, I guess. I was too, I was about to quit when the rabbit gave up. Then I kicked down on his head and smashed it. At last I'd killed a jack-rabbit. But I couldn't carry it, it was a great big one and heavy, so I dragged it along after the herd.

On my way home my father, Slim Man, met me. He saw the rabbit and laughed and asked me, "Who killed that jack-rabbit for you?" I said, "I got it out of a badger hole. I had a hard time killing this jack-rabbit." When he saw where the rabbit had scratched me and torn my shirt he started laughing; he laughed for a long time. He tied the legs together and put it over my shoulder and told me to carry it home. It was sure heavy. When I brought it home his wife cleaned and buried it in ashes, and when it was roasted we ate it.

About evening, a few days after that, my mother and father returned from Keams Canyon. They'd sold the wool and bought a lot of stuff, calico, green coffee, sugar and flour. Many of the sheep were lame, because they'd been driven a long way, and their feet were sore, and in places, where they'd been cut, they were swollen. While shearing some of the fellows must not have cared and cut them. My mother put medicine on the cuts.

The morning after they came back she killed a sheep. The meat was cut up, and while the others were starting to cook it she started roasting some coffee. She said, "The trader said, 'This coffee is unroasted, so you have to roast it first, and after you roast it you grind it up and put it in a pot.' " She put a pail of water on the fire, and after the green beans were roasted she ground them up on a rock and put them in the pot and poured the water over them. While we were roasting the meat on charcoals she started making tortillas. But there wasn't any baking powder. She put a rock over the fire and had it hot enough to bake tortillas on, but they were all as hard as a board, because there wasn't any baking powder in them.

When everything was cooked and the coffee was done they laid it out, and we started eating. About then Slim Man came over from another hogan where he lived. My father said to him, "Come get something to eat. Here's some coffee. Have some coffee." We dipped some out of the pot and tasted it; it was real bitter. Everybody was making faces and spitting it out; you couldn't swallow it. My mother said, "We have to put sugar in it." We did, but it was still the same. We put in more and more, but we never did sweeten it. It just got worse and worse. That was because she'd burned it. It was as black as charcoal. Slim Man said, "You must have burned it. Perhaps it should be cooked just right. I think you burned it, and that's why it's so bitter."

We put the coffee aside and tried to eat the tortillas, but they were thin and hard as a rock and had no taste, for she hadn't put in any baking powder or salt, just flour and water. It was so hard you couldn't chew it, and it didn't taste good. So we couldn't use that, we had to let that go too, and just eat our own food, meat and cornbread and other food we always had. After we'd finished eating we threw the whole thing away. We wasted all that food. They said, "It's no use buying any more of this stuff; we don't know how to use it. We won't buy any more coffee or flour, because they're no good at all."

One day in the fall, as I was walking in the middle of the herd, all at once the sheep saw something. I looked, and there was a rabbit jumping around, not knowing which way to go. I sneaked up to him, and when I was real close, not more than four yards away, I shot him with an arrow. I shot him at once, right through the heart, and he began jumping around and got caught in the grease-wood. I ran up and killed him there and took the arrow out of him and brought him home. I was proud of myself. I thought, "No one can do that. I'm great on hunting. I'm a man, now that I've killed a rabbit."

My mother had been telling me about bows and arrows, and I wondered what they were. I was thinking about it all the time. One day I asked her to make me a bow and some arrows, so she made a bow out of cedar and arrows out of rabbit-bush. She found some feathers,—I don't know what kind they were,—and tied them to the arrows. That was what I first carried around with me. When I shot those arrows they used to go whirling around, not one of them went straight. When my bow became bent she made me another out of the same wood, and when that one became real round she made me another. This time she made me a bow out of oak. But I had the same arrows. Then, when that bow was bent and round again, my father must have thought I enjoyed bows and arrows for he made me a bow out of oak. He made me a nice one, and arrows out of oak also. He found some crow and owl feathers and made me nice arrows. They were the ones with which I shot the rabbit. They all went straight, not one of them went whirling.

5 . *Who Has Mules spends the winter learning songs and prayers, and Blue Goat is cured of a disease.*

THAT winter, while we lived on Black Mountain at Willows Coming Out, Who Has Mules came to our place. I was out herding. When I returned with the sheep towards evening he came out of the hogan and rode away. He'd been with my father all day; they must have been talking about something. The next day he came again, and when the sun was pretty well down he began gathering up some wood. He gathered together a big pile and then went back to his home. In the evening he came again. My father was lying in the middle of the hogan. He put out a sheep pelt for his nephew, and Who Has Mules sat down at his right side. My place was always on the south side, my mother's place was always on the north, and my father's on the west.

Old Man Hat said, "I'll tell the stories first, then you'll know and remember. You can easily learn if you hear the stories first. If you want to learn about the horses, sheep, cattle and properties, if you want to have all these things, you don't want to be lazy, you don't want to go to bed early at night and get up late in the morning. You have to work hard for all these things. You have to fight everything, the heat in summer and the cold. Everything is hard to get, even little things. If you're lazy you can't get anything. If you do nothing but sleep and lie around you won't get anything, you'll starve to death. You must be lively all the time. When you've acquired stocks you have to work on them day and night. Especially during lambing season will you get only a little sleep. If you fight and resist it you'll soon be accustomed to everything. So you mustn't sleep too long, and you must not be lazy. If you wish to learn something about the stocks and properties, especially after you have learned something about them, you don't want to sleep too long. It will be no use. Even though you learn and know something about it, if you're lazy it will be just no use. You won't get anything."

Then he said, "When you learn about the stocks and properties you'll surely get them. If you go ahead and overcome all these hardships you'll soon have a big herd and property, and you'll have lots to eat. After you get all these things you won't have to go around and beg for them. You'll have everything for yourself. A lot of Indians may say you're stingy. You don't have to mind them, pay no attention to them, just keep on working. That's the way to become a rich man.

"Then, when you learn about all these things, there's a song for each one. Even though you know only one song for each of them everything of yours will be strong. Even if you have only one song for the sheep you'll raise them, nothing will bother them, nothing will happen to them, you'll have them for a long time, the rest of your life. You may live for a long time, you may die of old age, even though you're old you'll still have lots of sheep, horses and cattle. When you haven't a song for the sheep you may raise them for two or three years, maybe longer than that, and you may have a lot, but those sheep will not be strong. Something will bother them all the time. Something will happen to them. They'll get lost every day. Sickness will bother them, and they'll be dying off. Soon you'll have no more sheep. You'll raise them all right, for two or three years, but once it begins they'll go back and disappear, and you won't know what's happened to them. That is, when you haven't a song for them."

While they were talking I was sitting up listening to what they were saying. My father said to me, "Sit up and watch the fire. Keep the fire going." So I was sitting there listening, and I was glad he'd told me to sit up. I wanted to sit up and listen anyhow. Everything my father said I was kind of picking up. So I was glad to be keeping the fire going for I was anxious to hear what my father was saying. I always liked to listen when a man was talking. When the men started talking I always liked to hear them.

He said, "Where there's good grazing and good water, good streams of water and good springs, around those places you'll find good sheep, horses and cattle. When you get one sheep or a horse or a cow and start to take care of it, taking it around where there's good grazing and good water, you'll start raising them, and soon you'll have lots of stock. For there's a million in one. So you don't want to kill a young ewe or young mare or young cow, for there's a million in one of those.

"After you've raised everything, sheep, horses and cattle, and have gotten lots of property you shouldn't cuss and swear at your properties and stock. You shouldn't say, 'Horse of an evil spirit,' or, 'May the bear eat you!' or, 'Let the snake bite you.' If you cuss them in this way it will surely come to pass. If you say, 'Horse of an evil spirit,' they'll soon be dying off, and when you say, 'May the bear eat you,' it will happen. Perhaps a bear will get into your herd and kill them all. The same with the snake, one will be bitten by a snake and poison the whole herd. So you mustn't say anything like that. These things are like your children. You've got to go easy with them, then you'll have something all the time. Now remember all I've said to you. You want to be stingy. Even though they say you're stingy, be stingy. You don't want to give everything you have to the people. If you do that soon you'll have nothing. Remember what I've told you, you must not lose, kill or give away young ewes, young mares and cows, because, as I told you, there's a million in one of those. Keep them all for yourself, be stingy with them. The others, the steers and wethers, you can do whatever you want to with them.

"Well, my nephew, my little one, you said you wanted to learn something about the stocks and properties. If you want to learn, learn it right now. You're young. While you're a young man you've got to learn. Learn about these things and get them. If you learn about it you'll surely get them. You'll get everything, and soon you won't know what to do with it all. So it's up to you. You'll have everything, that is if you're not lazy. But you've got to go through hard summers and winters. If you fight against it, then you'll soon have all these things."

That was all he said to his nephew, and then he started singing. He started a song from here, from the earth, and went along up to the sun and around and back and came to earth again. There were four long songs. My father said, "You need learn only these four songs. If you learn these four, fix them well in your mind, the rest will be easy." Towards midnight, or a little after, while they were working on the songs I fell over and went to sleep. From there on I don't know what they said, nor how long they sang. Early in the morning my mother woke me and told me to go out and get some wood and build up the fire. She had the fire started. They were still sitting up. They said, "It's morning now," and Who Has Mules said, "I'd better be going back." My father said, "All right," and he went home.

78

That day I went out with the herd and was herding all day, but he didn't come. The next day my father and I were herding. When we came back in the evening there was a big pile of wood, but he wasn't there, he'd gone back home. After we had supper he came, and as soon as he arrived they started in. My father said, "Now, I guess, you remember all you learned the night before last. You should ask questions on anything you want to ask about. If you want to learn you don't have to be afraid to ask questions. So, if you want to ask a question, go ahead, because you want to learn all about these things, and I'm willing to teach you. I want you to learn all about them. This is a good chance, so you'd better stick to it, until you learn all that I know."

Then he said, "Now you can go ahead and repeat all the songs. Start from where we started and repeat every one. I'll just listen to see if you get it all." So he repeated all the songs; he started from here and went up to the sun and around until he came to earth again, to the middle of his hogan. My father said, "That's right. I know you've got them all now. Every song you repeated is right. You didn't miss anything. I think you got everything the first time. Once you learn it it won't go away from you. You'll remember them always. I know you won't forget them."

While they were working on the songs again that night I fell asleep. In the morning when my mother woke me they were still up, they'd been up all night again. From there on he came every two or three days. That winter we didn't do anything, nor go any place. Those two were working on the songs, prayers and stories all that winter. All that I did was herd, sometimes by myself, sometimes I'd go out with my father or mother, sometimes my mother went out with the herd by herself.

Late in the spring, after he'd been gone again for two days, when I came back with the herd in the evening, there was a big pile of wood. That night he came, and they started on the songs. After Who Has Mules was through repeating all the songs and all the prayers that go with them and all the stories about them, the stories about the sheep, horses, properties and other things, my father said, "Now you've learned everything. You remember everything from where we started to where we stopped. Now I know you remember things, and I think you're a smart man. There are lots of people who can't learn these songs, and now you've learned a few of them. When you start using them on your stocks and properties, if you do it right, you'll soon have everything. Now you can go ahead. You wanted to learn, and I told you you could. I promised you, and I've given it to you." He cupped his hands and spread them out before him and said, "You see, you think there's nothing in my hands, but my hands are full. Everything is overflowing, things are falling out of my hands. That's the way you'll be later on. So just stick to it and learn some more if you want to.

"You must remember everything I've said to you. I told you that I had a handful of things, and that you'd be that way sometime, but you'll have to have a hard time first. You won't get this way just as soon as you learn all the songs about them. You have to work for all these things, you have to go through many dangerous places, down in the arroyos, in the canyons, and climb up and down mountains. You have to kick sticks and rocks and get splinters in your feet and hands and be cut. You may think you'll get them all as soon as you learn the songs, but you must suffer a great deal before you get them. After you've suffered, then, for all your knowing you'll have a handful of things, and you'll look at them and won't know what to do with them. But you'll use them all the time. After you get all this stuff your children will have everything. They won't starve, they won't be ragged, they won't hunger for meat and other things. They'll have everything, if you have it on hand for them. And you can help the poor and others with it all the time. That's after you get all these things, but before that you must be stingy."

They were up all night. Early in the morning my father said, "Now you've learned all that I know, all the songs, prayers and stories. I wanted you to learn, for you are my only nephew. I know you wish to have lots of stock and property, and I know you need them, I know you have children. I don't want your children to go starving. So, now, you can go ahead, tend to your stocks and properties, and do it right. And don't talk roughly, because you've learned many songs and prayers. If you know the songs and prayers you don't want to talk roughly. If you do you won't get these things, because all the stocks and properties will know that you'll be rough with them. They'll be afraid and won't want to come to you. If you think kindly and talk in the kindest manner then they'll know you're a kind man, and then everything will go to you. So, now, just go ahead, this is all I want to say to you. This will be the end." That's what my father said, and Who Has Mules went home.

In the spring we moved to Aspens Coming Down. Two or three days after we got there my mother wanted me to go with her to where we'd buried our corn that fall. We started in the morning and that evening got to Lake Between The Shoulders, where we'd buried the corn. My mother told me to take some of the dirt off the hole while she went after water on horseback. When she came back we cooked some lunch and ate. The next morning when we opened the hole the mold came out like smoke. The corn was all moldy. It must have gotten wet somehow. My mother said, "Even at that we'll take it." We got out all the corn and put it in a sack and started home. We went back on the same trail to the top of the mountain and got home way late in the night.

Two men were sitting in the hogan. One was my father, the other was a man named Blue Goat. My mother cooked some meat, and she and I ate lunch. My father said, "We just ate a while ago." Blue Goat said, "I came here today. I didn't know where you folks were, but I just started and took the trail that goes by Water In Bitter Weeds. I came on that trail and arrived at Spring Under Pine. At that water I saw the tracks of sheep and horses. Right away I thought it must be you folks. But I knew you'd been living way down below Willows Coming Out all winter, and I thought you were still there. But when I saw the tracks I thought right away that's you folks, and I followed you for quite a ways. Then I turned around and went to Ruins's place and asked him about you. He didn't know, they all didn't know anything about you. They all thought you were still down at Willows Coming Out. But I said, 'There were some tracks around the water at Spring Under Pine, some sheep and horse tracks.' Then they said, 'Well, that's those folks. They must be at Aspens Coming Down by now, because that's the only place they can get water, and they always camp there. So maybe they're over there.' That's what we all said. That's why I turned around and came to this place, and sure enough you folks were living here."

He said, "I came here to you folks for help. I came here to have my uncle help me out, cousin," he said to my mother. "I got into some kind of disease, and I'm suffering from it. That's why I came here; I want my uncle to help me. That's what I came here for, cousin," he said again to my mother. She said, "Where did you get that disease? How did you get into it? You must have been with a woman. I told you not to go around with women. Every time I leave you you always go around with the women." That's what she said to him. This was just joshing, because he was a cousin to my mother. He laughed about it, he laughed and said, "Ha! Ha! Ha!" My mother said, "I told you to behave while I was away. Whenever I leave you I always tell you to behave, not to bother with women. Now I know you were with another woman besides me." He laughed again and said, "Yes, I was with a woman. It is a disease from a woman that I have. There was a young woman, and she was a pretty woman, I thought maybe I could get her and marry her. I met her, and I stayed at her place only one night. At that time I asked her about different diseases that a woman carries around. 'There are lots of women who are that way, and they're dangerous. Women like that, who haven't any husbands, are just spreading disease. I know you haven't a husband. How are you about disease?' She said, 'I haven't any disease. I don't know what you mean. I don't know anything about disease, so I don't know what you mean by it. I'm all right,' she said. That's why I stayed with her. From there on I started feeling kind of funny. Soon I was that way all over, and kept on getting worse. When I took a leak it began to hurt me, and I started suffering from it.

"I'd been that way a little over a month when she came to my place after me. I was mad at her. I said, 'Stay away. Don't bother me any more, and I don't want to bother with you. You told me a big lie, and you've got me in suffering, so go away and stay away with your disease.' She began begging me, saying, 'I haven't got any kind of disease. You must have gotten that disease some place from another woman, because I haven't any disease on me.' But anyway I told her to stay away. It's about a little over two months now that

I've been around with this disease, so I need help. Before I started she came to my place again, but I told her to stay away. 'That's what I told you before. I told you to stay away, and I mean it,' I said. She was begging me, saying, 'I want to stay with you, because I like you better than anyone else.' I said, 'I guess you feel that way, but I don't. I don't care for you at all. I don't like you one bit. Worse than anybody! If you want me to f— you again I'll f— your ass this time; maybe you haven't any diseases in your ass.' That's what I said to her, because I was so mad when she made me suffer like this. She was still around when I got on my horse and rode away. So that's why I came up here to find you folks, because I know you know about these different diseases from a woman. I want you to help me out and cure me." My mother said, "That's what you get when you run around with a woman. Maybe you like it. Maybe you like to suffer and are feeling fine. Maybe it's just like eating something sweet to you." When she said this he laughed again, but Old Man Hat was just lying there, he didn't say anything.

My uncle, Blue Goat, said, "That's what I came here for. I want you to do something for me, my uncle," he said to Old Man Hat, but Old Man Hat was lying there, he didn't say a thing for a long time. Then he asked, "How's your c— looking now? What's it look like?" "It looks all right to me. That is on the outside, but I don't know just how it is on the inside. All around there it's swollen and hurts me badly. On the outside it looks as though nothing were wrong with it." Old Man Hat said, "Well, that disease is from the women all right. They have different diseases. One is called syphilis, another is called the spanish pock, another chancres, another syphilitic sores. I think that's chancres that's bothering you now. When it starts eating around inside of you you'll be gone, you won't live long. But I don't think it's

84

started eating around the inside of you yet. Still it's a long time since you've had that disease. You said you've had it over two months now. However, I think I can cure you. If that bad stuff comes out you'll be cured. If it doesn't you'll be a goner. You know they're dangerous things to get into.

"Well, you'll have to suffer some more when you begin taking medicine. You've got to starve. You don't want to eat anything hard, meat especially. You can only take things that are soft, like mush. You'll be starving all the time. That's what I mean by saying you'll have to suffer some more. To-morrow I'll go out and get some medicine for you, and you can put up a small sweat-house for yourself. While you're in the sweat-house take the medicine, drink as much as you can stand, and drink a lot of water after it. You'll be p—ing every once in a while, and the poison will soon be out of you. All the bad stuff will break open and start coming out every time you p—. Keep on taking the medicine right along. You'll soon be well. As soon as the poison is out you're safe." That's what he said, and then we went to bed.

Early the next morning Blue Goat got up and went outside to where he was going to put up a sweat-house. He could hardly walk; his legs were way far apart. While he was away that morning my father said, "I guess he enjoys suffer-ing. I've told him many a time about those things. Not only that, but many things besides, about different kinds of trou-ble and different kinds of sickness and different kinds of diseases, like what he's got now, because that's the only thing he looks for and wishes for and goes for. He does nothing but go around after the women. So he's gotten into a disease now and is suffering from it. He ought to go and begin f—ing as hard as he can, because that's the only thing he wants to do. He's crazy about women. I tried to stop him once, but I couldn't. He and Old Man Spitter are both just alike; they want to run around with the women all the time. They're crazy about women, just as their mother used to be," he said, pointing to my mother. "She used to be running around with lots of men. She used to be crazy about men. Maybe they're that way because their mother was that way too." He meant my mother, his wife. She got mad at him and said, "What are you talking about? You must have become crazy or something. You think you're a sensible man, and you think you're a good man. You were worse than anybody in this world. You've been with every woman who has come around. You were crazy about them. You ought to be ashamed talking to me like that." My mother was kind of mad, but my father was just joshing her. He was lying there smiling. About then Blue Goat came back, and they quieted down about that.

We ate breakfast, and my father said, "I'll go out and look for some medicine. When I come back I'll take out the herd, so let them stay in the corral." He went out and was gone for just a little while and then returned, bringing some kind of weed and the roots. He pounded and mashed it up with a rock and put it in a dipper and poured some water on it. "Let it stand here and dissolve. When it gets good and strong let him take it. After he takes it he can go in the sweat-house. When he drinks it up he can put more water in it," my father said and then went out with the herd.

I went to where Blue Goat was putting up the sweat-house. He'd already chopped some poles, and I started gathering cedar bark to put over the sweat-house and inside. I gathered a lot of it, and after that I gathered up the rocks. He got the sweat-house up and put the cedar bark over it. There wasn't any shovel, so he took a piece of wood and made it flat and thin and used that to put dirt over the bark. The fire was going on the rocks. We started it before he put the cedar bark over the sweat-house. About the time he finished putting dirt over the bark the fire was out. The wood was all burnt, and there were only the rocks piled there, good and hot. He began putting the rocks inside and told me to go in and straighten them up. So I was in the sweat-house, helping him pile up the rocks. It was hot. I didn't see how he could stand all that heat. When I thought about it it made me shiver. After we had all the rocks inside he told me to go home and get the blankets. I got them, and he put them over the door. "Did he get some medicine?" he asked me. I said, "Yes, he has it setting for you, my uncle." "Go and get it for me," he said. I went back to the hogan again and took the medicine over to him. As I got there with the medicine he was starting to undress. While he was undressing I went back home and began dragging in some small wood.

Late in the afternoon, while I was outside, I saw somebody riding along on horseback. I looked at the rider for a while, and it was a woman, coming towards us. She came to our place and got off her horse and went inside. We weren't living in a hogan, we were in just a brush shelter, a corral like. My mother said to me, "Go and take your uncle's horse to water. Water your uncle's horse, it's probably thirsty by now. Take the bridle along with you. That horse is tame, but you be careful with it anyway." As I picked up the bridle she asked the woman, "Where are you from?" "I'm from way down the valley," she replied. "From where?" my mother asked again. "Oh, way from the foot of the mountain." "Where are you going? Where are you heading for?" "Oh," she said, "I'm just riding around. A man wanted to come up here sometime ago; I'm following him. I heard he's with you. That's what I'm after."

I was walking quite a way from the hogan when my mother called me back and said, "Take this horse along too."

The woman took her things off the horse and took off the saddle. She handed me a wool rope, telling me to hobble her horse with that. I went on and watered the horses and hobbled them together. When I came back home she was grinding corn. My mother said, "You ought to have taken the jugs along with you. There isn't much water for tonight." The woman said, "Go get my horse and put the saddle on it and take the jugs along. It looks as though it's a little too far for you to carry water." So I went over and got her horse and put the saddle on him. They put the jugs on the horse for me, and my mother said, "Leave the jugs on the horse and pour the water into them." When I brought the water home Blue Goat wasn't back yet. He was probably still over in the sweat-house. I took off the saddle and led the horse back to where the other was and hobbled him again. It was just getting dark. As I was coming home there was my uncle coming also, carrying the blankets over his shoulders. When we got home I looked at him, and he was looking mad when he saw this woman in the hogan.

By that time my father had returned with the herd. He came inside and said, "I see somebody has come and is visiting us. But I don't know you," he said, as he walked up and shook hands with her, "I don't know you, but I'm glad to meet you." The woman said, "So am I. I don't know you, but I'm glad, too, to meet you." "Oh, that's our daughter-in-law. She came after him," my mother said, pointing to Blue Goat. Blue Goat was sure mad. He said, "Daughter-in-law! I don't think so. I don't like her. You think she's a woman, you think she's a clean woman. She's a dirty woman. She's a nasty woman. Why do you want to call her 'my daughter-in-law'? For—" He was going to say something else, but it seemed he couldn't talk any more he was so mad. Then he said to the woman, "What do you want to come after me for? I

88

told you not to bother me any more. I told you, 'Stay away from me, evil spirit.' You ought to be ashamed of yourself, carrying disease around after me, carrying diseases around the hogans. What do you want to come after me for? You dirty woman, you." My mother said, "Oh, my son, don't say that to her. You mustn't say that to a woman, my son." He said, "I said it because I'm mad at her, and I don't like her. She ought to stay away. She ought to be ashamed of herself, carrying diseases around to the hogans." Again my mother said, "Don't say that to her, my son. It's your own fault. It's not her fault. She didn't drag you into her. You got after her yourself. I know that. So don't talk that way to her, my son." Then the woman said, she was sitting close by my mother, "That's the way he talks to me. He claims I've gotten him into a disease. He claims I'm carrying a disease, but I'm not, I'm all right, I haven't any disease. He must have gotten into a disease somewhere else. He must have gotten that disease from some other woman. But he always blames me. The blame is all mine." When she said this she began to cry. Her tears were running down. My mother said, "Don't talk that way to each other, my children," and then she started crying too. My father sat up and said, "Well, now, all of you, my children, don't talk that way to each other. You don't know what you're talking about. You don't think. Think first, and then, if you want to say something, you can say it. Now you're mad at each other, and you don't know what you're saying. Things like that, when you want to find out something about them, you've got to think it over first and talk it over after. In that way you can fix things up right. So with this thing, if we talk it over we'll soon find something about it. And if you want to fix it up we'll fix it. So don't just hurry to start trouble. I don't want any of you to start trouble here at my place. Now we'll forget about that and just go ahead and cook some lunch. We'll all eat, and after that we can talk about it."

My mother and the woman started cooking; my mother made some corn-mush and corn-bread, and the woman boiled some meat. After everything was cooked we started eating. My mother gave some food to her daughter-in-law and some mush to my uncle. When the old man was through eating he picked up his tobacco, and while he was rolling a cigarette he said, "Well, we'll talk about it now. I'd like to know about you both. I'd like to find out if you both have a disease. Both of you have got to tell me the truth. You don't have to be ashamed to tell, because the disease you're talking about is dangerous, a dangerous thing to have. When you have a disease like that you'll spread it all over, and it's not nice to spread disease. You've got to tell me the truth right now. There's no one around here, only we will know it. So you don't need to be ashamed to tell. After that, when you've told me the truth, I'll say something to you both. Now you can go ahead and tell about yourselves, about how long you've had that disease. Tell me right out. You don't have to be afraid to tell. I won't do anything to you for that. But, if you tell me you're diseased, I'll do something for you. I'll take all the poison out of you both. I'll cure you. So you've got to tell me right now. Don't be afraid or ashamed. I know, now, you both are diseased. And because, as I told you be-fore, it's dangerous to have a disease, it will kill you any time, if you want to live you'll have to tell me right now that you want to live long. If you don't want to live long, tell me that too, say it, that you don't want to live. But you must tell me your part first. My nephew, here, has told me all about himself. I know just how he is. You must tell me your part now. When one is diseased the other is diseased also. I know very well you have a disease too. So tell me now and say it, that you've got a disease."

Then the woman started telling about herself. She said, "I don't feel well all the time. Whenever I stop moving I get to aching all over. If I get up and go about or do something I'll be all right, I won't feel anything, but my arms and legs will start aching as soon as I keep still. Like in the evening when I go to bed I'll begin to ache all over, around my hips especially, and my back up to my head will be aching. I'll be sweating all over, even though I haven't any covers on me, and my pulse will be beating as hard as it can beat. My feet and hands will be just as though they were burning, and I'll move them around to cool places. I always get hot in between my legs, close to my c—. My legs will start aching, and soon it'll be hurting me badly. It gets that way only at night. When I move around I don't feel anything. That's the way I am."

The old man said, "I think you've got a disease all right. I know you have. So you'd better take some medicine too." My mother said, "You'd better hurry and get some medicine, because she needs it. I want you to go out and get some medicine for her." He said, "You're on your daughter-in-law's side, so you'd better pay for the medicine for her. It's got to be paid for first. So if you want some medicine you'd better pay me first, then I can get you some medicine for your daughter-in-law." My mother said, "Sure, I'll pay for it for her. I'll pay you for the medicine, because I want my daughter-in-law to get well." The old man said, "Well, we'll wait until this fellow's through with the sweat-house. We'll see about it later on. She'll be all right."

In the morning he said, "You'd better go and fix up your sweat-house again today. Make it good and hot, and take some more medicine. When you get it good and warm you can both go in together and take some medicine." He said to me, "You go over to the sweat-house with your uncle and help him gather up more rocks and wood. I'm going out with the herd again today. While I'm out I'll get more medicine for you two. You should take a lot of medicine before you go in and take some every once in a while and drink a lot of water after it. Soon all the poison will be out of you." My mother said, "I'm glad you said you were going to get more medicine. You told me to pay for it. I haven't got anything to give you, but, anyway, sometime I'll make you a single saddle-blanket." That's what she said to my father and laughed about it.

I went over to the sweat-house with my uncle, and we started to gather up some wood and rocks. I watched him walking around there, gathering up wood, he could hardly walk. It must have been hurting him badly. We got some rocks and piled them with the wood and built a fire, and then went home. My mother and the woman were butchering a sheep. After they were through butchering they cut it up, and my mother cooked some meat and made corn-bread and some mush, and we started eating. But my uncle didn't eat anything, only the woman ate a little. She just took a taste of the meat, and that was all. After that they both went to the sweat-house, and my father went out with the herd, saying he'd get some more medicine.

They went to the sweat-house for three days. In the evening of the third day, as I returned with the herd, the man was coming along and the woman behind him. They were coming back from the sweat-house. He was so awfully weak; he could hardly walk. He walked as if he were drunk; he almost fell. I thought that he must be hungry. But in three days' time all the bad stuff had burst through him. That's what he said, and that was what made him so weak. The woman was the same, but she wasn't very weak. That's what happened after three days of taking this medicine, but my father didn't say anything about it.

The next morning my uncle could hardly move. He wasn't able to gather any more rocks or wood or build a fire. My father said to me, "Go to the sweat-house and gather some small rocks and build a fire on them. It will be all right even if it's just a little warm." I went over and gathered some wood and rocks and built a fire and then came back. My uncle could hardly walk. They made him a cane, and he began to walk with that. When he stood up he was so weak he was shivering all over. My mother was scared. She said to him, "How are you feeling, my son? Are you any better? Or are you getting worse? How are you feeling, my son?" He said, "I'm all right. The swelling's all down, and the pain's gone. There's no more swelling, and I don't feel any pain. I'm all right. I'm not suffering from pain any more. But I don't understand why I'm so weak. However I think it's because I'm not eating anything. I must be starving. So don't worry so much about me, my mother." She said, "What a nasty thing you had, my son. You're suffering so much from it, and you're starving to death. I know you're so weak. You ought to eat something, my son." The old man said, "You just keep still and be quiet. Don't talk about eating. You make him starve the more. You make him wish for something to eat. So you just keep quiet about food. They'll be all right, and he'll get well soon. When he's well then he can have anything he wants."

My mother went over to the sweat-house to put the rocks in for them, and I went out with the herd. When I came back in the evening he was sitting by the door against the brush hogan. The woman was sitting inside. He tried to get up, but he couldn't. He tried his best, he was holding onto his cane, but he couldn't, he was so weak. Then my mother came out and helped him. He stood up, and while she was holding him he started to walk inside. He took a few steps, he was close to the fire, and he couldn't go any further, so he got down on the ground and crawled to his bed, and there he lay, quietly, without moving. I looked at him, and there was no flesh on him. He was as skinny as he could be. His ribs and hips stood out, and there were big holes around his shoulders and stomach. His face was just the same with large holes in his cheeks. I thought he was starving to death. He said, "The chancres is out. I'm weak now."

The next day they couldn't go to the sweat-house any more. My father said, "You two can stay at the hogan for a couple of days. I think all the poison that was in you is out, so you can stay here today and just rest. Perhaps the poisons are all dead now." Blue Goat said, "Something all mixed up of different colors passed me, and a whole lot of bad stuff with it that looked like worms." The old man said, "Yes, that's the poison. Those are the worms all right. When there are worms in you you get that way, as you are now. I knew you had worms. That's what you call chancres. Now you're safe. If those things were still in you it would be dangerous. If you hadn't come up here those worms would have killed you. When they start moving and eating around in you they'll surely kill you. But they're all out now, and you're safe. They're all dead."

The next morning I went out and brought in some dried meat. Those two couldn't get up any more. They just lay and p—ed and s— right there. My mother cooked the meat, and after it was cooked she pounded it with a rock and made it soft. She'd had the stomach of a sheep boiling all night, and it was good and tender. She poured out this stomach, that had been boiling, the soup was nice and fat, and gave it to them. She said, "Eat some of this soft meat with this soup, and eat some of the stomach of the sheep. Then you'll be all right." When my mother raised him up he was as bony as he could be. Nothing was left on him. All the flesh was gone, and big knots were around his joints. I don't know how the woman looked, my mother tended to her. When he started eating I went out with the herd.

In the evening as I came back with my sheep I saw him walking out of the hogan without his cane. He went a little way over a hill. He looked funny, he was so skinny. From there on they were getting better all the time. About three or four days after that they were well. The woman began carding and spinning wool, and she and my mother started the saddle-blanket for the old man. They made it in a day. Quite a few days after that they were both looking fine. The woman was looking better than the man, because he'd suffered so very much. But he was well. His body was kind of pale, and the skin was peeling off, but he was good and strong. He said, "I guess we'd better be going back now. However, we'll spend another day here with you folks, and tomorrow we'll go back to our place. We'd better go and work on our farm, because it's time to plant something." They stayed all that day, and the next morning he said, "Well, I guess we'll start back for our home now, my people."

When they left we gave them five sheep and five goats. Four of the goats were wethers, and one was a female. They started back that morning. They went around by Red Willow, past Two Valleys Run Together and on to War Trail. When they started down the mountain the sheep and goats didn't want to go down that trail. Soon the goats started to run, and soon they'd scattered in the woods. They went after them for a long way, but they couldn't stop them. They couldn't do anything with them, and so they just let them go and started driving down the sheep. They only took the five sheep with them to their home. About four days later the five goats were back in our herd.

6. *He romps in the corral with an old man's wife . . . His mothers quarrel, but he refuses to part from his sheep and goats . . . In the fall they move to Navaho Mountain where the coyotes kill the lambs and the sheep freeze to death.*

A FEW days after Blue Goat left a man and his wife came to our place. They said they started from Ganado and went down to visit Ruins. Next they went and visited Who Has Mules, then Choclays Kinsman and some other people on the west side of Black Mountain. From there they came to our place. The woman was a Bitter Water; her husband was a Many Goats. He was my father's nephew. He'd been with Old Man Hat when he was young. That's why they came and visited us also. He was an oldish sort of man, but his wife was young and slim. They were driving a bunch of sheep they'd gotten from their relatives, and when they arrived at our place toward evening they drove them in to our herd.

In the morning I went out in the corral with my mother, and we began feeding the lambs. A lot of them were hungry, because their mothers hadn't any milk, so we had to feed them. That's what we always did every morning and evening. While we were giving milk to the lambs the woman came and helped us. When we were through my mother milked some goats, and I went out with the herd.

Toward evening when I came back and put the herd in the corral, about the time I'd fixed the gate, this woman came out, and we began to feed the lambs. We were out there working on them until dark. There were always many of them that had to be fed. While we were doing that she began bothering me, running after me and when she'd catch me start to play, touching and tickling me all over. We had lots of fun that evening out among the sheep. The next morning she helped us again, and when we were through I went out with the herd. I came back in the evening, and just as I had the gate fixed up my mother came out, and we started feeding the lambs, and she came too, and helped us. When we were about through my mother went back to the hogan, and I was out there with the woman all alone in the sheep corral. As soon as my mother left she started chasing me and tickling me and touching me all over, and then I started touching her. I touched her around the breasts, I got hold of them, and I grabbed her between the legs. She liked having me touch her. She wanted to get down on the ground, and she must have wanted me to f— her, but I didn't know how to go about it. My c— was hard, and she must have felt the same way too, for in between the legs she was all watery. I thought perhaps she'd p—ed. I know she wanted to be f—ed very badly, but I didn't know how, so I didn't do anything but touch her. We were fooling around for quite a while and then went back to the hogan.

The next morning after we'd fed the lambs again I went out with the herd. I was herding all day. In the evening I came back, and as soon as I'd fixed the gate she came right out, and we fed the lambs. We did the same thing that evening. We fooled around, and it was just the same, her thighs were all wet. That evening I felt something on my legs. I felt of my c—, and there, on the end of it, coming out, was something that seemed to be like soup or gravy. But we didn't do anything to each other again that evening.

The next morning she was getting ready to move on. Her

husband, Old Man Gosh, said, "Get ready, quick, we'll go early this morning." After she had her things ready she began painting her face with red powder. When she was through she said, "Come here. I'll paint your face for you." I went right up to her, and she painted my face. They separated their sheep from ours, and my mother and father gave them ten more, and they started off, driving their sheep across a little flat. I was standing there, looking after them until they went over a hill and down in the wash. That was the last I saw of them. When they went over the hill I almost cried. I was so sorry that she'd left. I'd been playing with her, and her leaving made me so lonesome. From there on I thought about her for a long time. I don't know how long I thought of her, and I don't know when it was that I forgot her.

Around in shearing season my father and mother took part of our herd to Keams Canyon. They were gone for a long time, and I was all alone at home. They worried about me while they were at Keams Canyon shearing the sheep, and so they sent me my younger brother. My real mother had another husband, his name was Yishi, and this man's nephew came with my brother. He stayed with us one night and went right back the next day.

The day after my brother arrived we started herding together, and from there on we both went out with the sheep every day. He surprised me. Even though he was a small boy he knew a lot of songs. I didn't know any kind of song. While I was out herding with him he started singing, he was singing Nda songs, and I wished that I knew some songs also, but I didn't. I walked over to him and told him to sing some more, and when he began I tried to sing after him, but I didn't know the songs at all. We'd been herding for perhaps a week or ten days. The boy, my younger brother, sang all the time, all kinds of songs. He used to tell me how the singers sang. He'd sit down, fix up something for a rattle, and say, "This is the way the singer starts." He'd straighten himself up, put one hand below his ears and start to shake the rattle. Then he'd sing, he'd commence with, Hey Yey! "This is the way the singer starts his songs," he'd say.

One morning, while we were still at home, before we'd turned out the herd, my real mother came in. She walked up to us and sat down between us and put her arms around our necks and started crying. She cried for a long time and said, "I had a fight with my older sister. She's no more sister to me. I thought she'd put her meanness away, but she still keeps all her meanness with her, so she's not my sister any longer. I've come here for you both. I'll let her go by herself, let her go alone, the evil spirit. I'll take you both back with me right now." She'd come early in the morning, as we were about to turn out our herd. I was thinking about my herd, that there was nobody to take care of it, and I didn't want to go with her. She said, "I want to take both of you boys back with me. I want those two old things to go alone. That's what I told them when I left, I said, 'I'm going for my two boys. I'll bring my boys back with me, and you two can go alone.' That's what I told them, so we'll go back now, my children," she said to us. "Let them be alone, the evil spirits." But I was thinking about my herd and said, "I don't think I'll go. All those goats are mine. I can't leave them. I want to stay with my goats all the time. You both can go. I want to stay." When I said, "I want to stay with my goats," she dropped her head. She was sitting that way for a while, and then she said to the other boy, "Where's the horse you rode, my son?" He said, "I've got it here, over the hill where I hobbled it." She said, "Go and get the horse. We'll go right now." The boy went after the horse, and I said, "Maybe you did have a fight with your sister, even though you fought with each other and want me to go back with you I won't, because I've got goats here. I can't let my goats go." But I said to her, "Perhaps, when you get back you'll both apologize to each other again."

When I took out the herd I said to them, "Eat some lunch before you go." We had plenty of meat up on the trees. They were just starting the fire as I left. When I came back in the evening there was no one around. There wasn't any noise, no sound of anything. I looked all around and half the meat was gone, they'd taken half the meat with them. I made a little lunch for myself, and after I'd eaten I went straight to bed. In the morning I made a little lunch again, and after I ate I went out with the herd.

I'd been herding for two more days when, while I was herding, I thought about my mother. I felt as if she were coming. I thought, "Perhaps they're home," so I started back with my herd. I got home while the sun was still way up. As I put the herd in the corral I looked towards where they'd gone over a hill, and over that hill I saw dust. I looked a few times, and as I was wondering what caused it I saw a herd coming around the hill, and a woman riding on horseback. That was my father and mother. I recognized them right away. As soon as I recognized them I started running to meet them. I ran up to my father first. He was sitting on his horse, and he reached down and put his arm around my neck and said, "Alas, welcome, my baby, let's see my baby, welcome, my young one." When he said this to me I started crying. He let me go and said, "Come and sit behind me." I looked up at him, and he was shedding tears too. I sat behind him, and my mother was coming along towards us. She rode up and put her arm around me and started crying. She made me cry again.

When we got home we put the herd into the corral with the others, and right away they started up the fire, and my mother started cooking. Some meat was still left, and we used that. After we ate they opened up their packs. They had food from the store, and some from the pueblo people, such as the bread that's baked on stone griddles and sweet corncake and the rest of it. They brought me back a pair of calico pants, already sewn, and a shirt, already made, and a red silk hand-kerchief. I dressed myself up, and I was proud. I had on a nice pair of calico pants and a shirt and a nice silk handkerchief around my head. That's what they brought back for me, and they gave me a black robe. They'd brought lots of different colored robes and calico. I didn't eat very much at first on account of seeing my good clothing. Then, when I got off of it, I began eating some more. This time I ate the pueblo people's food. When I was through we put all the things away, and it was evening. I hadn't noticed the sun was down; suddenly when I looked out it was dark.

My father began asking me about the woman. "A woman started for this place. When did she come here?" I said, "She was here the day before yesterday." "What did she say to you?" "She was here early in the morning. She wanted us both to go back with her. She said, 'I came here for you both. I want to take you both to my home. I want to let the two go alone; I want them to be alone, the evil spirits. So we'll go back home right now, this morning.' That's what she said to us. But I said, 'I can't go, because I've got my goats here. I've nobody to take care of my goats for me. I've got to take care of them myself. You two can go home. I'm not go-ing. I'm going out with my herd.' She didn't say any more to me, and my brother went after the horse. While she was still around here that morning I went out with the herd. When I got back in the evening they'd taken some meat along with them." "When she first spoke to you, how did you feel about it? When she first said, 'I'll take you back to my home,' what did you think? Did you want to go with her?" I said, "No, as soon as she said that, right away I thought about my herd, and I said, 'No, I don't want to go, I want to stay with my herd.'"

My father said, "My dear, my baby, that's right, my poor boy, you're right. I'm glad you didn't go with her. I'm glad you didn't leave your herd. If you'd left and gone with her the herd would be gone by now. The coyotes would have killed them all. But you had sense enough to stay. I'm glad of it. So with anyone who comes to you and tells you to let the herd go. You musn't let the herd go, because as soon as you do there'll be nothing left of them. The same with the horses, if you let the horses go, if you don't tend to them for a few days, they'll all be scattered out. In that way you'll lose many of them. But you didn't let your herd and horses go. I'm so glad about it. The herd is money. It gives you clothing and different kinds of food. You know now that you have some good clothing; the sheep gave you that. And you've just eaten different kinds of food; the sheep gave that food to you. Everything comes from the sheep. So it's a good thing you didn't let the herd go.

"You and I, we have nothing to do with them." He pointed to my mother. "She had a fight with her younger sister. They were like dogs. It's a funny way to act. Even though they're sisters they fought. That's what I call a dog's way. But it's up to them. However, they'll soon forget it. Some day, when they meet again, they'll have their arms around each other, crying. They'll apologize to each other sometime soon. As soon as they get to see each other again they'll be crying one for the other."

He said, "I think they got into a quarrel about me, but

that's a crazy way to act. I don't see why they quarreled over me. I think of myself as being good for nothing, because I'm old, I'm no longer young, so I don't understand why they quarreled about me." The fight had started about goats. Years before my real mother had given me four goats. They were the ones we raised. It all started over them, and next came jealousy. First they talked about the goats, then about their husbands. My mother was jealous of her younger sister, because my father, Old Man Hat, had once been married to her.

In the fall when it got real cold we moved up on Black Mountain to Aspens Coming Down. There we lived all winter, and in the spring they took the sheep to Keams Canyon. A few days after they returned from that place they wanted to move, because there wasn't any grass on the mountain. The sheep had plenty of feed, but the horses were getting poor. So we moved, past Water In Bitter Weeds and on to Sweet Water. There wasn't any feed at all around there, so after two days we moved again. That night we camped at Two Red Rocks Pointing Together, and the next morning we moved to Dry Around The Water. But there wasn't much water there, so we passed that place and went on to Flowing Through Rocks and stopped and camped on top of that wash. There was plenty of water; the horses had water, and the sheep had water too.

We thought there'd be some feed, but there was nothing. The stock had nothing to eat, and so we moved again. They said, "We'll move down to In The Rocks. A little way from there's a place called White With Reeds. We'll stop and camp there." But we passed that place and kept on toward the San Juan. They said, "There's another store on the river. When we get close to it—we might even get there—we'll shear the sheep we haven't sheared yet." When we arrived at the San Juan, where all these washes end, we stopped and camped close to the river by a big rocky hill, called Coiled Mountain. All around upon that little mountain was lots of feed. They said, "Now we've come to a fine place with plenty of feed for the stock."

After we'd camped there some people came and visited us. They thought we hadn't sheared yet, but over half the herd was done; only a few, the ewes, still needed shearing. When they started in they killed a billy-goat and sold the skin at the store. They got a dollar for it and bought some grub. Skins were worth a whole lot, and after they'd sheared all the sheep they killed ten billy-goats, all at once, and the fellows who helped us got a skin apiece. We kept five and the wool. We sold the wool and the hides and bought more stuff, flour, baking powder, coffee, sugar and other food, and a lot of drygoods, calico and things like that, and different kinds of dishes. They said the wool wasn't worth much, but then stocks in the store were low too. Everything they had in the store was cheap. I guess that's why the wool wasn't worth much, but they'd bought a lot.

The day after they returned from the store they said, "We have our wool all sold now. I guess we'd better start moving back." We'd come by way of the canyon, but we didn't go back that way; we took a short cut over the rocks. We camped overnight among the rocks, and the next morning when the sun was pretty well up we moved to White With Reeds. It was hot then, early in the summer.

There wasn't any rain at all, or any cloud. It was hot and getting worse every day. Even at that we stayed at this one place for many days. Nobody did anything or went any place, and I did nothing but herd. Then we heard that my father, Choclays Kinsman, had moved down to the flat and was living at Hawohi Water. They wanted to move to where he was living, and so we started for that place. It wasn't very far, but when we got to Hawohi Water no one was there. They'd lived there all right, but they'd moved back toward Black Mountain. There were fresh tracks around, so we followed them all the way to Lines Of Thin Rocks.

The next morning we followed that little canyon to Solid Rocks Upward. They said, "There used to be water there." My father rode over, and when he came back he said, "I think there's enough for the horses." So he drove them over, and only the horses had water. We stayed until it got cool and then started again and got to Flowing Through Rocks in the evening. There'd been water in that wash, but there wasn't any now. The wash was dry. We camped there, and the sheep were thirsty. They were making a great noise, crying for water. So that evening my father and I took them to Black Rock Standing. The moon was shining, and there we watered the herd. There was plenty of water in that wash. When they'd had enough they all quieted down, and then we got some for ourselves and started back. It was close onto midnight.

There was no cloud anywhere and no rain. Everything was dried up, no grass, no weeds, no feed for the stocks, nothing green all over the flat and the valley. The sheep had enough, because they can eat anything, but the horses were poor. They were starving. My father, Choclays Kinsman, came to our place and said, "I'm living a little above Black Rock Standing. That's where we moved to. We couldn't find any feed at all any place. The sheep are all right, but the horses are starving. I don't know what to do about it. Do you know of any place where we can find feed for them? We've got to do something. We've got to go around and see where there's some feed." My father said, "I've been moving and riding around, looking for feed for the stocks, and asking the people I get to see about grazing, but it's the same all over, no rain and no green spot, no place at all. There's a little grazing down close to the river, but it was too hot to stay in that sand. The horses' hoofs were sore from going around in the sand and rocky hills." They talked about the stock and grazing for a long time.

We stayed at this place many days. Then all at once they said, "We'll move again." We moved, passing Many Streams, and on past The Lake, past Anything Falls In to Flowing From Tassel Rock. From the mouth of that little canyon out into the valley where the water spreads was a nice level place all sandy. There my father, Slim Man, lived. He had a farm in the valley, and the corn was ripe. My mother went over to the hogan where he lived and brought back some corn. She used to call his wife, my daughter. She said, "My daughter said to me, 'You can come and get corn and make yourself some corn-bread whenever you want to. When you come just go into the field and help yourself. Take all the corn you want.' That's what my daughter said, so I must go and make us some corn-bread. Slim Man wasn't at home. I asked for him, I said to my daughter, 'Where has my son gone to?' She said, 'He's staying with another woman.' " He'd married another woman, who was a Red Clay, and from there on he had two wives.

There we located all during the fall and had corn right along. When fall came we helped them take it in off the field and lay it out to dry. About then my father, His Horse Is Slow, came to our place. Old Man Hat said, "I can't think any more. I've been thinking and worrying about the stocks all summer, but now I've given up, because I can't find a place where there's any feed for them." His Horse Is Slow said, "That's the way it's been with me too, but I've found a good place to go. I heard there's lots of feed for the stock down at Navaho Mountain, and that's where I'm going. Some fellows from there had nice fat horses. They said there's lots of feed over there. So that's where I'm going soon. I was figuring on going to Blue Wash, but they say there isn't any feed around there, that place is still worse, all the stocks are starving to death. That's why I think I'll go to Navaho Mountain." Before he left he said to my father, "We'll start moving for that place together."

The next day we moved to Mouth Of The Canyon, close to his place. They had their corn all in too, and put away, buried in a hole. He came to our place, and they started to talk about the grazing. That was all they were talking about. Finally they said, "We'll all start moving together for that place where they say there's good grazing." Early next morning he came again and said, "You folks can go ahead. You can move today, or you can stay two or three days more. It's up to you." Right away my father said, "I guess we'd better start this morning, because we'd like to get to that place as soon as we can. The stock is getting poorer all the time." His Horse Is Slow said, "All right, you can go ahead, and we'll go just as soon as we get ready. Once we start we'll go right along. So you people had better go now."

We moved that morning. In the evening we got to Two Streams Run Together. A little way below there we camped. The next morning we got the horses and started moving again, and that night we camped at Trail Through The Woods. In the morning, after we'd eaten, we packed our horses, and when we had everything ready we started on. We passed Trail Going Over Rocks and Solid Rock Places and got to Many Streams Coming Out At One Place where we camped that night. In the morning my father brought back the horses, we had everything ready, and after we ate we packed them and started when the sun was pretty well up. We got to the foot of the cliff and started climbing. It was a bad place, but it was the only place where there was a trail. We had a hard time getting the sheep and horses on top. They were slipping and falling on the rocks. We were climbing all forenoon. From there we went on through a wood and beyond the wood was sagebrush. We went quite a way through that to a lake, called Lake Between The Rocks, and that's where we camped.

Giving Out Anger was living there, quite a distance from the lake. His son and his son's uncle were young men, and they used to run a race to the lake early every morning. By that time it had frozen a little on top like crust. We used to hear them go. They said to me, "Don't lie in bed too long. As soon as morning comes get up and put on your moccasins and run a race to the lake. Get in as your brother and uncle are doing." So I'd get up in the morning and put on my moccasins, and when I'd hear them coming I'd start for the lake too, and I'd be hollering. When they'd get to the lake they'd take off their moccasins and jump in, and I'd do the same. But I never stayed in the water long. It was too cold for me. I'd get in and roll a while and then put on my moccasins and start for home. Those two would still be swimming in the lake.

We stayed at this place a few days, and then moved again. We'd waited long enough for the other people. We went down the valley towards Tall Mountain and on to Lower Valley where we camped that night. The next morning we started down the trail of a canyon on the east side of Navaho Mountain. Fresh tracks were coming up. That was Giving Out Anger's herder who'd been down there with the sheep. We went down the trail to the foot of the canyon and camped.

In the canyon was lots of salt-weed, and that's where Giving Out Anger's herder had taken their sheep. They'd been down for salt-weed, perhaps the day before; the tracks looked that way. As I was walking around, not far from where we'd camped, I got to a hole where they used to bury corn. It was about four feet deep, and down at the bottom stood a great, big, black wether. I called my mother, and the two of us began taking it out. We had a hard time. When we got it out she undid her red belt and tied it to one of the horns, and then we chased it towards our herd and turned it loose.

While I'd been walking around out in the salt-weed a man had come to our place. He was a Bitahni. My mother said, "A man came to our camp, your grandfather, Old Man Won't Do As He's Told. He took his horse to where he wants to hobble it." After we'd turned the wether into the herd we went back to camp, and he was back from where he'd hobbled his horse.

That evening when it got dark my mother said, "Let's kill that wether. It's good and fat." My grandfather got some cedar bark and softened it, that's what we used for a light, and all of us went out and rounded up the herd. We could tell that wether easily, because it was black, and it was running around in the herd. While Won't Do As He's Told held up the light my mother caught the wether, and we took it back to camp and killed it. It was sure fat. Old Man Won't Do As He's Told butchered it, and that's what we had that night, nice, fat meat for lunch.

The next day my mother said to my grandfather, "Put the meat up on a tree. When you go back you can take it all with you, my uncle." He took the meat and put it on a tree and gave my mother and father thanks. "Thank you very much for the meat. I'll have nice, fat meat with me when I get home. That's what I want and like to have, and now you've given it to me, and I've got some meat now."

He stayed with us all that day and night again. The next morning he went home, and we started moving again that morning also, following the canyon down towards the north.

As we were moving along close by the trail called Trail Going Towards Navaho Mountain a Paiute came driving some horses towards me. I was riding at the head of the sheep, holding them back, because we wanted them to go slowly, and my father and mother were way behind me. The Paiute let his horses go and rode right past me and started chasing back the sheep. He was waving at them, saying, Shah! Shah! Shah! The sheep were scared and stopped, and some of them turned back. About that time my father and mother caught up with me. Then the Paiute let the herd go and rode up to them and said, "What do you want to drive your sheep down in this canyon for? This isn't your place. This is all mine. So take your sheep back on the canyon, and stay upon the canyon with your sheep. I don't want any Navaho to come down in this canyon. I don't want any of them to live around here." I was going along slowly at the head of the sheep and could hear them talking to each other. They were both talking as loud as they could.

My father said, "Maybe you think that way. What do you think you are? You're just a Paiute, that's all. I'm not a bit scared of you. You think you scare me, but you can't scare me at all. All around here, all over around Navaho Mountain, belongs to me. It doesn't really belong to me, it belongs to all the Navaho; so you've got no business riding up to me like this. You didn't make this canyon. You didn't make all those rocks. You didn't plant all these trees, brushes, weeds and grasses. So you've got no business talking about this place. Somebody made this whole world, and it's put up for everybody, for all the animals and birds and other creatures, whoever wants to get on it. If he wants to stay he can stay anywhere he wants to."

As I went over a little hill with the sheep I could still hear him talking. I went quite a way with the herd before they caught up with me again. My mother said, "We had a quarrel with Nabahadzin. He didn't want us to stay in this canyon, so we quarreled and cussed each other." My father said, "This canyon has water quite a way below here. We'll camp by that water." From there on it was good grazing. Where the sun struck some of the grass and weeds were still green. We went down following the canyon, around I don't know how many points, and there was a spring, coming out of the rocks. That was plenty of water for the stocks, and there was lots of feed.

We stayed at that place three days, and those people caught up with us. The day after they arrived we all started moving again. They said, "Quite a way below here's another spring, and there's a little bigger space than this. We'll move down and live there for the winter." It was a long way, way down close to the San Juan. It was quite a space, but still it seemed small when the two herds scattered out over the canyon.

While we were living there we had a little snow. A few days later my father, His Horse Is Slow, said, "I want to go up on the canyon to look around and see if there's any feed." He rode his horse on top of the canyon and was gone all day until the sun was almost down. When he came back he said, "Up on the canyon the snow is about a foot deep, but there's plenty of feed, lots of grass for the horses and lots of different weeds for the stock. It's a big space, so we'd better move on the top, because it's a better place." Right away my father and mother said, "We'll do that." The next day we all started to move. We took our sheep and horses up first, and afterwards the other people took up theirs.

It was a big point between two canyons running north to the San Juan. It was a big space with lots of trees and plenty of wood on the east side and on the west. Between was sage-brush and different weeds and grass. There we stopped and camped and lived, right in this space. Ten days after we got on top we took the herd down in the canyon for salt-weed. We took the horses down also. After we brought our sheep back they began lambing. It was cold, about the middle of the winter, but the lambs were getting along fine. Giving Out Anger and his sister and another outfit of his had moved above us.

After many of the lambs had been born we took the herd in the canyon again for salt-weed. The mothers of the lambs went down all right, but the lambs wouldn't go, because the trail was too narrow there at the edge of the canyon where it started down. My mother said, "Stay there with the lambs, and I'll take down the sheep." She went on, and I stayed with the lambs, and they all lay down.

When the sun was low my mother called me, and I went down, and we started driving up the sheep. My father was in the canyon with the horses. When we were close to the top I went ahead to where the lambs had been, but they were gone. When all the sheep came up I said to my mother, "The lambs have gone." The sun was almost down. We'd figured on camping at the edge of the canyon. She said, "They may have gone back home. I'd better go after them." She left, and I was herding around waiting for my father. When he came up with the horses I said, "The lambs went back home, and my mother's gone after them." He began to track them. He hadn't gone very far from where I was, and there two of them were lying. The coyotes had been after them. It was like that all the way to our home. The coyotes had killed nearly all of them. Only about twenty got back. In places two, three and four of them were lying, some still alive and walking around, pretty well chewed up. "It's that way all the way to our home," my father said when he returned.

We started back, but it was a long way to where we lived, and we didn't get very far before it was dark. We took the sheep down in a little hollow, and there we stayed, walking around them all night. They were making so much noise, crying for their little ones. It seemed like a long night. By midnight I was so tired from walking around them, and weak and hungry. It was sure a long night. Early in the morning we went on. As soon as we started they wanted to run. My father got on his horse and tried to stop them; he got out his robe and waved it, but still they wanted to go. I couldn't do anything; I just walked behind them. When we got close to our camp he let them go, and they were running around there, looking for their little ones, making an awful noise.

I was walking way behind the herd. I tried to run, but I couldn't, I was too weak and so hungry and tired. I hadn't slept all night. Close to our home I was about to cry. My mother met me, and I said, "I'm weak, and I'm starving." She said, "You'd better hurry back. The food is cooked and ready to be eaten." I said, "I can't go any faster, I'm so weak." She grabbed me and shed a little tear and took hold of my arm and started back with me. Everything was ready, some meat was cooked and other food. My father was just beginning to eat. My mother said, "Only about twenty lambs came back. I got home when it was real dark and found only a few of them running around. I've been taking care of them all night. I didn't sleep either, for I thought if I let them go they'd run away, or the coyotes would get after them again."

We lived there for many days. Then we heard Giving Out Anger's outfit had been shaking their hands. They said they'd found out by hand-shaking that we'd have a bad winter. This winter it would start snowing early. The snow would be deep, over above the sagebrush. But we didn't believe them. They worked a few days making a trail and then moved down into the canyon on the east. We stayed on top with His Horse Is Slow.

The first snow that fell was only about six inches deep. Then we moved about four miles north, close to the point, where there was lots of wood, but His Horse Is Slow lived on at that same place. After we moved my father herded the sheep while my mother and I put up a small hogan. In a few days the clouds gathered from all over, and soon they were right close above us. It was that way all day, and that night it started snowing. In the morning when we got up it had snowed about a foot. It snowed all that day and all night, all the next day and all night again. In the morning it stopped. It had snowed from two and a half to three feet. It was over the sagebrush. The herd couldn't go very far, so it stayed around the hogan. Those people were right, but, I guess, it snowed that deep all over, even down in the canyon.

It stopped snowing early in the morning. As soon as it stopped the clouds broke up and moved away. By daylight it had all cleared off, and the sun was shining, and a warm breeze came up, and the snow began to melt. By afternoon the snow had almost turned to water, but when the sun was pretty well down it began to get cold. We thought the snow would be gone the next day, but that night it was cold, and the snow turned to ice. For two nights it was bitter cold, and the sheep were getting on top of one another and killing themselves that way. We tried to stop them but we couldn't, it was too cold for them. When we took one pile apart there'd be another. Soon we just gave up, we couldn't do anything with them, so we let them go. In those two nights a lot of them were killed, smothered, crushed and squeezed to death.

My mother was crying, but my father was quiet; he didn't say anything about it, only my mother was crying. Then he said, "Well, you mustn't cry. You mustn't cry for the sheep. You shouldn't cry for them. They belong to someone who made them. He gave them to us, and we've been using them for many years. Now who made the sheep wants his sheep back, so he's taken them. He took them away from us because we've had them and used them for many years. Perhaps he thought we were satisfied. So you stop crying and don't think about it, don't worry about it and don't be sorry. Even if we lost every one we'd soon get them all back again."

We hadn't put up a corral, and that day we took all the dead sheep and made a corral of them. They'd quit squeezing one another, but they were starving to death, because there wasn't any feed, only the sagebrush, that was all they ate, nothing besides. So they died of starvation. They kept on dying, we couldn't do anything. The ice was as hard as a rock and a foot thick. I tried to chop through it, but I couldn't. We couldn't do anything. We couldn't move to any other place, and so we just stayed there.

This happened the middle of December. Toward the end of January, all at once, it began to blow. It blew a breeze all day and night. By next afternoon the ice had melted away. Only in places where there was shade, as under the trees, under the rocks or sagebrush, there was still a little left. And so the ice melted away after we'd lost nearly all our sheep and goats. They were lying all around where we were living, about a half mile from our place. Anywhere you went you found dead sheep and goats lying close together. The horses were all right, for they'd been going around for grass in the wind-swept places against the hills where there wasn't any snow.

About that time His Horse Is Slow came to our place. He was so surprised. He said, "I'm sorry for you folks, that you've lost all your sheep. We lost some, but not many. We lost only a few head, because where we're living there's a thick wood, and in that wood it didn't snow deep. It only snowed on the trees, not on the ground. That's why we didn't lose very many. You should have stayed with us," he said. "I'm so sorry for you folks."

Then we moved to where we'd lived before, close to His Horse Is Slow. We stayed there at that place several days, and then they said, "We'll move down in the canyon again for salt-weed." We went down, and His Horse Is Slow came after us. We stopped and camped a little while and then started back up the canyon. We'd stay at one place for a few days and then start moving again. We kept doing that the whole month of February, all the way up the canyon, moving a little way and camping for two or three days.

We got to where the Paiute had met us, and where my grandfather, Old Man Won't Do As He's Told, visited us, and finally we got back to where we'd lived for a while, where the lake was. The lake didn't have much water in it, even though it had snowed deep that winter. It had just soaked into the ground, and so the lake was pretty well down. The grass was getting green. It was early in the spring, and I was happy about it. I was so eager to see the green grass.

There we lived for a little while. It was nice and warm. In a few days the grass was about three inches high, and there was enough feed for the horses and sheep. His Horse Is Slow came to our place and said, "I went to Water Under The Rocks where we buried our corn. At that place it's pretty dry.

It looks as though it didn't snow over there. But in Another Canyon and at The Middle Wash it's nice and green, everything is getting green. I think there's enough feed for all the stock. It looks better than around here, so we'd better be all moving to that place." Right away they wanted to go.

7. *His uncle advises him to get married . . .*
He is kicked by a horse and cured . . . They
move again from place to place in search of
grazing . . . No Neck tells them of the tall
grass at Cedar Standing near Lake Oraibi.

A FEW days after we'd moved back to above The Middle Wash, where some of our hogans were standing, a man and his wife came to visit us. His name was Walk Up In Anger. He was a Bitahni. His wife was the niece of Giving Out Anger. She was a Red Clay. We started shearing, and His Horse Is Slow and his wife came also and helped us shear for many days. I did nothing but herd. Then they stopped, they were through shearing the sheep that had good wool, and my father said, "Let the others go the way they are. Those poor ones haven't much wool, and their wool isn't any good." But Walk Up In Anger said, "I want to shear some of them yet."

I used to hold the heads of the sheep for this woman while she was shearing. While I was holding a sheep's head for her my uncle, Walk Up In Anger, said, "My nephew, you ought to get yourself a woman. You'd better get one, so you can have a good time with her. When you get yourself a woman she'll help us around too." His wife said, "If you want your nephew to get married why don't you get a woman for him?" "I'll get a woman for him," he said, "so he'll have a good time." She said, "Your nephew doesn't know anything about women. He doesn't know how to get at one, and he doesn't know how to work at one." Then he said to his wife,

"Well, you're staying with him right now close together, and you'll be the one to show him and teach him how to work at a woman. You'll show him everything. You'll show him how the thing has to be done." She said, "If I tried to teach him you wouldn't like it. You'd sure be mad." But he said, "Even if you start to teach him, even if I see you teaching him, I won't say anything, I won't do anything, because I don't care. All that I want is for my nephew to learn. That's all I care about. I want him to learn about women. So you can go right ahead and teach him how." They were talking to each other that way for a while, and my uncle said, "Now, my nephew, you can go ahead. You mustn't be bashful, and my wife will teach you how to get at a woman. She'll teach you everything." That's what he said, and I was afraid of her. I thought she'd sure get after me. I thought they really meant it, but he was only joshing. When they were through shearing they gave them some wool and a sheep too, and they went back to their home.

My father said to me, "I want you to stay at home while your mother and I take some wool to the store at Keams Canyon. You stay here with the sheep and take good care of them." He said to my mother, "Start packing the wool tomorrow morning. I'll go around the hogans to see if I can find a boy to stay with our son. There's one at Lost His Moccasins' place, and another at His Horse Is Slow's. He's herding sheep. If they haven't started shearing I'll bring him. If I can't get a boy here I'll go down below and get my grandson."

My mother started packing the wool the next morning, and my father got on his horse and rode to where Lost His Moccasins was living. There he got two boys. He took them to His Horse Is Slow's place and said to His Horse Is Slow's mother, "Come over to our place in the morning and stay with the boys and watch our place. While the two boys are herding you can stay at home with the little one." That morning, while my mother started packing the wool and my father rode off after the boys, I went out with the sheep. My mother made me some lunch, and I was herding all day. I had lunch at noon and came back in the evening. My mother had the wool packed and ready to be put on the horses. They'd borrowed some blankets from His Horse Is Slow and with our own there were four big blankets full of wool.

Early in the morning they woke me and told me to go and get the horses. They weren't very far from our place. I brought them back and put them in the corral, and there was my grandmother and the two boys. She was Old Man Hat's real younger sister. They used to call her Loud Voiced Woman. She was cooking some food. They'd killed a sheep and were boiling the meat for their lunch on the way to Keams Canyon. They sent the little boy out with the herd, and the rest of us led the horses out of the corral and put the saddles on them and started packing them with wool. We had it all packed and tied down solid before noon. Then they started off, leading a pack horse. They said, "We could take the short cut over the mountain, but it's too rough and too much climbing, so we'd better go the other way." They'd intended to leave the boys with me, but they took the largest one and left the little boy and my grandmother at home. When they left I went after the little boy and was herding with him all day. That evening when we came back with the herd the old woman, my grandmother, had everything cooked and ready. She had the insides washed and had some cooked for us. All we did was walk up to where she'd set it out.

The next day I took out the sheep and was herding all

day. The next morning the little boy went with me. We were herding in the little canyon when we saw a big herd coming towards us, two boys and a girl and quite a big bunch of sheep. The children were on foot and carrying packs on their backs. I met them and asked where they were going. They said, "We're going way up in this canyon with our herd. We'll stay up there a few days. That's what our mother told us to do." I said, "We have our horses up there in the canyon. Don't chase them around." The girl, who was older than the boys, said, "We're not going up for the horses. We're just going up with our herd for a few days." So I let them go.

When we got home that evening I told my grandmother about it. I said, "Three children were going up the canyon with their herd. They said they're going to stay a few days." Right away she got mad. She used to have a loud voice, and she said, "Whoa! They ought to know better than that. They know you have your horses up there, and they know it's the only place you take your herd. Their sheep will eat up all the grazing, and there'll be nothing left. Tomorrow you tell them to get out. Chase them back out of the canyon, because that's the only place you go with your herd, and the horses are up there too." I said, "I don't like to chase those children around. They said they'd be staying in the canyon just a few days." "Even at that," she said, "when you go up there to-morrow tell them to get out."

The next morning the little boy and I went out with the herd again. I picked up a braided rope that was made of wool and took it after the sheep. When we got in the canyon I said to the boy, "I'll go up and look at the horses. I'll get a couple, and we'll both ride a horse after the sheep." There were two horses just as tame as they could be. I got one and put the rope around his neck and tied it around his jaw.

Then I led him into a little arroyo and got on. I thought I'd chase the other one back to the boy, so we could both ride. I got a little way chasing that horse when, all at once, he kicked up and struck me right on the knee. As soon as he struck me I fell to the ground, and the horse I was riding walked away. I was crawling around, crying, and it was getting worse and worse every minute, hurting me so badly. Soon I couldn't move any more. I just lay there crying for a long time. After a while I crawled over to a stick that was lying close beside me and raised myself up. I had a hard time. The horse was walking around eating grass, and I went over where he was and led him into the arroyo again and got on him. It took me a long time. Then I started back to where the boy was herding. I said to him, "The horse kicked me. I can't walk, and it's hurting me so badly I've got to go back home."

When I got home and told my grandmother the horse had kicked me she got mad. That's the way she used to be, always getting mad over any little thing. "Why do you want to get after the horses? You know very well they'll kick, even though they're tame. There's nothing wrong with you. Get off that horse. I don't see that there's anything wrong with you. Get off the horse, I tell you." I said, "I can't move, grandmother, it hurts me so." She got up and said, "What's the matter with you? I don't see anything wrong with you." She came up to me and stood right by the horse and said, "Put your other leg over the horse towards me and put your arm around my shoulders." I put my leg over the horse and grabbed her about the neck, and as I got down off the horse I hit her again with that same knee. It sure hurt.

She let me down on the ground close to the hogan, and my leg got stiff, as it got cold, I guess. It hurt awfully. I couldn't stand on it. I began crawling to the hogan, and I was crying because it hurt me so. She was running around, talking to herself, I don't know what she was talking about, and there I was, suffering and sitting against the hogan. She gathered some wood and built a fire and put in some rocks, and then she went off up on the cliff. She was gone quite a while.

When she returned she had a great many different weeds. She said, "These are all medicine, different kinds of medicine." She dug a small hole, the rocks were good and hot, and she put them in and covered the hole with all these weeds. She chewed up some and spit that all around my knee. Then she said, "Put your leg over the hole, right on top of the weeds." I lay there, with my leg over the weeds, and she covered me with a blanket. Soon I felt the heat, and it was fine. After a while she said, "Lay your leg the other way." So I rolled over. Both sides of my leg were pretty well cooked. When it cooled down she took the blanket off me, and the pain was gone. But my leg was stiff, I couldn't move it, and it was swollen. It hurt a little bit, but there was no feeling to it. When I touched it it felt like nothing, as though it were dead.

I lay in bed all day. Every now and then she asked me, "How are you feeling?" and I'd reply, "I'm feeling all right." At times I never answered her. I hated her because she kept on talking to me. Then she'd get mad at me every once in a while. "I know you did it on purpose, because you don't want to herd. You don't want to do anything, you just want to lie in bed. That's why you let the horse kick you. I know you're glad to be doing nothing. I know you're glad to be lying in bed, and I bet that's not hurting at all." I was mad at her, but I couldn't say anything.

The next day I never said a word to her. I was mad because she'd spoken roughly to me. When she talked to me in the morning I just didn't answer her. After a while she began to speak to me in the kindest way. She said, "How are you, my little boy? I'm sorry you're suffering. I'd better do something more for you now." She built a fire and put in five rocks. The first time she put in three. Then she went out and brought in more weeds. "This time," she said, "I got some medicine to put on your knee. That's red-medicine." She had a bunch of it with roots and leaves. She pounded that up with a rock until it was just like adobe. Then she plastered my knee with it and bound it up with a rag. She dug another hole, a bigger one this time, and put in the five rocks and covered it with weeds. She said, "Lie on your belly." I laid my leg over the weeds, and she put something under my foot. It hurt as I lay there on my belly with my leg over the weeds, and I was crying. When the heat struck my knee it sure hurt. I couldn't stand it any longer. Still I just lay there, and all at once there was no feeling left. I quieted down then and lay for a long time. I began to like it. My leg felt fine as long as I held it over the hot rocks.

After a while she took off the cover, and I was all sweat. She took the rag off my knee and took away the medicine, and the swelling was gone. It was down, and the skin around my knee was all soaked up. She said, "Lie on your back this time." She poured some medicine down into the hole on to the hot rocks, and the steam felt fine. She covered my leg, and I lay there again for quite a while. When she took the covers off I rolled to my bed, and there she washed my knee with medicine, and after that she put some more all over it. This time she wrapped it up as tightly as she could. That felt fine too. She put a rag around it, and then there was no more feeling to it.

Late in the afternoon she asked me, "How are you feeling?" I said, "I don't feel any pain. It hurts a little, but the pain is gone." She said, "Try to stand on it. Try to walk on it." She handed me a stick—she'd made me a cane—and I stood up. I walked a little way towards the door and back to my bed, and it felt all right. It hurt a little, but the pain was gone. "Now, I think, I've cured you. You'll have to give me one of your big wethers for that," she said to me.

One afternoon the three children who'd taken their herd up in the canyon were going back home. They were passing close by our place, and my grandmother saw them. She got up and said, "I'll go and meet those children. Maybe they've got some of our sheep in with their herd." She went over and stopped them, and I was looking at her running around in the middle of the herd, looking, I suppose, for ear-marks. Then she went up to the children and was standing there with them. When she got home I said, "How many of our sheep were in with their bunch, grandmother?" "I don't know. I looked at all the ear-marks, but there weren't any like yours. They were carrying something on their backs. I thought they might have stolen one of our sheep and were carrying the meat with them, so I searched them, but it was their bedding and a little grub. That was all I could find. But I know very well they've stolen some of our sheep, and I'll bet you they did and have used it up already." She was running around, talking to herself about the sheep.

When my father and mother left they told me to take good care of the sheep and horses, but there I was, lying in bed all that time while they were gone. The little boy was herding alone every day, but even though he was small he was a good herder, he stayed with the herd all the time. Even so my grandmother was always worrying about him. She used to be that way, worrying about every little thing, and she used to talk all the time. Every once in a while she'd get up and stand around outside and look and watch to see if anything happened. She used to be on the lookout for anyone who went into the canyon. She was always looking towards the canyon. She was that way. She used to worry a great deal. Sometimes she worried about me, and sometimes she got mad at me. She'd say, "You're lying there for nothing. You ought to be herding. That poor boy is with the herd all alone. He must be hungry or thirsty or tired, and you, here, now, are staying in bed doing nothing." That's the way she used to talk to me, but I just let her talk on to herself. She was great on anything.

After I'd been lying in bed for six days I began to walk, but only around in the hogan. In eight days I walked outside. It still hurt me a little, but I walked with it, and in nine days it was all right, I could walk, but if I stopped walking it hurt.

By the ninth day my grandmother was pretty mad, because my father and mother and the boy had been gone that long. "They ought to have been back long ago," she said. "I know that place. I know just how far it is. It should take them two days to get there and the same coming back. They ought to have been back four or five days ago. They think I'm taking care of everything for them. They're away all this time just because I'm staying here." She began to worry about herself, about me and about the little boy who was herding, worried about her children at home, and about the boy who'd gone with my father and mother. She was worrying about everything. She said, "The poor boy must be lonesome by now. They ought to have been back with him a long time ago." She was talking to herself again a long time.

The next day they came back. They arrived at noon while the herd was home, and as soon as they'd taken their stuff off the horses and turned them loose, while they were still carrying the things inside, my grandmother said to the boys, "We'd better be going home now." I looked at her, and she was mad. She said to the boy, "You've been gone from your home a long time. You should have been back long ago. You ought to be herding at home. Your poor sister's been herding by herself all this while." She was running around, talking to the boys. She grabbed her robe and the little things she had, she grabbed them up and said, "Come, children, we'll go home now." "Wait a while," they said. They were talking to her outside for a while, and then she came in the hogan and began to talk about me. She wasn't looking angry then. She said, "He's been kicked by a horse. I treated him twice and cured him. He was suffering badly; he couldn't walk at all. I put some medicine on his knee and got him well. Now he's all right." My father said, "Well, that was fine. I'm pleased to hear that. I'm glad you cured my boy. And for the medicine you gave him—" he said, and reaching for the sack he got out the calico and gave it to her. "You can make a dress out of that, my younger sister. I'm very glad you put the medicine on my boy for me. That was nice of you, my sister," again he said to her.

My mother began to tell about their trip. "We got to Keams Canyon and sold our wool, and from there we went to my sister's place. We stayed a couple of days, and they loaned us horses, and we went to the Hopi village. We got some corn and cornmeal and other food from them. When we got back to my sister's place we stayed two days more and then started for home." That's what she said about their trips. She just made a quick story of it for my grandmother.

They'd brought back about fifty pounds of flour and about the same amount of cornmeal, and lots of coffee that was roasted, and some sugar and lots of calico and two robes. That was from the store. From the Hopi there was more cornmeal, some corn, different foods, dried peaches and salt. My father gave the boy some cloth, and my mother gave my grandmother some grub, flour, cornmeal of both kinds, coffee, sugar, dried peaches and some salt. She had quite a bundle, and she was giving thanks. She was as happy as she could be. Then she and the two boys went home.

After we ate my father said, "I'd like to see how my horses are getting along. Maybe they're fat now." He saddled a horse and drove the other three back into the canyon. About sundown he returned, riding another one. That one was looking fine. It was fat, and he was happy. "All the horses are looking fine. They're all fat now. I'm glad of that," he said. "His Horse Is Slow's horses are looking fine too." He was walking around his horse, looking at it, and he seemed happy. He said, "I'm very glad they're all looking fine. Now I can go somewhere on any of them." He turned the horse loose, and it went back in the canyon.

Then he said, "There isn't any feed from the top of Black Mountain all the way to Black Mountain Sitting Up. The winter before, they say, it didn't snow, and last summer it never did rain, and now, this last winter, it didn't snow either. So everything is dried up. There isn't a green thing sticking up all the way down to Black Mountain Sitting Up. Nothing at all but dust and dirt. From Black Mountain Sitting Up on towards the Hopi, and all around where we've been is plenty of feed. Everything is green over on that part. I don't know what we'll do about our stock. The only place it snowed was where we lived last winter, and from the foot of the mountain down into this flat there's quite a bit of grazing. But after they eat it up I don't know what to do."

We lived at that place a long time. Then we heard a number of people had moved down from Black Mountain, and some were still coming down. My mother said, "They'll soon be out here where we're living. And they'll be moving into the canyon too. We'll move closer to the mouth of the canyon, so that when they come here we won't let them in, because we can't let them use it. There's lots of grazing in the canyon, but it's just enough for our own stock. So if they move here we'll tell them to stay out." My father said, "Everyone thinks like us. We moved to many different places for grazing, and, now, all those people are that way; they're moving to different places to find grazing for their stocks. That's the way we were too. I don't like to turn anybody out of this canyon. I'm not Nabahadzin. I don't care to act like him. It's no use for us to turn the people down. Let them go wherever they want to."

Several days later some people moved into the canyon with a big herd of sheep. That was the woman who used to live out in the flat. Her name was Woman With No Teeth. She was of the Salt Clan. They located a little above us. Five days later another outfit moved in and located a little above the others. They had a big herd too. That was a fellow named Hairy Face. He was a Reed People. It wasn't long after these people moved into the canyon that there was no more grazing. So Woman With No Teeth moved out.

My father said, "I guess it's no use for us to live here any longer. The horses are looking pretty bad because they haven't any feed, and the sheep are just the same. In that canyon there's nothing. Even under the cliffs there's no grazing. So we'd better move to Hill Across. I think it rained some there. It looks like it's been raining a lot up there. It seems to me from here that it's always cloudy there. I know it rained, because lightning flashed around, and we could hear the thunder way out here. So we'd better move. Maybe we'll find some grazing for our stock, and I'm sure lots of water's there by now."

The sun was pretty well up when we started. We camped that night on the way, and the next morning we moved again and got to Water Up High by noon. There the horses and sheep had water. We stayed two days, and my father said, "I'd like to ride around to see where there's some grazing and water." He was gone all day. When he returned in the evening he said, "There's nothing. I've been to Thief Rock and around Many Coyotes and way down in the valley to Hill Across. The other side of Hill Across is the only place where I could find a little feed. The grass is just about an inch high. That's the only green spot." The next day we moved to that place. There were some trees coming out from the foot of the mountain, and a little lake, and a little grass just getting to be an inch high. We camped close by the lake. Every evening and morning my father and mother talked about the grazing, water and stock, about various locations and about moving. My father and I herded every day.

One day, as we were herding at the edge of the woods, a man came riding out in the flat on the trail going to the northeast and southwest. When he'd almost passed by he looked up and saw us, and so he turned his horse and started riding towards us. My father said, "Who's that fellow? Do you know him?" I said, "No, I don't know him." He rode up, and it was a fellow named No Neck. They called him No Neck because he had a big, round, short neck. He was an Along The Stream. His father's name was Little Wife Beater; he was a Reed People. My father recognized him and got up and shook hands with him, saying, "Where are you from? I haven't seen you for a long time, my cousin. I'm very glad to see you again." He said, "I'm from below Oraibi." "Where are you heading for?" my father asked him. "I'm going to my older brother's place. They say he lives

131

around here somewhere, and I'd like to visit my relatives who live here. That's where I'm going." My father said, "When did you start?" "Yesterday morning I started from my place." Then my father said to him, "Tell me how the places are towards your home. Tell me how the weather is and what the land is like, the grazing, the water, the feed for the stocks. Get down off your horse and tell me all about those things." As he got off his horse he said, "I've got nothing to tell." But when he sat down beside my father he said, "There's nothing from here on all the way down to Popping Rock Point. A little beyond there is good feed; that's where the feed begins. From there on this way there's nothing, but from there on over towards Cedar Standing, down in that flat, there's plenty of grazing and water. Lake Oraibi has lots of water, about a mile across. So there's plenty of water and large tracts of grazing too, and not much stock."

My father said, "Tell me just how much feed and how high the grass is, my baby." He pointed to a brush about two feet high. "The shortest grass," he said, "is about that tall, and the highest is about three feet. And it's mixed with all kinds of weeds. The weeds begin at about the same height as the grass and are up to five feet high. So there's not much feed to tell about." He was riding a nice, big, fat horse. My father said, "Is that right, my baby?" And he said, "Yes, that's all the feed there is." "That's a whole lot," said my father. "Around here, as you know now, there's nothing. It's that way all over. I can't find a place for my stock. I'm worrying about my sheep and horses. My horses are all getting poor, they're starving, and so are the sheep. I'm glad to hear you tell me all about it. And how is the corn and other food, melons and peaches?" "They're about getting ripe now at the Oraibi and Hopi places."

My father said, "Well, well, that's the place for me. I'm

going there. That's what I've been looking and listening for. Maybe you don't believe me, but I'm there right now." And he asked, "Are many people living there?" "Nobody's living in that whole valley, except one outfit. That's Smoker, who's living below Lake Oraibi. Old Man Black Of Many Horses used to live there, but he moved to Onion Spring." My father asked him about the trail. "There are two trails. One goes by Trail Up Blue Mesa and around Big Mountain Pointing Up; but that's way off. Another goes by Ruins and Many Cottonwoods straight to Scratch Out Water and Big Flat House, meeting the other at Big Mountain Pointing Up. I came over this straight cut. There's plenty of water not far apart all the way down to the valley. But in the valley you'll find water wherever you go."

My father was so anxious to know about the grazing, water and trails. He said, "Well, well, I'm very glad you told me all about those things, and I'm glad I had my herd here close to the trail. I think it was luck. If I'd turned my herd out the other way I wouldn't have found out anything about that place. I'm glad you didn't pass us. I'm glad you turned your horse around and came up to us. So I'll go now. I'm going right now to where you came from. I thank you very much. Thank you, my little one, my baby, for telling me all about the good things."

Then he asked for his older brother. My father said, "There isn't anybody around. I haven't seen him, so I don't know where he is. Do you know where he used to live?" The man said, "Well, he used to live at Many Coyotes." "Nobody's living there," said my father, "and I don't know where he's living now. Maybe he's way down in the valley, maybe he moved to Cheek. You can't find a fellow now at this time, because everybody's chasing around to different places." The man got on his horse and said, "I'll try and look for him. Maybe I'll find him somewhere."

We always brought the herd home in the evening, but this time we started back when the sun was still way up. As my father was walking towards the hogan, where my mother was sitting, he said, "I'm happy and pleased to know about the feed. I'm so anxious. I thought I was there right now at that place." My mother said, "What are you talking about? What's the matter with you?" She was looking at him, "You must be dreaming about those things." He sat down and said, "A fellow was riding on the trail out here at the edge of the woods. When he saw us he turned his horse and rode up to us. He said he's from way beyond Oraibi, and he said there's lots of feed around Lake Oraibi and Cedar Standing, lots of grazing that's there for nothing. There's no stock around. And he said that at the Oraibi and Hopi the corn and other stuff, peaches and stuff, were getting ripe. I'm thinking, 'I wish I were there right now.' So you get ready, start making lunch. We could move right now, but it's getting late."

The next day we started moving. We moved right along, and at noon on the third day we got to Big Flat House. They said, "This is the place called Big Flat House." I looked all around, but I couldn't see a house, and I never did find one. When it got cool we went on towards Big Mountain, on the trail going up the west side towards the east. We went over the mountain, and as we got out in the flat the sun was going down. A long distance off towards the south were the Oraibi. They said, "The Oraibi live way over there." We kept going along until after midnight, and then we stopped and camped.

Soon it was morning again. While it was still real dark my father woke me. "Wake up," he said. "We'd better be going now, because there's no water around here. So while it's still cool we'll go on. You get up and go ahead with the herd. After I get the horses we'll go after you. There's only one trail to Popping Rock Point, and that goes toward Oraibi. You just go ahead on this trail, and we'll catch up with you somewhere." So I started off with the sheep. It was still dark; I could just see the trail. I went a long way, and as I went over a hill, kind of round and flat, it was daylight. There a trail branched off, but I kept to the one that went straight ahead.

A long way from where the trail branched off they caught up with me, and it wasn't the trail I should have taken. I was way out in the valley. They said, "You should have taken the other trail, the one that passes by Popping Rock Point. If you'd taken that trail we'd be by the water right now. Instead we're out in the flat, and it's getting hot." But it was their own fault, because they'd been slow, and that's what they said to each other. They were blaming each other about the water, and my father said again, "You ought to have taken the trail that goes by Popping Rock Point. We'd be right at the water now." My mother said, "It's your fault. It's not his fault. He doesn't know about the trails. He's never been here. You should have told him a trail branched off at a certain place. If you'd told him that he'd have taken it." My father said, "Well, I guess we'd better just keep going. There's lots of green stuff around here, and lots of juices in it, so I don't think the sheep will get very thirsty." Even though it was getting hot there was a breeze, and it was fresh and cool. I was so eager to move to that place. All sorts of weeds and sunflowers were blooming that smelt so sweetly.

We were traveling through the valley all forenoon. A little after noon, as it got hot, we arrived at Cedar Standing. Long ago two cedar trees stood there, they said, but they were dead. The two stumps were standing upright by the water, but they still called it Cedar Standing. We were pleased that we'd moved to that place. We unpacked our horses, and my mother started cooking. The sheep and horses were lying around, they didn't know what to eat they had so much to feed upon. My father said, "We'll go and camp where those trees are. After we eat lunch, when it gets cool, we'll move to that place. That'll be a good place to live." Two children were bringing a herd up from the west to water. After lunch my father put the saddle on a horse and said, "I'll ride around and look for a place. If I find a good place under those trees we'll move there."

When he returned he said, "That's a good place up on that hill where the trees are. You can see all around. From there I rode to where the two little children went with the herd, I got to their place, and that was Little Wife Beater." "Oh, yes," my mother said, "I know him. He's my older brother." My father said, "They were so thankful when I got to their place. They said, 'We're living here alone and are so lonesome for our relatives. But now you've moved here. That was nice of you. We're so thankful.'" When it got cool we left the sheep and horses in the valley and moved up on the hill and camped under the trees.

8. *The way of a man and a maid ... Horse racing and wrestling ... The last quarrel ... He beats the Oraibi at running ... How they find out you've been with a woman, and what to do about it.*

EVERYTHING was ripe, peaches, corn, watermelons and other crops were all ripe at the village of the Oraibi. Two days after we camped my mother and father wanted to go to that place. They killed two goats, butchered and cut them up, and took over the meat and skins. They were gone all day and stayed one night. The next day they returned with two big sacks full of peaches, and some corn and a few watermelons. They said, "The pueblo people whom we visited were kind. They want us to visit them every once in a while. They'd like us to come again soon."

The day after they returned Lost His Moccasins and his children arrived at Cedar Standing. They found out that we'd moved to that place. A few days later another outfit moved there. That was Mexican Blanket; his clan was Red Clay. His wife was Bitahni; her name was Dlosh Woman. They camped against a hill across from us. We stayed there at that one place all the rest of the summer and all fall. By that time the horses and sheep were looking fine. I went out with the herd every day. I'd start out with my sheep in the morning and go to where the horses were. I'd catch a horse and then round up the others and start them towards the water. From there I'd herd on horseback.

Little Wife Beater had four grandchildren, three girls and

a boy. One day I saw the girls herding sheep. They came up to me, and we began to herd together. From there on, every time I went out with the sheep, they'd be coming after me. Soon we became acquainted, and after a while they wanted to ride with me, and so we began to ride one horse. All three would sit on the horse behind me, first the oldest girl and then the next, and the youngest sat behind us three. Once I let the horse trot a little, and he shied. We were holding one another around the waist, and as the horse shied we all fell off. Only one of the girls got hurt, and she cried. That's what we did every day. I always got the horse and rode bareback, and they always came after me with their sheep. As soon as they came up to me they wanted to ride, and so they'd sit behind me.

Each had on just one dress, and their dresses were short. When they'd get on the horse behind me their dresses would be above their hips, and their white legs would be hanging down. They didn't care. I used to turn around and touch their legs. That's where I began to think of doing something to them. But I didn't know about women, and I didn't know what to say. I only thought and wondered if they had teeth as my mother had told me. But I found out by touching them there were no teeth. Whenever I touched them they didn't do anything; they liked being touched.

This was in the summertime, and all summer I'd been herding with these girls. We had lots of fun. In the fall their mother and father and everybody went to trade with the Oraibi, and my father and mother went also. The girls were alone, and I was all alone too. I started out early in the morning with my herd, and as I went out in the flat I saw them coming with their sheep. As soon as they caught up with me they ran up and got behind me. I began to touch the older girl, and wherever I touched her she didn't mind it;

she enjoyed being touched. But I just didn't know what to do and what to say. Then we all got off the horse and began to play, building a rock house. We wanted to make a house like those of the Oraibi.

While we were doing that their sheep had wandered far away, and the oldest girl wanted her two sisters to go after them. I let them have my horse, and she said, "Get on this horse and ride over there after the sheep and bring them back." So they got on the horse and went after the sheep. While they were away we two began to play, and soon we were touching each other. She didn't care about anything. But I didn't know what to do, nor how to do it. I was wondering how it could be done. I thought about the sheep, "I'll do as the sheep do," I thought. But I changed my mind, "Maybe it's a different way," and I thought she might know something about it. I said, "I'm wishing for something, but I don't know how to do it. How do they do, a man and a woman, when they're wanting to marry each other?" She said, "I don't know how to do it either. I've never been with a man before." After a while she said, "I saw a man and woman doing that. They were on top of each other. That must be the way they do. The woman was lying under the man, and he was lying on top of her. That's what I saw once. I told my mother, and she said, 'That's the way a man works on a woman.' So it must be that way. Let's try it."

Then I made up my mind I'd try it. She lay over and pulled up her dress and said, "Take off your pants." I took my pants off, and she spread her legs, and I got on. As soon as I stuck it into her she started moving with me and kind of crying, but still she was holding me to her. She said, "Do it easily, because it hurts." I worked on her easily, and soon I got it in a little further, and all at once I stuck it all the way in, and suddenly something happened. But I didn't notice anything. I was like in a faint. I was paralyzed. She must have felt the same. She lay there, shivering all over, not moving, her arms and legs dropped down. I wondered what had happened. It felt as if somebody had poured real cold water on you. I was afraid to move for a long time. When I got my senses back I got up and put on my pants, and she rolled over and lay there a while and then got up and put down her dress. We didn't say anything to each other; we were both bashful.

About then the two girls were returning with the sheep. I said, "Let's go and meet them." We met them about halfway, and they gave me back my horse. She went over to her sisters, and they started off with their herd, and I got on my horse and started home. I was wondering what she'd done to me. I was weak and kind of sorry for myself, and I was scared, thinking of all I'd done. I was worrying and sorry about it, sorry for what I'd done to her and wondering if she'd tell on me. I wondered if, when her folks came home, they'd find out about it. I thought, "Maybe they'll track us." When I thought of that I got all shivery. I went out the next day with the sheep, but they didn't show up. From there on they didn't come near me any more. I only saw them herding from far off.

Sometime in the fall a man named Bad Eyes brought over two racehorses. He wanted to exercise them. A Night Chant was going on, and he wanted his horses to race over there at the dance. My father had a racehorse too, and so we started to race them every evening. On the third to the last day of the dance another man came. This man's name was In The Rocks; his clan was Many Goats. He said, "I'm going to the dance. I always race with a man named Gamaha, so I'm taking this horse over to have a race with him." My father said, "We're planning to go and take the horses over too."

The next morning five of us started from our home. We got there about noon. As soon as we led up our horses they called for In The Rock's horse, and he and the man named Gamaha got their horses out on the track, and they started betting, some with money, some with silver buttons, bracelets, robes, double and single saddle-blankets, buckskins and all the other things they bet each other with. When they were through the horses started off. It was quite a distance, and when they went over the line In The Rock's horse got beat.

Then they called for my father's horse, and His Horse Is Fat got his out too. His clan was Mexican People. When the horses were on the track they started betting again. This time everybody bet more. When they were through I went out and began taking off my clothes. I was going to ride this horse. But everybody said, "That boy hasn't ridden a horse yet on the track. We've never seen him before riding a racehorse." They didn't want me to ride my father's horse. They got a boy, they said, "This boy rides racehorses a lot, and he knows about it." So I put my clothes back on, and the boy got on the horse. They started off, coming right along and went over the line together. My father's horse was ahead, the head of it was sticking out a little, but they said, "We don't count by the head. By the step, that's what we count by." The tracks were about the same on the line, and so they started arguing about it. They were talking about it for a long time, and then they just returned the things to one another, and nobody won.

After that they called for a man named Big Red Clay and another man, but I didn't know his name. They were both tall and big around, about the same size, height and weight. They had all their clothes off, not even moccasins on, nothing, just a G-string. When they stepped out they both looked just alike. That was for wrestling. They began betting one another again, and when everyone was through they made a big circle. They said, "We want plenty of room for them." There was a big crowd all around, some sitting, some kneeling, some standing, some on horseback. When everybody was ready the two men got up and went toward each other. At that time they didn't shake hands. They came up and held each other and started wrestling. It wasn't long before Big Red Clay had thrown the man flat on the ground. He just gave one swing and got him on the ground as hard as he could throw. When he let go the man lay there a while. He must have been hurt.

About then the sun was almost down, and everybody went back to the dance. In the evening they started dancing, one right after another, and pretty soon I fell asleep. Early in the morning my father woke me. "Let's go," he said. "We'll go home now." We went to where we'd tied our horses and started home while the dance was still going on. We were back before the sun was up. As soon as we got back we turned the horses loose and went to sleep. When the sun was way up my mother woke us, and after we ate I went out with the sheep.

A long while after that my real mother came from Keams Canyon. She said, "I heard you'd moved here, and I said I'd like to go over to see you people, because you'd moved up here close to us. That's why I started off, and now I'm here, and I'm very glad to see you." She stayed with us five days. Then she said, "I just wanted to come over and visit you. I know now my son is growing up. He'll be married soon. Soon, I know, I'll have a daughter-in-law." I didn't tell her she had a daughter-in-law already. She said, "When I get one I'll be here again." That's all she said while I was home, but I guess they'd been telling things to each other while I was out herding.

I was herding all the time. I didn't have to look for grazing, it began right at our door. One time I went with the herd to the water at Cedar Standing, and there was the man named No Neck and a boy. We three got together at the water. Pretty soon we two boys started wrestling, and No Neck threw us in the water with our clothes on. Then we both got after him and dragged him in the water too. We were covered with mud. After that we washed our clothes and spread them out to dry.

Quite a few days later we moved down into the valley to Lake Oraibi. It was late in the fall. Several days after we'd moved the other two outfits, Mexican Blanket and Lost His Moccasins, moved back. Then another outfit came to that place. That was Grey Hairs' Children. They had many small boys and girls, all younger than I was.

One evening, after I'd returned with the herd, I said to my father and mother, "I'd like to go over where that new outfit is camped. There are a lot of children there; I'd like to go over tonight and play with them." They said, "You're too big to play with those children." But I said, "I'd like to go anyway." Then they said, "If you want to go, go ahead." So that evening I went to their place. It was about a mile and a half to where they'd camped. Little Wife Beater lived between us, about a half mile from our place.

I got there, and we started playing the moccasin game. While we were playing two women arrived. They were from Little Wife Beater's place. They said to me, "We came over to tell you the old folks got into a quarrel. They fought, and the old woman is lying there crying. It looks like she's been hurt badly, and the old man's gone away." Right away I went back, and the two women came after me. When I got home my mother was lying there; it sounded as though she had quite a pain. The old man had gone away. "What's the matter with you?" I asked her. She said, "I don't know. It's your father. I don't know what he's done to me. I fought with your father, and he's left and gone away. So I don't know what he's done to me, and I don't know where he's gone to." I went out, and on the other side of the sheep I saw a light. He'd made a fire and was lying there. The two women went over to him. When they came back they said, "The old man wants his herd separated for him. He said he wants to leave."

In the morning he went after the horses, and we started to separate his sheep. He had quite a bunch. My mother said to the women, "Take one, take the biggest wether and kill it. He won't notice it." So they did, they caught one and took it away and killed it. Just about when we'd separated all his sheep he returned with the horses, and that morning he got out all his stuff and packed it and started off with his sheep and horses. My mother didn't say anything. She just lay there in bed. After he left the women brought the wether over to the hogan and butchered it, and I went out with my herd. I was herding that day out in the valley. Every once in a while I looked around for my father. As I was looking towards the hogan I saw a man riding across the valley towards my home. His horse was standing at our place all afternoon until the sun was pretty well down, and then he went away.

I came back in the evening, and there was only one side of the ribs and a hind quarter hanging in the hogan. The rest of the meat those women had taken home. I asked my mother, "Who's that man who came here on horseback?" She said, "That was my older brother." She meant Smooth Man's Son. His clan was Walk Around You. His father and my mother's father had been brothers. Their clan was Salt. She said, "He came and scolded me about your father. He said he met your father and asked him where he was going. He said your father said, 'I'm going home. I've left the old woman.' So that's why he came, and he gave me a good scolding. He asked me 'Are you having a good time now by yourself? Do you think from here on you'll have a good life? And do you think from here on you'll have everything you didn't have before? I know you're acting now as if you're suffering from a very bad pain, but I know you're just making believe. I know you haven't got a bit of pain. Maybe you have a little, but that's nothing, because everything is all your own fault. It's not the old man's fault, and I'm not blaming the old man. I'm sorry for him. I'm sorry for him for your sake. You may not be sorry for him, but I am, because soon you won't be like you were before.' This is the way my brother spoke to me, and a lot of other things besides. What do you think about it?" I said, "I'm thinking about my father. I've been thinking about him and looking for him all day, and I'm sorry for him, because there's no one around here I can call my father." She didn't say anything for a while. Then she said, "Well, you go after your father tomorrow and bring him back." The two women had brought some medicine for my mother, and she said, "I got some medicine from Little Wife Beater's wife."

The next morning I went out with the herd and came back a little after noon. On the way I caught a horse. When I got home I ate some lunch, and then I went after my father. I got to my mother's brother's place and asked about the old man. He said, "He went out with his sheep this morning." Then I tracked him all around back to the water at Cedar Standing. From there he went over a hill. Back of that hill he was camping with his sheep. The sun was down, and he was just making a fire.

I got off my horse and walked up to him just about the

time he had the fire going. He sat back and told me to come over. I walked up and sat right by him, and he put his arm around me, and I put an arm around him. "Where do you think you're going, my baby?" he said to me. I said, "I've come for you." "What do you think? Are you sorry for me, my baby?" I said, "Yes, I'm sorry for you." When I said this I almost cried. He said, "I'm the same, I'm sorry for you, my baby, because I didn't say anything to you, I didn't say to you, 'I'm leaving here.' I was going along with my sheep when that man came up to me and asked, 'Where are you going?' I said, 'I got into a quarrel with my wife, and I left her. But I don't know where I'm going.' He said, 'I don't like to let you go. Stay around here first, and I'll go over and talk to her for you. I mean it, I don't want to let you go. No, no, no, indeed, I don't want to let you go. I'm going over to her right now, and I'll tell her something that she'll take too.' That's what he said to me, so that's why I'm still around here."

He asked me, "How's your mother?" I said, "I don't know. She seems to have a pain somewhere." He said, "She's just making believe. I didn't do anything to her. I didn't hit her, or anything. When she started to come after me I just gave her a push away from me, and she made believe she fell. That's all. She's just making believe she's got an awful pain. Don't believe her, because that little push didn't do anything to her." I said, "She wanted me to come after you. She said she wants you to come back." "Well, my baby," he said, "you go back to her, because she's all alone now, and to-morrow you meet me with the herd somewhere out in the valley. I'll be back in two days. So tomorrow be sure and come and meet me some place in the valley with the sheep."

Then I started back. It was evening. Just as I was going to get on my horse he said, "Wait a while." He came up to me and said, "I took the sheep to the water today, but they didn't take much, so tomorrow I'll take them again." He pointed over a hill and said, "There's some water back of that hill. It's quite a way from here. I'll take the sheep over there tomorrow, and I guess I'll be gone all day. So don't start off with the sheep this way tomorrow. You can come the next day and meet me in the valley, but not tomorrow." Then I started back and got home that night. I told my mother what my father had said, and I asked her, "How are you feeling now, my mother?" She said, "I'm feeling all right, just a little pain still, since I took some medicine. That got me well." But I didn't believe her. I thought she was just saying that.

The next day I was out with the herd all day. In the evening after we'd eaten supper my father came. He walked right in and sat by me, a little way from my mother. My mother was lying against a great big pillow and started to groan, making believe she had an awful pain. "What did you come back for?" she said. "I thought you'd left for good." My father said, "I thought you wanted me back. And that groaning, you're just making it, making believe you've got an awful pain." She said, "Yes, you killed me. But now you can kill me right now. Kill me instantly. Then you can go wherever you want to go and wherever you wish to. So kill me right now. From there on you'll enjoy life." My father said, "I'm not killing the people, and I never did anything to you." Again she said, "Kill me, I tell you." He said, "I thought you'd put everything away out of your mind, but I see you're still thinking the same." She said again, "I told you to kill me. After you kill me you can get someone else and live well from there on." Then my father said, "If you're still thinking the same then it's no use for me to stay." When he said this he got up and started to walk out. He'd taken just one step when she grabbed him and held him. She said, "I told you to kill me first, then you can go. I won't let you go unless you kill me." My father didn't say anything; he just stepped back and sat down.

She was talking to him for a long time, begging him not to leave, not to go away, but he didn't say anything. At last he said all right, and they apologized and made up again. They both put the trouble away and said, "We'll forget about it now, and from here on we'll be the same as ever." They talked a long time. My father started talking, saying lots of things to my mother about himself, about me and about everything. When they made up I cooked some meat and gave it to him along with other food. After he ate he left and went back to his sheep. He said to me, "Take the sheep out tomorrow morning, and we'll meet out in the valley."

In the morning I took the herd way up in the valley, and there he was, coming along with his sheep. We put them together, and I had a big herd once more. He said, "Start back and herd toward home. I'll go and get my stuff. I left all my things where I camped. From there I'll take the horses to water, and I'll be back some time this evening." I started the herd towards home and got back just as the sun went down. He'd come back already. His horses were out in the valley, and he was there at home.

I was herding the next day, and when I came back in the evening a horse was hobbled out in the valley. I didn't recognize it, and inside the hogan a man was sitting by my mother. He had his medicine-outfit with him. He was a singer named Red Hair. My father had gone after him that day and brought him back. He sang over my mother three days and three nights; by that time she was good and well. Then the man went home. From there on they were good to each other. They didn't have another quarrel. But before that they used to get mad every once in a while.

One day, as I was herding out in the valley, I met the girl again. She was with the sheep by herself. Just as we were getting together I saw a fellow coming on horseback. "Who's that?" I asked her. She looked and said, "It's my father." We separated right there. When he left I went over again and asked her, "Who was it?" "Sure enough," she said, "that was my father." "What did he say to you?" "He's going after the horses." "Did he see us here together?" "No," she said, "he never said anything about it. I don't think he saw us." I'd been wishing for her all the time, and she must have felt the same. I said, "I want to do just the same thing again we did at first." Right away she said, "All right." This time we knew what to do, we didn't wait for anything, and it gave me life, and I felt good.

When we were through I said to the girl, "You shouldn't tell about this." She said, "It's up to you. Maybe you'll tell somebody about it." And she asked me, "Did you tell on me?" I said, "No, I never said anything, and they never said anything to me." She said, "I'm the same. But every once in a while they ask me if I've been doing something with you, because they know we always herd together. But I say, 'No, I don't know what you're talking about. I don't know what you mean.' So from here on you mustn't tell on me," she said. I said, "No, I won't tell anyone. But it's you, maybe you'll tell. I know you will, because you said they've been asking you about it. If they keep on asking you you'll tell on me." "No," she said, "I won't. Even if they ask me I won't say anything."

That was the last time we did anything, and that was the last time I saw her. Five days later they moved away towards the north, and I never saw her again. I sure did miss her. Every day and night I thought of her and wished she were with me always. But we were far away, and there was no way for me to go and see her.

Two years later I heard she was married. After they held the wedding the boy who married her found out she wasn't a virgin, so he went back to his home and told his father and mother. His father went to where the girl lived and took back all the horses she'd got in marriage. They began asking her who the one was she'd been with, but she wouldn't tell. They tried and tried, asking her for a long time, but she never told anything at all.

In the fall, after those people left, we moved to the foot of Black Mountain Sitting Up. We came to a hogan and stopped and lived there. Near by lived a man named Grey Streak Going Up. His clan was Red House. He came to our place and was glad we'd moved there close to him. A few days later he came again. My father said, "I'd like to go to the pueblo people, because we haven't much grub." The man said, "Is there anyone who wants to go to that place? If there is I'd like to go along. I've been wanting to go for a long time. I think I'll go with you. I want to go anyhow. I'd like to get some food for myself." My father said, "All right, we'll go then, my younger brother. Tomorrow we'll get ready. We'll kill some goats and have them ready for the day after. You get ready, too, tomorrow. Have your horses ready and everything. We'll go in two days." The next day we killed four goats and butchered them. My mother and I worked on the meat while my father was herding all day. When he got home in the evening he changed his mind. He said, "I want you to go with that man tomorrow." I said, "All right."

The next morning he came, and we started off. He knew the way, and I just followed him. When we got there we stopped our horses before a house, and he pointed to two places. "Every time I come here," he said, "I go to those two places, besides this one here. I wonder where we'll stop?" I said, "It's up to you." Just about then a man came down from the second story and said, "Unload your horses." We got off the horses and unloaded our stuff, and they carried our things inside. While we were standing around two women came up to us. They had their sleeves rolled way up to their elbows. They said, "Come inside." They'd been cooking, and as soon as we came in they gave us some food. When we started eating two boys went out. "Those two boys are going to take your horses down where there's feed for them," they said.

After we ate we sat there inside the house. They were hollering and screaming outside, so I went out to see what was going on, and they were having a foot race. I went downstairs and over to the bunch, and they told me to run a race. This boy was smaller than I was, and I beat him. They told me to race another one, so I ran with another and beat him. As soon as we went over the line they told me to run again. This time I almost got beat. They wanted me to race another boy, but I said, "I don't want to run any more, I'm tired." So they wanted to wrestle with me. I said, "I don't want to." They wanted to wrestle, but I kept saying no. A lot of them were coming after me. Pretty soon one jumped on me. I just gave one swing and threw him on the ground. Then another jumped on me, and I threw him. By that time they were mad. A man, a kind of an old fellow, wanted to wrestle me, but I said, "No, I don't want to. You're older than I am, and you're too big for me." He was coming after me, trying to grab me, but I dodged away and pushed him off. Then I left them and went back to my partner. He'd gone out, so I stayed around waiting for him. He came back when it got dark, and we stayed there overnight.

In the morning I went with one of the boys to where they'd taken the horses. When we got back my partner was trading with the people. He got me a lot of corn, beans, dried peaches and other foods, and the same for himself. Then we took our stuff and put it on the horses and started off down to the trail that runs along the slope. On that hill were a lot of great big rocks. I asked him, "What are those rocks standing up for?" He said, "They're traps. They kill coyotes with them. There's a catch under the rocks and when the coyote gets underneath, as soon as he moves that thing, the whole rock will fall on him." So they were rocks for killing coyotes, and I'd thought the boys played with them. We came down off the hill and went along, riding all day, and in the evening we got home. They cooked us some food, and we started eating, and they were eating the stuff we'd brought. The man stayed at our place overnight and went home the next morning.

Then, after many days, they said, "We'll move to where there's more feed, more grazing for the sheep." Down in the valley stood another hogan, and we moved into that. We cleaned it out and put a little dirt on top and lived there. A corral was up already, but it was small, and we made it larger. Just about that time the sheep and goats all started lambing. We had many kids and lambs at that place. Some of them had twins. My father said, "Kill one of the twins, so they won't starve to death." My mother said, "Don't kill them," but he said, "If they're twins they'll be starving. If it's only one then it won't starve." So I killed one and left the other with its mother.

We lived at that place, tending to our sheep and horses, all the rest of the winter. While we were still living there the snow was gone and spring had come, and everything was getting green. They said, "We'll move again. There's lots of green stuff up against the hills where the sun strikes, and it's warmer." We moved from the valley towards the hills to a place called Green At The Foot Of The Rocks.

That spring I noticed my voice was changing. One day when it was windy I tried to scream and holler at the sheep, but my voice was gone; it was changed and low. I was wondering what caused it. I didn't have a cold. Only a cold does that, but I never had one. When I started singing it was just the same, and it was the same when I talked. One day my mother said, "Say, what have you done with your voice? Your voice is changed. What have you been doing? You must have done something, we never hear you holler at the sheep any more, and you don't talk much at all. We know what you've been doing," she said. "You've been going around with a woman, haven't you?" But I never said anything. "I know some woman has put you on top of her. Your father and I both know who the woman is. It's Slim Man's wife." I always called that woman my older sister, and they claimed I'd been with her. But that wasn't the one. They tried to make me tell, but I never did. My mother was talking about it for a long time, wanting to find out, but I never told her.

I was that way for a long time. I could hardly talk. One day my father, Choclays Kinsman, came to our place. He said to me, "Go and build a big fire on the rocks." I did what he told me to do and then went over with him in the sweathouse. There he asked me about my voice. "What's the matter with your voice? It sounds kind of funny to me. You must have f—ed it away. I know you've done that, haven't you?" he asked me. I said, "I don't know. I don't know what's wrong with my voice." He said, "You'd better get into the sweat-house every once in a while. And you'd better get up early in the morning and run a race. While you're running you must holler and scream. By doing that you'll get your voice back."

9. *They trade their wool for cattle . . . The adultery of Quiver's Wife and Giving Out Anger and the trouble that followed . . . His father goes out in the snow to pray for the horses, and is so delighted in spring to see them again.*

WHILE we were living at Green At The Foot Of The Rocks a man came to our place. He was the son of Old Man Thankful. He said, "I've been to Many Streams Flowing All Around, and I heard the Mormons who live around there are going to sell some cattle. They want a lot of wool for them. They said they'd have lots of cattle there this spring, and the Indians should take their wool to that place if they want some. They said they'd trade the cattle for wool."

My father said to us, "We'll move, my children. Even though it's a long way we'll take all our sheep and horses to that place and get some cattle. It's getting warmer every day now, and the grass and other things are getting green. In places there may be lots of feed for the sheep and horses. We'll take our time, and when we get there we'll start shearing. By that time it'll be good and warm. If we shear here it'll be hard carrying the wool to that place back and forth. It won't be very much work if we move and shear our sheep over there. We'll do that, my children." I don't remember what time of day we started, whether it was in the afternoon or in the morning, but, anyway, we traveled along with our herd and horses, and in three days we got to

Covered Water. It's a long way, between sixty and seventy miles, yet it only took us three days to get there.

Some Paiutes and Navaho were living there, and my father went among the Paiutes and asked them to help us shear. He told them each one would get two head of sheep for helping us. Eleven Paiutes and one Navaho started shearing. This Navaho was a nephew of my father's. His name was Black Streak. He was the only one who had shears; the others had only knives, and that was my first sight of a pair of shears. I stood beside the man, and it was interesting to me and made me surprised the way the blades worked.

After they were through my father took some wool to where they were trading off the cattle and got a yearling. While he was chasing it home he met a fellow on horseback. He said to him, "Go to my place and tell my wife I'm driving home a calf." The fellow came to our place and said to my mother, "The old man's on his way chasing a cow." It was towards evening. So she got on a horse and went to meet him. I waited a long time, but they didn't show up, and so I went to bed. During the night they got home and put the cow in the canyon. In the morning my mother woke me up and said, "Wake up, my boy, you've got one head of cattle in the canyon. Get up and dress yourself and go over and see if it's still there."

Two days later my father went to that place again. This time he took two Paiute boys along to help him. They stayed there overnight, and the next day he started trading and got three head of cattle for his wool. Some of his relatives were there buying cattle too, and so he let the Paiute boys go home with the pack horses, and he came back with his relatives. When they got to our place they stayed overnight, and in the morning my father separated his three head from the bunch and put them in the canyon with the other. At first we thought these three were bulls, but we found out after a while they were all steers. The next day he went again with more wool, but this time he went by himself. At the end of two days he came home with one more. This was a female. She was real tame.

In about ten days, when we thought the cattle were rested, we started moving back to the place called Another Canyon. Every time we stopped and camped the tame cow would go among the pails and dishes, bothering us all night, throwing buckets around, looking for water. When we camped we put up a little shade for our home, and she would come inside and walk around and toss the things about. We'd chase her away, but as soon as we turned our backs she'd be after us again. One of us had to be awake and watching her all night, otherwise she might come in and step on us.

This cow had been given to my mother, and I got the first one we bought. My mother and I had females, and my father had three steers. Somehow he got to thinking about the cattle, and, I don't know how, he got to thinking that he had only steers and we had the two females. One day he said to us that we both had females and his were all steers, and he couldn't get any little ones out of those. So he begged us, saying he wanted one of the females back. He said, "You can have one of the steers, anyone you like. In that way later on we'll all have cattle. You'll have some, and I'll have some too. If we do that we'll be fixed right." So we gave him back one of the females, and we got one of his steers. He asked my mother, "Which one of the females will be mine? And which one of the steers will be yours?" She said, "You can have the tame one, and I'll take the steer without the horns." But somehow I thought she meant the tame one and the steer without horns belonged to us. I liked this steer, because he hadn't any horns.

I didn't find out until fall that the tame one belonged to my father. One day I was out herding and found a bull on top of her. I was so glad to see the bull on my cow. As soon as I got home I said to my mother, "The bull was on our tame cow." She said, "Oh, that isn't ours, that belongs to your father." I almost dropped over. She said, "The other female, the one we got the first time, is ours." I began to think about it, and it made me sorry, thinking she'd soon have a calf, and we wouldn't get any, because the bull wasn't bothering ours. But I kept it to myself; I didn't say anything about it.

In Another Cayon, where we located, the grass was green, and there was plenty of feed. Lots of cattle were in the canyon that different Navaho had bought. Some had one head, some two, up to fifteen. Giving Out Anger was the only one who had fifteen. The others had only a few apiece. They had them all in the canyon together, and we put ours in there too. That's where the bull was. They made so much noise. When I went there with my herd I used to be afraid. I never went near them. But after a while I found out all the cattle in the canyon were tame; they wouldn't do anything to me.

One day, while I was herding in the canyon with my sheep, I saw a little spotted calf walking in my herd. I thought to myself, "I wonder what that is?" It was so cute. I went over and caught it and put my arms around its neck and thought, "What a pretty thing it is." It was real young. As soon as I grabbed him he hollered, and all at once I heard a noise, and there was the mother coming out of the brush, right close by and running at me. As soon as I saw her I let the calf go and started running. Not very far off was a stone wall and I ran for that wall as hard as I could go. I ran a little way and looked back, and there was the calf, and the mother right behind her little one. I started running faster, but the calf kept right behind me, and the mother too, coming closer all the time. I was hollering and screaming and running as hard as I could, but when I got to the wall it was too high for me to climb, so I just fell over behind a rock. I couldn't go any further. I was out of wind, and my heart was beating. After a while I stuck up my head, and there was the calf and its mother right close by me. I just lay there quietly; I didn't dare move. I was all shivery. I thought, "If I get up, when she sees me, she'll sure get after me."

After a while I stuck my head out again, and the cow and the calf had gone. A little way off was a lot of brush, and they were just going into that. When they went into the brush I couldn't see them anymore. Then I got out from behind the rock and started for my sheep. While I was going along I looked in every direction, thinking the cow might be laying for me somewhere. I went around behind bushes and stopped and looked, and when there was no sign of anything I'd run for another. I kept that up all the way to my herd. I was so scared I was all sweat, and my clothing was soaked.

At last I got to my sheep and drove them as quickly as I could out of the canyon. While I was driving the herd I looked around in all directions to see if the cow was after me. After I got out of the canyon I knew I was safe. From there I took my time. When I got home I told my mother about it. I said, "I found a little calf in my bunch of sheep, and I went over and caught it. As soon as I caught the calf it hollered, and the mother heard it and chased me a long way." My mother scolded me for that. She said, "You mustn't bother with the calves, because the mothers will surely get you. It's a good thing the cow didn't catch you, because if she'd caught up with you you'd have been killed. You mustn't touch the calves any more. If you bother with the calves again some day your guts will be on the horns of the cow. So now you leave them alone."

One day my mother, Quiver's Wife, rode up to our place. It was evening, and we were sitting outside. She said, "Where's your ax? Let's kill this horse." That wasn't her horse. It belonged to Giving Out Anger. He'd got after this woman, and so she'd taken away his horse. It wasn't given to her. She just took it away from him because he'd f—ed her. She took the horse and everything, saddle, bridle, rope and saddle-blanket. I guess my mother recognized the horse, and she must have been afraid to kill it. She said, "We haven't got an ax. We had one, but a fellow wanted to borrow it, and we loaned it to him. So we haven't got an ax. I'm sorry." But the ax was lying inside. My mother said, "Why don't you put a rope around his legs? Tangle him up, and when he falls to the ground get a rock and kill him." Then the woman left. She didn't go far from our place, and there she killed the horse.

Someone was walking along, it looked like a person carrying something on his back, and that was she, carrying the saddle. The next morning my mother found the horse lying there. She came home, picked up a knife and walked over and butchered it. She cut off the front and hind legs and the ribs. It was good and fat. One side of the ribs she gave to a Paiute woman who came by on horseback. But they don't like horsemeat, they never eat it. We didn't know that. The woman went behind a brush and threw the ribs away. My mother and I took the meat to our home, but we didn't eat it all, because it was summer, and it spoiled on us.

Two days later a man came to my father and said, "They want you to come to Quiver's place. He and his brothers and nephews are there. On the other side is Giving Out Anger and his clansmen. They are after one another. They want to fight. They all have bows and arrows. So they want you to go over." My father went over and was gone all day and night and all the next day. When he came back he told us about it.

On one side were Quiver and his brothers, Small Bitahni, Big Bitahni and Walk Up In Anger. On Giving Out Anger's side were Old Man Black, Old Man Gentle, No Sense, Wounded Smith and Big Red Clay. They were all brothers of the Red Clay Clan. They were all saying the same thing, they wanted to fight, they wanted to kill one another, they didn't care to live. Between the two parties were Old Man Hat, Choclays Kinsman, Who Has Mules, Slim Man and Pounding House. They were Many Goats. They were on Quiver's side. On the side of the Red Clay was a man named Whiskers, he was an Along The Stream, and a fellow named Big Chancres, he was a Bitter Water, and some others. They didn't want to let them fight.

Whiskers made a long speech. He said, "All of you Red Clay, you've done wrong, and you're trying to do more wrong things by doing wrong. What I mean is you got after this man's wife. He was living with this woman, and they were living well. They had lots of stock and properties, and you poor Red Clays got after his wife, because you were jealous. You all hated him, because he's the only one of all us Navaho who has a great many sheep, horses and cattle and a lot of property. That's why you poor Red Clays got after his wife, because you wanted to spoil him. You wanted to destroy his things, and now you've done it. What you wanted to do you've done, you've spoiled them. They were living together and lived well, and you spoiled them. You've all done wrong, but you don't see it. You want to fight over this one horse. That horse isn't anything to them. They've got lots of horses. They have lots of everything. You don't want to make trouble for yourselves. You'd better keep quiet about it. Let it go. Drop it right now. You poor Red Clays, you certainly will be killed, because if that outfit once gets hold of you, or even touches you, you'll be a goner. So you just let that horse go. Don't talk about it anymore." Then they quieted down, and he sent them away. He said, "Go away. Leave this place right now."

After that they talked over the stocks and properties of Quiver. Whiskers began talking about it, but they didn't know what to do. Quiver said to my father, "I'll leave it up to you. Even though you all don't know what to do about these things, think about it and fix it the way you want to. How do you want to fix my things for me? There are sheep, horses and cattle, and the two slaves of mine." He had a boy and a girl, Paiute children. The boy's name was Wild Ram. The girl was Ugly Girl. "Now you think about it and fix the things up for me." My father said, "I've got nothing to say about it. And all the rest of us are the same. All these men here have nothing to say about your things, because it all belongs to you. None of us helped you; we didn't help you buy them. You bought all these things yourself, and you raised them. So fix it up yourself, and nobody will bother you. We've got nothing to say, and we won't say anything about it." They said to him, "Now you just think about it yourself. You have a little boy, a son, think about him and fix your things the way you want to."

He lived with his wife another year. One day two fellows, Bitahni and Old Man Small, were herding his sheep. They each had a rope, and while they were taking the sheep to water they tied their ropes together and tied on a rag. The sheep were thirsty and started to run as hard as they could for the water, and a good many of them were behind. Then the two men ran into the middle of the herd and waved the rope with the rag tied on it, and the sheep that were behind got scared and stopped. Those that they scared they turned around and took back. The others went to the water. Those that went to the water belonged to Quiver, and the ones they took back were given to his wife. Over half went down to the water. She got only a few out of that big herd. The sheep Quiver got were all strong and young. His wife got the old ewes and old wethers; almost all of them were poor. He took the horses that had been used, all that were broken and tame, and the rest, all the wild ones, he gave to his son. And he gave him all the cattle.

They separated, and she took her herd way over to where we were living at the time. There she brought the small herd she got, and there we found out what had happened to her. Quiver took his sheep and the two Paiute children to his younger sister, Old Man Hat's daughter, Moving On. He was already married to another girl, a sister of Big Mexican, and that's the outfit he went with.

We lived in the canyon all summer until fall. We never did move out, because it was a good place with lots of grazing for the stocks, and it was nice and cool, just like up in the mountains. Many people moved there after they'd planted. Some passed us and lived all the way up in the canyon, and some lived below us all the way down. It was a big place. Even though they had lots of stock there was plenty of room for them all.

In the fall I discovered I had hair on my lip and under my arms and on my c—. I wondered how it happened, and I began pulling them out. But in two places I couldn't pull any more, it hurt awfully, so I only plucked them out on my lip. I was bashful when I had a mustache and kept pulling them out. I didn't let it grow on my lip, but in the other two places I let it go. I tried to pull them out, but I couldn't stand it, so I never bothered with them any more.

When it got cool we moved out of the canyon and up on Black Mountain to our old place at Willows Coming Out. A big hill points out close by there, and out from behind that hill comes a wash, called Yellow Water. That's where our old place was. We had a hogan and a sheep corral there already. When we moved back I fixed up the hogan; I cleaned it out and put more cedar bark and dirt on top, and we lived there again. There used to be water about five miles from where we located, and every morning I started out with my sheep and cattle for the water. I used to get the tame cow and ride her behind the herd down to the water and back. I used to ride her all the time. I did all kinds of things to her.

Many days after we'd moved back to Yellow Water it snowed a little. About that time Slim Man came. He said, "I'm rounding up all the horses that I see, and some of yours too. I'm going to take them on the mountain. There's lots of dry grass up there and plenty of snow." My father said, "I'm glad you're taking the horses on the mountain. Be sure and take up all you see." Then he left. After he'd taken the horses up on the mountain, his horses and Choclays Kinsman's and my father's, he came back to our place and said, "I took up all that I saw. There's plenty of grass for them and plenty of snow."

Then, after many days, they wanted to move again. They said, "Down below here is plenty of feed for the sheep." So we moved to White Rock Sitting Up. While we were living there it started snowing. It snowed all day and all night, all the next day and night and all day again. When it stopped the snow was about three feet deep. While it was still snowing a bit my father, Slim Man, came. He said, "I was on the mountain all day yesterday, but I didn't see any of the horses, and I didn't see any tracks. I stayed up there last night, and this morning I started looking for them again, but I didn't see one, and I didn't see a track. But I couldn't see anything because it was snowing so thick. You could hardly see ahead. The snow is deeper up there." He was all wet. The snow had melted on his clothes, and he was icy. My mother said, "It's a good thing you weren't frozen, and a good thing you started for our place. Now you're safe." He took off his clothes and hung them up inside the hogan. He dried and warmed himself, and my mother gave him warm things to eat. She was saying, "Oh, it's a good thing you didn't get lost or frozen to death, my son. If you'd happened to get lost in the thick woods you'd have been frozen to death. A good thing you didn't get lost. Why do you want to go after the horses anyway? They'll go around and find themselves a place where they'll be safe."

He stayed with us overnight, and the next morning he said, "I'll just start back for home from here." My father said, "Don't try to go up on the mountain again, my nephew, because it's dangerous right now. It's too slippery to ride a horse up there. Just let them go. They'll find their way and come down off the mountain out here in the flat. When one starts they'll all go. If the snow's too deep for them on the mountain they'll be out here soon. So don't try to go up again," he said.

After he left my father said, "I'll go out in the snow and say a little prayer, so that the snow will go down quickly." He went out that morning towards the south, and there he was, standing way out in the snow for a long time. When he came back he said, "I hope the snow will go down quickly." I took out the sheep, but they didn't go far, the snow was too deep. That day it went down pretty well. The next day it got down to about a foot, and about then the sheep started lambing. I cleaned the snow away from under the trees and built fires all around, and there I kept the lambs. Even though the snow was all over the ground it wasn't cold, and the lambs were all right. I kept them warm, and none of them froze on us. We kept the fires going under the trees all night.

We stayed there the rest of the winter. Nobody came around all that time. While we were living there the snow had gone, except for a little where there was shade. But out in the valley there was no snow. About then my father, Choclays Kinsman, came to our place. My father asked him, "How about the horses? Do you know anything about them?" He said, "That's what I came here for. I'd like to know about them myself. I never went out in the snow, I haven't been out since the snow fell. After the snow fell I was afraid to go out. I was just lying in the hogan, where it was warm, like a jack-rabbit. All at once I thought about you; I thought I'd come and visit you. I thought you might know something about the horses." My father said, "No, I was the same. I didn't go any place. I've been tending to my sheep, that's all. My nephew was here when we had that big snow and said he tried to look for the horses, but he didn't see any of them, so he just quit and came here. He was almost frozen to death. I said to him, 'Don't try to go up on the mountain again. You might get lost and freeze to death.' He went home from here, and that's all I know. But I guess some of them are still alive."

They were talking about that the rest of the day. Choclays Kinsman said, "I just came over to visit you. I'd like to stay with you a day or a night." My father said, "That's the way I've wished for you at times. I'd liked to have gone over to your place and stayed with you a day, but I just couldn't get away. I had so much to do with my sheep. But I'm glad you've come. I'm very glad to see you." They were talking and sitting close beside each other.

He stayed with us that night, and the next morning I brought his horse back for him, and after he ate he went home. My father said, "Get me a horse; I'll ride up to Yellow Water. Maybe some of the horses got out there. I want to ride around and see how that place looks." I went up on the hill where the horses were and brought one back for him, and then, right away, I turned out the sheep. I returned with the herd in the evening, and a little while after he came back also. He said, "I didn't see any of the horses. There are none around Yellow Water, and I didn't see any tracks. But our cattle are still there. They're looking fine, all still fat and lively. They were running and jumping around. But that's all I saw."

We lived there, and the snow was gone, except for a little on the hill. The lambs were good and strong. I was herding with them down in the valley. One day my father, Slim Man, came again. He asked, "Did you ever go and look for the horses?" My father said, "No, I haven't been upon the mountain. I rode to where we lived before, but I didn't see any of them. I don't know what's become of them." Slim Man said, "Some of them came out, but those belong to Choclays Kinsman. But only some of them came out from the mountain. They're on the other side of Willows Coming Out, near Fire Stone Burning. When I was up at his place the other day he said, 'I've been over where the horses are, but it's just a few of them. A lot haven't come out yet. I missed many of them.' And none of my horses are out yet. I don't know what's happened to them." My father said, "I don't know either. I don't know where they are. Maybe they're all frozen or starved to death. If they were still alive they ought to be out around in these valleys by this time."

After that Slim Man said, "Do you know anything about some fellows having killed two white men?" My father said, "No. How would we know? We're living here all alone, and nobody comes around." Then Slim Man began telling us about it. "It was before the snow fell. Two white men were traveling, crossing over Black Mountain, but nobody knew what they were after, or where they were going. Three fellows went after them, Little Mustache, Has Done It and Has A Hat. Has Done It killed one of them, but the other got away and hid himself behind something. From there he shot Little Mustache, but he only wounded him a little on the cheek bone. Then they went after this white fellow and tracked him a long way. They found him on top of the mountain, and there they killed him. That's the way everybody knows about it now, and everybody says, 'Soon, when the white people find out about it, they'll be around here after us.' That's what everybody thinks and says."

He stayed overnight, and the next morning my father said to us, "You two go up on the mountain and look for the horses. Go up on foot, because there are many bad places for the horses, and I don't think there's much feed for them. So you'd better go up on foot, my children." That morning we killed a sheep and boiled a lot of meat to take along for lunch. After it was boiled we let it cool, and then we put it in a sack along with some other food and started off. A little snow was still on the ground at the foot of the mountain around under the shade. Just as we got on top the sun went down, and a little way in the woods it got dark on us, and there we stopped.

The next morning when the sun was up we started off again. Here the snow was deep, but it was hard, and we could walk on top of it. Only in some places we broke through. We kept on for a big bare spot way up on the mountain. When we crossed that spot there was nothing, and no tracks of anything. Then we turned south, back into the woods, and made us a walking stick with three prongs, so we wouldn't break through the snow. He said, "We'll go for that point. Maybe some of them are over there." In that point was an old track, just a little hole in the snow. We kept going, and finally, way in the end of the point, we came on the tracks of horses, and there we found them lying all around. They'd been eating cedar bark and other brush, but yet they were dead. Many of them were lying there. Only one horse was still alive, a white horse belonging to Choclays Kinsman. We walked to all the dead ones, but none of them were ours. They belonged to Choclays Kinsman and Who Has Mules. We caught the white horse—it was about dead too—and led it around to where there wasn't so much snow. We had a hard time. It almost gave out.

When we got to the bare spot we started a fire. Slim Man had a bunch of matches and started lighting them, but he must have got them wet for none of them would light. They just smoked and went out. So there we were, out of matches, and it was far to where we'd had a fire the night before, and we were both tired too. Then we looked for some soft wood, and when we found it we made a fire drill and started drilling. At last we had a fire. He said, "Now we've got a fire, and we're safe. Nothing will kill us now." We warmed ourselves and dried our socks. These were rags that we wrapped around our feet. We made a big fire and gathered a lot of wood, so that it would last us the whole night. Then we dried our clothes, and after that we put some rocks into the fire. When they were good and hot we took them out and put snow over them. We'd scooped out a place by the fire, and soon that whole place was full of water. That's what we used for making coffee and for drinking. After we ate we sat by the fire smoking and talking about what we'd do tomorrow, and then we went to sleep. We didn't notice the cold or anything that night.

We woke up early in the morning. The white horse was looking fine. He'd been eating sagebrush and dodge-weed all night, and his belly was full. After we ate lunch we left him in the sagebrush and started off for another place. There we found more horses. And the trees were the same as in the other point, all the bark was peeled off, chewed by these horses. In places the branches were white where they'd been chewing on the wood. Way in the end of the point one horse was still alive. This was a bay, belonging to Who Has Mules. This horse had no hair on the tail or mane on the neck. All the hair had been eaten off by the starving horses. Many of them were lying around like that. But none of them were ours. We caught the bay and started back, but after we'd gone a little way we got hungry, and so we stopped and made a fire.

I'd been carrying a fire all morning long. I'd fixed some cedar bark, softened it and made it into a roll, tied in a few places, and I'd lighted one end and was carrying that all morning. We made a fire and got some water too, and after lunch we started off again, leading the horse. We had a hard time taking it back. It was about to give up just as we got there. We led it up to the other one and turned it loose. It was evening then, and we went to where we'd slept the night before and gathered up more wood and built a big fire. Then we dried our clothes and made some water and ate our lunch.

In the morning we started off with those two horses. We wanted to take a short cut down the mountain, but when we got to that place we found no one could go down that trail. It was on the shady side of the hill, and the snow was as if it had fallen the night before. So we passed on to another. That trail was better. In the shade the snow was up to our hips. Finally we got out of the snow to the foot of the hill. At the edge of the woods my father pointed off into the distance, "There's a horse standing way up on the other side of that point," he said. We left the two horses and our blankets there and started over, and behind the point we found a lot of them. Some were looking fine, some were poor, but they weren't all there. He said, "Two of Choclays Kinsman's horses are in the bunch, but the rest are mine." He was so glad and happy to have found them. He said, "Maybe the others are still alive. They may be out somewhere. I'm glad I've got all my horses."

We roped two and rode back to where we'd left our blankets, and he said, "Well, I guess we'd better go back, my son, we haven't any more grub." So we left the two we'd brought down from the mountain and started home. It was a long way. We rode all the rest of the day until late in the evening. When we got home he said, "We'll just turn them loose. They'll be all right. They'll go back to where the others are."

As soon as we walked inside he said, "We only found those that belong to me. Some are looking fine, some are not, but I'm very glad I've found my horses. Almost all of them are there. We didn't find yours. We found some on the mountain in two points. At the end of two points we found a lot of them lying around dead. But we didn't find one of yours among them. So I don't think any of yours are dead. I think they all got out to some place." Right away my mother had the food cooked for us, and we started eating. My father said, "I wonder where they are? If they were up on the mountain you'd have found some lying around there dead. But you said you saw none of them up there anywhere. I think they're out some place. If they did go out they're safe." They were talking about the horses while they were eating. Slim Man said, "If they got out they must be in the valley, because there are no tracks on the mountain, only of those we found dead. All of your horses can't be up on the mountain. I think they're out in the flat. I'm sure they're all safe." They were sitting and talking about them a long time.

Then my father said to me, "Tomorrow, early in the morning, you should get up and take the rope with you and go over where we used to camp in winter." We had another winter camp at a place called Among The Black Rocks. He said, "Go all around there and look for our horses. Just take a rope with you and go on foot. I don't want you to lie in bed all morning. You want to worry about your horses. You know you didn't find any of them, and you ought to be worried about it now. That's the way I am; I'm worrying about them, and I'm anxious to see them. So get up early in the morning. You want to start off and just take the rope with you." My mother said, "You don't want him to go on foot. There are horses around here that can be used, and you know he's tired. He's been going around upon the mountain on foot for three days, plowing through the snow, and he's tired. He ought to take one of the horses." My father said, "He doesn't have to have a horse. And he's not tired at all. He shouldn't be tired. He ought to enjoy walking. That's the way I used to be when I was young. I used to get up when I knew the morning was on its way and run around after the horses the rest of the night. I used to enjoy walking and running around on foot. He ought to be that way, and I want him to be that way too. So you do what I tell you.

You shouldn't act like a little boy. You get up tomorrow, early in the morning, and go over where our winter camp is. I'm sure the horses are out there."

Then we went to bed. I went to sleep, and all at once I woke up. I went outside to look for the morning, but the morning hadn't come yet, and I went back to sleep. All at once I woke up again and went outside, and morning had come. I had the rope all ready. My mother had made me a little lunch, a little meat that she'd wrapped in a skin sack, and I had it tied on to the rope. It was cold, but I didn't mind the cold at all. I put on my moccasins and the one thin pair of calico pants and shirt I had and started off. I didn't take anything along, just the rope and a little lunch. I didn't say anything; everybody was sleeping. The two old men were sleeping there close together, snoring as hard as they could. They didn't notice my leaving.

It was cold when I started out, but I ran a little way, and soon I was warm. I kept on running for about fifteen miles, and by then it was daylight, and I started across the valley for the trails that come from Scratch Out Water. When I got up on the hill, there, on the other side, were the horses, walking around in bunches. I ran up to one bunch, and they were looking fine. They were good and fat; none of them were poor, because they were in lots of different kinds of feed. Some was dry, like different grasses, but some of the weeds that the horses eat are green all summer and winter. They were in this good feed and looking fine.

Four good horses were in this bunch. They were gentle and tame. I drove those four in a corral and put a rope around the racehorse that belonged to my father and got on it and rode all the way up in the valley. It didn't take me long to round up all the horses. They were all there, all three bunches. We had three bunches, each with a stud, and all three were in this valley. I was glad and eager to see them. When I knew they were all there I was full of joy and happiness. I drove them out of the valley through a little woods and over a hill. On the other side was another valley. I drove them across that and over against another hill, and there I let them go and started home.

I went over a big hill and down in the valley, and there was my father herding the sheep. I rode up to him, and as soon as he saw his horse he said, "Well, my dear horse, I'm very glad to see you again, poor horse of mine. I thought you were lost. I've been wishing for you all this time, my poor horse. I'm very anxious to see you again." While he was saying this he had his arm around the horse's neck. He hung his head a minute and almost cried. He said, "Well, my son, how are the horses? And where are they? Are they all there?" I said, "Yes, they're all there, all three bunches. Not one is missing. They were all right together in the same valley, the one we call Last Valley. And they're looking fine. They're all lively. The young ones and colts were running and bucking and playing around while I was driving them this way." "That's fine," he said, "I'm glad to hear that, and I'm glad they're all there. I'm glad none of them are missing." Then he said, "You go back home, and after you eat put the saddle on the horse and come back to me. I'd like to go over and see them. Where did you drive them?" I said, "I drove them to the first valley, against the hill, this side, on our side." "Well, then, as soon as you eat be sure and put the saddle on the horse, and I'll ride over and look at them."

When I got home my mother had the food all ready for me, and I started eating. She went outside to the horse, and I heard her saying, "Welcome, my horse, I'm very glad to see you again. I knew you had sense enough to get out of the bad snow. I know you're like a human being. I know you're all safe too, and I'm very glad. I know you all know what to do about yourselves." That's what she was saying to the horse outside while I was eating. I didn't eat much, because I was so very glad about the horses. I was thinking about them more than eating. Then I took out the saddle and put it on the horse and said to my mother, "My father told me to put the saddle on the horse, because he wants to ride over where they are." She said, "Well, you hurry and go back to him. I guess he's anxious to see his horses. That's nice that he's going over. Are you sure they're all there?" I said, "Yes, none of them are missing." "That's nice," she said, "You go over to your father, I guess he's waiting for you."

I got on the horse and rode back to him. He was walking along like a young man, straightening himself and walking lively. I heard him singing—I don't know what kind of song —because he was glad and happy about the horses. When I rode up to him he looked happy, and he was smiling. Then I got off the horse, and he got on, quickly, like a young man, and rode away, and I started herding.

That evening, as I was returning with the herd, he came riding back on another horse. This was a big mare. When he got home he took off the saddle, and as soon as he turned her loose she started running back, and while she was running she was neighing every once in a while. They were both so glad and happy about the horses. They were laughing while they were busy inside the hogan. They were both laughing while my mother started cooking and the old man was fixing up his saddle, taking it back in the hogan, talking about the horses and about the ride he'd had that day. They were so happy about it.

In the evening after we ate he said, "Someone, whom we live by, is still taking care of us. When the snow fell I went out in the snow and begged it would go down quickly and all my horses be saved. That prayer of mine was taken for me. I found that out now. If my prayers hadn't been taken my horses would be dead. But they're all safe, so I know we're still being taken care of right along by someone we live by. When Choclays Kinsman was here the other day he said there was no spirit of any kind that would take care of us, and nothing would save our horses. But he's mistaken. If there were no spirit he wouldn't be alive. He's alive and living by someone, so he's mistaken. I'm very glad to see all my horses."

10.
They start a farm at Anything Falls In . . . Rumors of War . . . The Utes pass by, and he trades a horse for a gun . . . Flight before the troops . . . Old Man Hat heads a party of peace.

SOON spring had come, and the grass began getting green, and the weather was warm. Then we moved toward the mountain. Against the hills, where the sun struck, different weeds and grasses had got green. Around the base of the rocks and under the trees, wherever there was a warm spot, the things were good and green. I had the cattle there, and every time I went out herding I rode the tame cow. Sometimes I put the saddle on her. Not long after we moved this cow had a calf, and the calf was a female. That belonged to my father. I was sorry for the calf, because it didn't belong to us. I wondered if our cow would have a calf just like this one. I was wishing for a calf that was still to be born and praying she'd have a female. A few days later our cow had a little one too, and that was a female, and that was ours. I was happy that we had four females. But even though we had a calf of our own I was still sorry for the other one and the cow, because that was a good-looking cow and calf, and the cow was tame.

When the calves were good and strong they said, "We'd better move down off the mountain to the valley, because our moccasin soles won't last long up here. It's too rough; there are too many rocks. We'd keep on making moccasins all the time, putting back new soles, and we haven't any. So we'd better move down to the flat. The moccasins last longer out in the valley." They set a date, they said, "In two days we'll start moving." My mother said, "We'll take the cattle with us." But my father said, "No, we'll leave them here, because they know the country, and there's plenty of feed for them, and it's cool. They like to be under the trees. They like to rub themselves against the bark. So we'll leave them. They'll be all right. Lost His Moccasins' cattle are up here, and his boys will look after ours." He said to me, "Take them back to Yellow Water." I got on my horse and drove up to that place and left them by the water.

When the two days were up we started moving. We took the valley that comes out from Valley Coming To The Edge. The sheep knew where to go. They started right along, because they were hungry for salt-weed. We always took them to the salt-weed on that trail, so they knew where they were going. They were going right along, making a lot of dust, and we were driving the horses behind them. We followed the sheep all the way down to Valley Coming To The Edge. About sundown we got to Flowing Out Of Narrow Canyon. My father said, "Take the horses down to Woods Coming Into Water and let them go there. We'll camp there. You two can go ahead with the horses, and I'll take down the herd." So we went on. It was just getting dark when we got there.

Early the next morning, while it was still dark, I went after the horses. It was a pretty place where we'd camped. Everything was green, everything was just beginning to grow. My father was out that morning too, walking around there, just looking it over. When I came back with the horses he said, "What a nice place we've come to. Everything is green. I walked all over, and every place I went there was grass and different weeds just starting up. But they're good and high now, high enough so that the stocks will get plenty of feed. Out in this flat is a nice level place where the water has spread. It's still wet from the snow. When the snow melted on the mountain the water came down and spread out over the valley. It's a good-sized place, all smooth and level. We'll plant something here. We'll go and look for seeds. We won't let it go, because it's a good level place and still wet." My mother said to me, "You go over there today and clear off some of the brush."

After we ate lunch I took over the ax—we didn't have a grubbing hoe or mattock or shovel—and started chopping the greasewood roots and cleaning off the land. I picked up a stick about four feet long and stuck it into the dirt. I stuck in almost the whole stick, and down at the bottom the ground was still muddy. That made me work more, when I found out it was still wet under the ground. I played with the stick for a while, sticking it in the ground at different places, and it was the same everywhere. That made me wish for corn and other stuff and made me work the harder, and so I started clearing off the greasewood.

Several days after we moved there Blind Mexican came to our place. He said, "Some white people camped below here the other day. Some fellows killed a white man and buried him there, and these white people opened the grave and took out the body. They put everything in a gunny sack over a big black mule and carried it away. I don't know where they're from, maybe from Fort Defiance."

My mother said to him, pointing the while to me, "You help him. He's cleaning off a piece of ground, and we're ready to plant now. You stay here and help him plant, my grandson. I want you to stay here with us a few days. Help us on planting." He said, "All right, I'll stay and help you, and you let me have a piece of land, and I'll plant something for myself." My mother said, "You don't live near here. You live far off. It's no use for you to plant here, because it's too far for you from where you're living." But he said, "No, it's not far for me. You think it is, but it's not. Even though I'm living far away from here I can run back and forth. So you—you—you let me have a piece of land," he said and laughed. He used to stutter.

We began clearing away the greasewood while my father and mother took turns herding. My mother made us lunch every day, and we took it along with us to where we were clearing off the ground. After we'd been working for a few days my father went after some seeds and brought back corn, melon, squash and pumpkin seeds. We planted the corn and then the squash and pumpkins and after that the melons, muskmelons and watermelons. We had quite a patch of different kinds of crops. Then we cut down some trees and put up a brush hogan close to the little farm, and after that Blind Mexican wanted to go home. My father gave him a sheep, and he killed and butchered it and cut the meat into thin strips and dried it. He'd planted a little patch of corn for himself, and he said, "I'll be back when the corn gets ripe." Then he put his meat in a sack and went home. About then the corn was up. It could just be seen. The rest of the seeds were coming up too. It was nice and warm every day, and so they came up quickly.

Many days after, when the corn was about two feet high, my father, Slim Man, came. He said, "I heard the troops will be out here against us all for that murder. But, they say, they'll give us a chance. They want us to catch the fellow who killed the white men. If we catch him they won't get after us. So they're waiting for us to bring him in. If we take him in then the troops won't get after us. If we don't they'll be out here killing everyone they see. Giving Out

Anger is going to take Little Mustache and Has A Hat to Fort Defiance, but his son, Has Done It, doesn't want to go. He said, 'I don't want to go. I'd rather be dead right here on my land. If they want me so badly they can come and cut my head off and take it.' That's the way he's talking. But another man, Hairy Face, has joined him. So there are two of them. They both want to be killed right here on their land."

By that time the corn was pretty high. It was looking fine, and we were glad about it. While we were living at the cornfield some Ute Indians passed by. They were running away from their reservation because they'd killed a great many troops. They said, "We did wrong, and we're pretty sure we'll all be killed." They were carrying guns and bullets which they'd taken from the soldiers. Has Done It traded one of his horses for a rifle and a whole lot of cartridges. He was the only one who bought a rifle. The rest the Utes took away with them. They moved towards Flowing Out Of Narrow Canyon. They said, "We don't know where we're going."

After that we heard Giving Out Anger and the other two didn't return from Fort Defiance. They'd said to him, "Go back and get your son and bring him over here." He didn't want to come for his son, so they kept him. They put him and the other two in a wagon and took them to St. John.

When the corn had ears, just as it was getting ripe, the Utes were moving back. They were coming along in bunches. A bunch stopped at our place and wanted some corn, so my mother went in the field and got some. I was outside sitting under a horse. It was a bay with a white spot under the belly and a white face and red eyes. One of the Utes, a young man, came up to me and said, "I'll give you this rifle and some cartridges for that horse." I said, "I don't know how to use it." He took the rifle down from his horse, he had it already loaded, and took out all the cartridges from the magazine. After he took them out he put them back again. I counted them, and there were ten that he put back in. "It holds this many," he said. He took them all out again and gave me the rifle and told me to load it. I filled the magazine, and then he told me to work them out. I took them all out and tried it again. Then it was easy to do. That was a .44 rifle. The points of the cartridges were all soft lead. He loaded it up again for me and showed me everything. Then he gave me a leather belt and a small sack and two boxes, all filled with cartridges.

I went over to my mother and told her about it. She said, "What do you want to have a rifle for? You don't know how to use it. You might kill yourself with it." But I said, "I'd like to get it anyway, because I'd like to have a gun. And he showed me everything. I know how to use it." She said, "Go in and tell your father about it." Just then he came out. He came up to me, and I said, "I'd like to have this gun. The man wants the horse for it." He looked at the rifle a long time. "It's a good rifle," he said. "It's a good thing to have. A man has to have something like this with him all the time. And they're scarce. They're worth a lot. This is a good chance to get it, right now. We haven't a gun of any kind, only bows and arrows. So you can go ahead and give him the horse."

Two days later my father, Slim Man, came. Right away my mother told him about the gun. "My son's bought a gun. I don't think he knows how to work it. I don't think he knows how to use it, but he bought it anyway." He said, "Let me see the gun. Where is it?" I went and got it for him. He looked at it and said, "Where are the cartridges?" I brought him some, and he put them in the magazine. He knew how to work it. He took the cartridges out again and said, "Well, you got a nice gun. I wish I had one. Now you've got something. It's a very nice gun. Give me two cartridges, and, let's see, I'll try it." He put in two and told me to set a piece of rock against the hill. I put the rock against the hill, about 200 feet away, and he shot it. He told me to set up another a little further off. I put one way off, about twice as far, and he shot at that. He almost missed it. He just shaved it a little right on top. He said, "It's a good rifle. You can't miss anything with it that far. When you know how to use it you can shoot a man's eye out. You ought to practice with it. It's a very nice gun you bought. You got it cheap too. You gave only one horse for it." I showed him all the cartridges, and he liked it very much.

Then he said, "I heard the troops were on their way. They want us to catch Has Done It. If we catch him we're safe. If we don't the troops will be after us all. But Has Done It and Hairy Face are away. Nobody knows where they are. They heard the troops were coming after them, so they left. They said they wanted to be killed right on their land." My father said, "I wonder if they'll start killing anyone they see. That's the way with the Utes. When they start after us they kill anyone they see. And the Mexicans are just the same. I wonder if the troops will start in that way? If they do I don't think we'll all be alive long." Slim Man said, "I don't know anything about it. If they want to kill whoever comes along they'll do it. If they only want to get this one man, then they'll just get him. But I don't think the troops are after us all. They're different from the other tribes."

Four days later we heard the troops were coming up from Water In Bitter Weeds. Everybody had got word that the troops were close at hand, except us. We didn't know anything about it. We looked down in the valley, and there was dust all over the flat. That was the people, chasing them-selves towards the mountain, and here we were at home. A boy rode up to us, he was White Horse's Son, and said, "They told me to come here and tell you the troops were coming. They said, 'Go over and tell your grandmother about it.' That's what I've come to tell you. That dust down in the flat is lots of people going for the mountain. Many of them have gone up on the mountain already."

Then my mother started getting mad at us. She was so ex-cited she didn't know what to do. She started running around, saying, "I want to go right now. I want to save my-self." She was so scared when she heard this, and she was mad at my father and me. She said, "You both ought to have got up early this morning and gone after the horses. You both knew very well the troops were coming. You ought to have had the horses ready all the time. Now we haven't any horses. Not one of them standing around here. What shall we do? We can't get away quickly. Shall we let all the things go and run for the mountain?" My father was lying there, he didn't say anything, he was just lying there smiling a little. She turned to the boy and said, "Lend us your horse. We'll get our horses with it." Right away the boy got off, and she said to me, "Quick, go after the horses." I got on the horse and rode way up around the other side of Where The Ar-royos Stop. It was early in the morning. The sun was just up, and there was dust all around the valley. The people were moving for the mountains, driving their horses and sheep.

I rounded up the horses and started back. When I got home my mother had already left with the sheep, and all our stuff was piled around outside. My father said, "The old woman has left already. I don't know where she's going." He sad-dled the horses and said, "Fix up those things lying around there." I piled the things in one place and covered them. The sheep pelts and blankets that we used for bedding, a few dishes and grub were all we put on the horses. It took us quite a long time to fix things there at home.

Towards noon we started off. The boy had gone. We went on, driving the horses, and caught up with some people driving sheep. They were running, throwing ropes and waving blankets, and the sheep were going right along. We passed them and caught up with another outfit. They were doing the same. From there on they were in bunches close together. There was dust all the way down from Narrow Canyon and Anything Falls In. We went along, passing them all, and began to miss my mother. But way ahead of us was more dust. We went for that, and there she was, running around. She was all sweat, and the sheep and goats had their mouths wide open; they were about to give up. She'd gone a long way. There was more dust ahead of us, but that was some fellows driving horses.

We let her have a horse and started off again. About then a bunch of horses and cattle were coming along behind us. The cattle were almost smothered to death. They had their mouths open, and the fellows were beating them with long sticks. When they caught up with us the three old men, my father, Old Man White Horse and Stutterer, rode along together talking about these things. White Horse said, "Take your time. I don't think the troops are after us. So everybody take your time. We don't want to kill ourselves and all our stock. We must all go easily. Has Done It isn't with us. He's off somewhere. So everyone go slow. Take a rest, and give the stock a rest." Then we started going slowly, taking our time. The three old fellows rode together and talked.

We stopped and camped at Sweet Water in the afternoon. We'd gone a long way from home. They were all catching up with us there and camping close around the water. Late in the afternoon, when it was cool, when everyone was good and rested, we started off again, down toward the flat to Thief Rock. There everybody stopped and camped. My father said to the people, "Now we'll just stop and camp right here, and all of us men will go back tomorrow morning. We'll leave the sheep and horses with the women. We'll let the women stay here with the sheep, and all of us men should go back. So tomorrow, early in the morning, get your horses. We should go back and see what's going on."

Everybody was awake that night, and early in the morning they all got their horses. My father said to me, "Get me my big horse. That bay Choclays Kinsman gave me. I want to ride that big horse of mine." I got the horse and led it back to him, and he put on the saddle. When he got on he said, "All of you people stay right here. Don't any of you try to move. Some of you young men get on your horses and ride around the hills and watch. The rest of you stay right here. Don't try to move again. I'm going back. I want to see what's going on. You just wait for me here. When I've discovered something I'll come right back." He rode away; he took only his bow and arrows with him. A lot of fellows got on their horses and rode after him. The sun wasn't up yet when he left.

The day before this the troops had camped at Bank Caving Down. They'd heard that Has Done It was with the Utes and Paiutes at Flowing Through Rocks. They had quite a village there. That night half the troops moved up and camped on every side. While it was still dark in the morning they surrounded the village, but the Utes and Paiutes had moved out up on to a big round rock. There they were working on a wall all night, putting up a wall around themselves with little holes through which they could shoot. The other two, Has Done It and Hairy Face, went up on a black rock standing on top of a big hill. They had their horses up there, and they'd built a wall too. When the troops found out nobody was in the village they stayed around a while and then went back to their horses, and before daylight they returned to Bank Caving Down.

Way late at night, as soon as the old man came back, he told about his trip. He said, "On top of the hill close by Flowing Through Rocks was a big crowd of people. Some had camped there last night; some had come this morning from different camps all the way back to White Ledge. I rode up on the hill where the crowd was, and some of the fellows came after me. I rode right into the crowd and asked about the troops. I said, 'What do you know? Where are the troops?' They said, 'The troops returned to Bank Caving Down.' I rode up to Old Man Gentle, Giving Out Anger's younger brother, and said to him, 'What do you stop here for? You may be thinking one way, but I'm not. I want you all to go over to the troops. We want to talk with them. So every one of you, let's go. Nothing will happen today. When we get there we'll find out what they're thinking. They'll talk to us, and I know they won't do anything to us. So let's all go and ride up to them.' He said, 'All right, we'll do that.' Then I rode up to Friend Of Once He Had A Child and told him the same, but he didn't say a word to me. I rode around the crowd at different places on the hill telling them we'd all go over and talk with the headman. Some said, 'All right,' some didn't speak at all. I said, 'Let's go. This way we can't find anything. We want to know and find out something from the troops. So come on and let's go. Hurry up. Everybody come right after me.' When we started off I looked back, but only a few of them were coming, a lot had backed out. We let those go, and the few of us started off for where the troops were.

"While we were moving along one fellow said, 'What

shall we say if they ask us about those two and about the Utes?' Some fellows said, 'We'll let them go. They'll be caught anyway sometime. Let them get caught themselves. We'll say we don't know anything about them. And the Utes, we'll say, moved back to their country.' We said this because we didn't want any trouble started; we didn't want any of the troops to get killed. If they'd gone after them they'd have been killed for sure, because the Utes and Paiutes were up on the big rock and had everything ready.

"As we rode along the fellows said to me, 'Well, our clansman, sing us a war song, a safe song for us, so we'll all be safe, and nothing will happen today. The troops will shake hands with us. They won't try to start trouble. They'll all be kind to us.' I said, 'All right, whatever you say I'll do for you.' I told them to get in a row. 'Even up all your horses. Don't any of you get ahead of me. Have your horses about on a level with mine.' They stretched out, and we let our horses walk, and I began singing, begging that nothing would happen. When I was through with my song we went right along and got to the top of a hill.

"From there we saw the camp. There were a great many tents all in a row. They'd camped by the water at the edge of the wash. We stopped, and I said, 'All stretch out again.' We evened the horses, and it was quite a stretch when they got in line. But there were only a few of us, all the others, the big crowd, had backed out. I counted the fellows, and there were only fifty. We went right down. There was nobody around the tents. When we got close to the edge of the wash they started running around, making some kind of noise, whistling or something. As soon as that noise started up they were all running out of their tents. They were in a hurry. It didn't take them long to line up. When we stopped by the wash they were ready with their guns.

"Then, from a tent standing in the middle, two of them came out. They got in front of the troops and said something and then turned around and went down in the wash and came right up to us. One was Chee Dodge. The other was the captain of the troops. Chee Dodge said, 'Who's headman?' Everybody pointed at me. I was in the center of the line. He said, 'Come down off your horse.' So I got down. I was thinking about shaking hands. I was thinking, if he just gives me the end of his fingers I won't call that shaking hands. If he does that I'll let his hand go and go back and sit on my horse. From there I was going to make a little motion to my crowd. But he gave me his whole hand and was holding me a long time, shaking as hard as he could. That made me feel lively and happy, when he shook me for a long time. That's what I call shaking hands. I asked about the white man. 'Is he headman?' The interpreter, Chee Dodge, said, 'Yes, he's headman.' Then I turned to my people and said, 'Get off your horses.' The headman said, 'I want to shake hands with all the crowd.' So I said to them, 'Come one by one and shake hands with our headman.' Everybody shook hands with him and the interpreter. I said to the crowd, 'Sit down.' When they'd all sat down I said, 'Keep quiet and listen. We all want to know what our headman will say to us.' Then I sat down too. He turned to his men and said something, and then they all turned in quick order and went back to their tents and stacked their guns.

"After that he said to us, 'What do you want? What did you come here for?' I said, 'We came here to shake hands with you, and we came to talk in the kindest way to each other. We came here for peace. And now we've shaken hands and are talking to each other in the kindest manner, we're all friends now. That's what we came here for. Even though I'm old—you look at me, and you know I'm old; you look in my mouth, and you know I haven't any teeth, and I'm about blind and about deaf; you see my hair is white, and my skin is wrinkled, my whole face is full of wrinkles; you know I look ugly—but even though I'm this way I'm thinking about myself that I'll live many years yet. I want to be safe always. I don't want to die right now. Even though the death of my old age is coming soon I'm thinking about myself that I'll live for a long time yet. That's why I was chasing around, chasing away from you. I thought you were going to kill me. But here I've found out you're a kind man.'

"He said, 'Why are you chasing around? Did you kill a white man too?' I said, 'No, I didn't know anything about it. I lived way on the other side of this mountain, out in the valley. I was living all alone, and from there I moved to the foot of the mountain, and there I heard someone killed a white man. Even though I didn't know anything about it I was scared. I knew right away something would happen. When I moved to the foot of the mountain I got on to a piece of wet ground and planted some corn for myself and other little things. Then I heard you were coming and got scared and hid myself away. I let my crops go. I turned it over to crow and coyote, because I was so scared of you. I've been chasing all over the mountain. Some of us fled from here all the way down to the other side of the mountain.'

" 'Well,' he said, 'I'm not after you, nor am I after a man like you. I'm not after a man who lives a good life. I don't want to harm anyone who lives well and talks nicely like you. I'm after just this one man. I'm only after Has Done It. That's all. I thought we had him. We were up all night last night at the place where they told us they were, but when we got there this morning nobody was there. We only saw the tracks. We didn't find anyone, so we came back here. Now you should all look for him and try to catch him. You all think about it now.' About then four fellows came out from a tent. That was Who Has Mules, Smith, Red Wife Beater and Standing House. They were with the troops. They all live up on Black Mountain, and they'd been called down. They walked up and sat down by us.

"I said to him, 'This, my crowd, and all the others of my people are thinking just the same. We all want to live a long life. We don't want to be killed. We don't want to start trouble. Not one of us here now ever thinks about trouble. All we think about is that we'll live long, and about eating and sleeping, and about raising stock, raising something to get something. We all want to do something for our living. That's the way we think. You said to us, "Try and get Has Done It," but none of us would dare go near him, because we're all afraid of him. We don't want to bother with him. If we did he'd sure start killing us. And, as I said, we don't want to be killed. I don't want any of my people to get killed for nothing. I want all my people to live long. Even though their time may be coming up close, still, even at that, I want them to be alive for some time yet.

" 'So, if you want to get Has Done It, it's up to you, if you want to go after him. But he's hard to find. Nobody knows where he is. If you want to go after him you won't know where to go. From here on it's pretty dangerous all over. When a person doesn't know the country he'll surely get lost or die of thirst. It's dangerous to travel around here, crossing the desert and the many canyons. A person has got to know where to get water, and water is scarce. There's no water for miles and miles. So I think it's dangerous to go after him. If a person knew something about him, knew how to go after him and knew just where he was, then he could easily be found. But as it is nobody knows where he is. Maybe he went across the desert with the Utes. Maybe he's with the Paiutes. So it's up to you. But you won't find water for yourselves or your horses. If you get out in the desert your horses will surely die of thirst. And it's hard on your horses' hoofs, traveling on these rocks.'

"Then Old Man Gentle said to me, 'My older brother, please ask him about Giving Out Anger. Ask him to turn him loose, because we're all anxious to see him again. We all know he didn't do any wrong. So, please, my older brother, beg him for Giving Out Anger. Ask him to let him go. Ask him to turn him loose. We want him back very badly.' Old Man Gentle was sitting right by me, and Slim Man was sitting by me too. I said, 'How shall I beg him? I don't think he'll be turned loose unless we catch Has Done It. If we don't get Has Done It he won't be turned loose. So if you want him you ought to get Has Done It.' But he said, 'Even at that try and beg for him. Beg him anyway. He might turn him loose.' When Old Man Gentle said this to me I said, 'If you wanted to beg for him, how would you beg? It's no use. He can't be turned loose, unless we get Has Done It first.'

"Then I turned around and said to the headman, 'A little while ago I said that we're all thinking about a long life and about getting something to eat all the time. We all want to raise more stock. We all want to raise more children. It's the same with Giving Out Anger. He's thinking as we're thinking now. He wants to live long. He wants to enjoy life. He wants to get more children, more stuff, more stocks, more of everything. But now you're holding him way off somewhere, and he doesn't know what to do about himself, all because of his son, Has Done It. He's the one who took his father away, and he's out here someplace. He ought to be where his father is now. His father didn't do any wrong. Giving Out Anger didn't tell his son to do bad things. He didn't know anything about it. And there you've got him and have him off somewhere. We all know he's a good man. He always wants to do something for himself and his children. That's the way he is, but now you've got him far off.'

"The interpreter told him what I'd said; then he replied, 'It's that way. I know just how it is. I know how Giving Out Anger is, because I have all his words. What he said is all on paper. I know he's a good man. I know he's innocent, and I know he didn't tell his son to do bad things. I know just how he raised his son. It's that way with all of us. When we have a son we tell him not to do bad things, we tell him to do the right thing all the time. But, even though they were good, all at once they'll do something like that, and then we'll be worried about it. They'll worry us. That's the way with Giving Out Anger now, he's worrying about himself and his son. But don't worry about him. We're holding him, but he's being taken care of. He's not treated badly. He gets enough sleep and enough to eat. We won't do any harm to him. We've got him, but we don't want to kill him. He's not suffering. He'll be back sometime. We'll try to get him out as soon as we can. So don't worry about your brother. He'll soon be back, because we know how he was living here. I know you're all anxious to see him, but now don't worry about him. As I said, he'll be back soon.

" 'I said to you I'm looking after all who need help, all who live well. I'm trying to help them. I don't want to harm anyone who lives well. I'm only after the ones who do wrong, like murdering people, like this one man. That's the only one I'm after. Those who live well are my partners, they're all my friends. Like these four fellows. There's Who Has Mules sitting there, and Standing House and Smith and Red Wife Beater. I know them very well. I know them very well, that's why I sent for them, and right away they came down off Black Mountain and up to me. They weren't afraid of me, because they're innocent men. So that's why they're my friends and partners. And now you and your people are the same. You came here and brought your people right up to me. Right away I knew you were all innocent men. I knew right away you were all my friends. I'm so very glad you brought your men. That's the way I like to see it.

" 'You said you left your cornfield. Now you go and bring your family back. Come right back to your cornfield tomorrow. Don't let it go to waste. And if any time you hear the troops are coming again don't get alarmed, don't run away from your farm again. Even though the troops come right up to you, stay right with your field. As I said, they're not after a kind man. So you must stay with your cornfield all the time.'

"Then I got up and shook hands with him again. 'I'm very glad we've met each other, our headman,' I said, and I gave him thanks. 'Thank you very much, our headman. Thank you very much for your talk and all your kindness. That's what we came here for. We came for good talks and for kind talks, and we've been talking in the kindest way to each other all day. I'm very glad now, and my people will be the same way too. I know they're all glad nothing has happened. They're all thankful for the good talks we've had.'

"While I was still holding his hand the interpreter told him what I said. He laughed and said, 'Thank you very much. I'm just the same. I'm feeling just as you are. I'm thankful too for your good talks and for all your kind talks. That's what I like to hear. Thank you very much,' he said and shook me more and let me go. 'Now you go right back to your people and tell them to come down off the mountain. Tell them to go back to their places, to their homes and to their farms. Maybe some of them have farms, let them go back to their farms, because otherwise crow and coyote will get after them. You don't want to let the crows eat all your corn. As soon as you get back to your people send them all down to their homes.' I said, 'I will.'

"Then I said to the fellows, 'You all shake hands with him now.' So everybody got up and started shaking hands with him. When they were through I thought about tobacco. I said to him, 'Well, how about it now? We said we were friends. You didn't see me smoking all day. I just saw you smoking, and I was wishing for it. I almost died for a smoke. I didn't smoke because I haven't any tobacco. Have you got any tobacco with you? I'm about dead for it.' When I said this he laughed again and turned and hollered across the wash to where the tents were. He said something, and there a fellow ran into one of the tents and out and across the wash, holding something in his hand. That was tobacco, a big, wide, long strip. 'Here now, smoke it all,' he said to me. 'Smoke all you want.' Then I walked up to him and shook hands with him again and said, "Thank you very much. This will last me many years.' He laughed and said, 'That's all right.'

"That was all about that, and we started back. As soon as I got on my horse all the fellows got on theirs and came right after me. They were all after my tobacco. Old Man Gentle was the first one to ride up to me. He said, 'My older brother, my old older brother, please give me a piece of your tobacco.' I turned around—I had it tied on the back of the saddle—I untied it and got out the tobacco and cut him off a piece. Then everybody wanted some. They all said, 'Give me a piece too, my grandfather, my uncle, my brother. Give me some too.' I got mad at them. I said, 'I didn't get this tobacco for all of you. I asked for it only for myself. If you wanted tobacco why didn't you ask the headman for it?' Then I just started cutting pieces off, giving a piece to each one.

"We went along, and Old Man Gentle said to me, 'I know

how you are now, my older brother. You weren't afraid to talk, and all the rest of us were dead like. We were so scared of the troops we didn't even draw our full breath. We were about dead when you were through talking with him, and you weren't a bit afraid. It seemed to me as if you were talking to a child, and all the rest of us were shivering. You were the only one who talked for us. We know now you are ahead of all the headmen. All the other head fellows just went to sleep. They were afraid to talk. You were the only one to talk for us. I'm very thankful for that.'

"We passed Where The Little Arroyos Stop, and from there some of the fellows branched off, going down towards the flat, towards Anything Falls In. From there on they were branching off bunch by bunch every little way. We passed Woods Coming Far Out Into The Valley, and we passed where my cornfield is. I just gave one look. Then we passed Flowing Out Of Narrow Canyon and went on up to White Ledge and then passed Sweet Water. So, I guess, tomorrow we'll go back to our cornfield."

My mother was glad to hear that. She said to me, "I don't want you to stay in bed and sleep all morning. Tomorrow morning I want you to get up early and go after the horses. We'll start back tomorrow morning. I'm very glad to hear nothing has happened. I'm very glad to hear they want us to come down to our homes. So you must get the horses early in the morning, so we can go back to our cornfield. Perhaps, by now, something has got after our corn. So we want to go back to our farm right away."

She kept on saying thanks every once in a while. She was thanking the headman, saying, "Thank you very much, our headman." She kept on saying thank you every once in a while that night after my father was through with his story. It was way late in the night when he was through, and from there on she kept giving thanks. She said, "I believe it, and I know they're kind. When they took us away from here to Fort Sumner the government gathered us up at Fort Defiance. He took us away from these different tribes of Indians. If he hadn't taken us away from them we'd all have been killed and starved to death. But he took us away and fed us and took us to Fort Sumner. He fed us all the way, giving us flour and coffee and other different foods, killing cattle for us all the way. And he took care of us there and on our way home, until he brought us back to Fort Defiance. And he's kept on helping us from there on. He gave us sheep that we've raised, and we got cattle and horses. Even though he didn't give us that still I always think he's given us everything. If he hadn't given us sheep we wouldn't have horses and cattle. And we began raising children, and he did that too, and he's still helping us today. I know he's kind to us all and is trying his best to help us. That's the way with the government." Then we all went to sleep.

11. *The Nda that was given for Stutterer*
. . . Snakes and string figures.

THE next morning, while they were still in bed, I went out and brought in the horses. My father said, "As soon as you eat take them back to our cornfield. We'll come right after you." Everything was cooked, and he said, "Hurry and eat and go down with the horses. Don't take your time. Get down as quickly as you can." After I ate I got a horse and put the saddle on it, and my mother got one for herself and one for my father. She said, "Go down there as quickly as you can and take your gun along. When you get out to the cornfield, if you see any crows shoot and scare them away." So I got my gun and tied it to the saddle and put the cartridge belt around me, and then I started off, driving the horses over a hill and across the flat. They were going right along. At Sweet Water I got some rocks and began throwing rocks at them, making them run as hard as they could go, and I was riding right behind them. Soon I got to the foot of the mountain, and soon I was back to our cornfield. Then I let them go towards the foot of the hill. They were all sweaty and white with the foam of their sweat.

I rode over to the farm, and a lot of crows flew up out of the corn. I got off my horse and took down my gun. A bunch of them were sitting on a hill. I put some cartridges in the gun and shot at them, but I only scared them away. Some others were sitting on a tree, and I took a shot at them. I saw the feathers fly, but none of them fell. At our home were the two dogs of ours that we'd left behind. They were still around the hogan. They'd been barking at night, I guess, and that's why the coyotes didn't get after the corn. I walked around in the field, but the corn was all right. I broke off some ears and took them to the hogan and built a fire, and there I sat, roasting myself some corn. After that I got another horse and went to the woods and started dragging in some wood. When I had enough I went after water.

About that time a lot of dust was coming along out from Mouth Of The Canyon. It was a hot day, and the people were camping there, waiting for it to get cool. But there was one cloud of dust coming on towards me. That was my mother and father with their herds. They hadn't stopped to camp. They came right along and got back in the afternoon and drove the sheep under the trees, where there was shade. I had lots of corn roasted for them, and they began eating.

My father said, "How's the corn? What has the crow and coyote been doing? Have they been after the corn much?" I said, "No, there were no tracks of a coyote. Only the crows have been after the corn. But they've been picking on just a few. The rest of it looks all right." "That's fine. Maybe it was on account of the dogs that the coyotes didn't get after our corn. Maybe they're hungry. Give them something to eat. I thought they'd be lost, but they're still around here. Go over and get a two-year-old wether and butcher it. Quick, so we'll have some meat." I rode over to the sheep and got one that I put across the saddle and brought back. My mother took it down and tied the legs together and cut the throat. She said to me, "Go ahead and butcher it. I'll go over and get some corn. I'll make some green corn-bread. I know there'll be a crowd here soon. There are lots of people who haven't any corn, and they'll be here to get some." While I started butchering she went to the farm and brought back some corn and began grinding it up. After I'd cut up the meat—it was good and fat—I built a big fire, and when she'd made the corn-bread she put it in the ashes and covered it up and built a fire over it.

About that time, sure enough, the people began riding up. There was lots of dust going off in different directions, some going along the foot of the mountain, some down to the flat. There was dust all over. Everybody was moving back. Some were passing us, and a lot of them stopped. Soon there was a big crowd at our place, and they all wanted to eat corn. My mother took out the corn-bread and laid it out for the crowd, along with lots of boiled meat, and everybody started eating. Some of them wanted corn. She said, "You can just go right in the cornfield and help yourselves." They built a fire at a few places and began roasting ears of corn.

They were sitting around and talking about the troops, and Old Man Hat said, "Those two fellows, Has Done It and the other one, ought to get on their horses and go out in the flat. As soon as the troops saw them they'd sure go after them. They ought to ride way out in the flat and then start riding away and keep going out in the middle of the desert where there's no water. I don't think those big horses could stand the desert. I know they can't stand the hot sand, and the troops can't either. As soon as they ran out of water, way out in the desert, they'd all die of thirst. These little ponies of ours can stand anything. They can run all day out in the sand." But some of the others said, "If they did that they'd be killed right there, because the troops are all crack shots. They'd be killed if they got out in the flat for them. The guns the troops have are powerful. It's a good thing they didn't do it." They were talking about it for a long time.

Old Man White Horse and his older brother, Stutterer, had come to our place. They were Many Goats. White Horse said, "We were just going to start the Nda. We were all ready for it, but instead we started running away. But now we'll have it, since the headman talked to us in a kind way yesterday, and we have our good mind and thoughts again. When we got back last night we talked about it. At first we were going to have it way down at Thief Rock, but we talked it over last night among ourselves and decided we'd come over here to you, my older brother. What do you think about it? Where shall we have this Nda? I want to hold it for my older brother. He's not feeling well, and we all think the Nda is bothering him. So I want to put it up for him. Think about it for us. Where shall we have it? And when shall we start it?"

My father said, "Well, if you want to have it done quickly we don't want to talk about it over and over. When a man begins to talk about something he won't stop for anything, he'll just keep on talking of one thing all day. So now we'll all stop talking about it and just say we'll have it now. And we'll have it around here close by, because there are many cornfields around here close together. There's lots to eat now. The people have lots of corn, and we've got lots of sheep and horses that we've been chasing around with. I'm sure everybody will help."

While he was saying this our sheep had wandered far away. It was late in the afternoon. When it got cool, while he was still talking, I went after the sheep. From there on I don't know what he said. While I was out in the flat with the herd there was still a crowd at our place, until about sundown, and then they began riding away. Everybody had left by the time the sun had set. I came back in the evening, and my mother'd made some more corn-bread. She said, "There's no meat left. A crowd's been here all day. They left only a little while ago. They ate up all the meat, all the insides, all the feet and head, liver, heart and lungs. They ate up everything, and we haven't any meat now. They said they're going to have the Nda soon. They set a date, they said, 'In two days we'll all gather at

201

Anything Falls In, and there we'll decide where to take the decorated-stick.' They're going to have the Nda right here, at Anything Falls In, up on the hill there."

When the two days were up I went out with the herd to the water at Anything Falls In. A big crowd was on the hill and around the water there, dragging in poles and branches, going back and forth to the woods, making brush hogans. I was at the water for a while, but I didn't go up to the crowd. When I started home they were still going back and forth to the woods, dragging out poles, branches and wood. That evening when my father came home he said, "They've put up one brush hogan already, and they're about finished with another in which they're going to cook. They may be through by now. I told them to go to a fellow named Always With The Rams. He's living at Coyote Water. I said, 'Tell him we'll bring the decorated-stick to him. Tell him to put up a date, but don't let him put up a date too soon. Tell him we'll bring the decorated-stick over to him in seven days, or a little more than that, because we want to let all the people know about it. We'll send word to Bunch Of Whiskers. He lives far away from here, at Country Of The Cheek. He's got lots of people living with him. We want to let them know about it. They'll all help us, and all those on the mountain and out in the flat and around the foot of the mountain. So let him put up a date from seven days on or a little bit more.'" Bunch Of Whiskers was Stutterer's brother-in-law.

Two days later my father went to where they were going to have the Nda. When he came home that evening he said, "The man who went to Coyote Water is back. He said, 'I got to this fellow's place in the evening. He was home, and he treated me well. Then I told him about the Nda. I said, "We've all decided we'll bring the decorated-stick to you. They want you to say, 'In seven days, or a little more, you bring the decorated-stick to me.' " He asked me, "Who's the fellow who said that?" I said, "It's Old Man Hat who wants you to put up that many days. Old Man Hat said, 'We'll have the Nda for five nights.' " Right away he said, "Well, it's all right with me. He's my son, Old Man Hat's my son. So if he says that to me I won't say no to him. From tomorrow on it'll be nine days. Bring the decorated-stick to me nine days from tomorrow. I'm not counting this night. I'll be going around too, to my people. We'll take our time on it." ' So in nine days we'll take the stick to this man. They've got a Ute bone already. Mexican Blanket brought it. So from tonight on they're going to have an Nda every night. There'll be a crowd there all the time. In two days a fellow is going to take word to Bunch Of Whiskers. When he hears about it he'll let all his people know, he'll let all his neighbors know about it. In that way everybody from there will help us, because they all have lots of things to help us with."

Three days before they were going to take away the decorated-stick the people started moving off the mountain. They kept on coming out with their sheep and horses, making lots of dust. It was just like when we were chasing away from the troops. They all went down to Anything Falls In and camped around there close to the water. A great many people moved out and camped all around there. They were making so much dust you could hardly see a thing. I went over the evening before they were going to take away the stick, and there was a big crowd. I was there part of the night and then came back. Early in the morning they rounded up their horses and started off, just as the sun was up. Many of them went. It was a long way to where they were taking the decorated-stick. The next morning they started back from there, and the day after that the visiting-party from Coyote Water moved up to where the troops had camped, at Bank Caving

Down. Everyone was going over there, going along, passing us in bunches.

In the afternoon my mother said, "We'll go over now." She meant to where they were having the Nda, at Anything Falls In. We were living only a little way from that place. My father had been over there for three days and nights. She said, "Gather some corn, and we'll take it over." I got a lot and tied it up in a blanket and put it over the horse. It was quite a load. Then we fixed our things, put everything away and covered it up, and she said, "Tie the two dogs out in the field, so they'll watch the corn." I put a rope around their necks and tied them up, and then we started with the sheep.

There was a big crowd all over the hill at Where The Gray Hill Comes Out. That's where we camped, close to the Nda. My mother took over the corn, and I stayed with the sheep. She came back in the evening when it got dark. "It's a big crowd," she said. "You can hardly get in between them. I never saw such a crowd. They say they're going to start dancing soon." I said, "I'd like to go over and see the dance." She said, "Be sure and come back tonight when you begin to get sleepy. Don't try to sleep over there, because they might run over you. You must come back as soon as you get sleepy. And tomorrow I want you to get the horses. I want to use one for herding, and I want you to use one to go over to the farm with and get some more corn. So be sure and come back tonight." Right after I got there they started up the dance, beating the drum and singing. They were dancing all night. While they were still dancing I started home, even though I wasn't sleepy.

In the morning I went after the horses, and while I was gone my mother killed a sheep. When I came back she said, "I'll go out with the herd, and you go to the farm and get some more corn. And take something to the dogs." I took along a little feed for the dogs and got some corn and started back. About then she was coming in with the herd. It was almost noontime. The party from Coyote Water was just coming along. About three miles away was a hill, and as soon as they moved up on this hill we could see them start running their horses and shooting and coming towards the Nda. When they were close the fellows from the Nda started out and met them out in the flat, and they began chasing one another back and forth. Then they rode around the hogan, shooting and making a lot of smoke. Dust and smoke were just like a rising cloud. Back and forth four times they went around the hogan. Then they stopped and camped where a brush hogan had been put up for them, and everything was quiet.

My father rode out from where they'd camped, he'd been there among those people, and as he started riding back to us some people came after him. That was Who Has Mules and his wife and some others with him. Then some more started towards us; that was Choclays Kinsman and his wife and some people with them. And some more came. They were all from Cheek. That was Wounded Smith and Big Red Clay and others that were with them. Then some more started towards us. They were from the mountain, from Scratch Out Water. They were all Mexican People. There was a bunch of them. One fellow's name was He Crosses His Legs. As soon as he rode up he said to my father, "Well, my grandfather, we're all hungry. We didn't have anything to eat all day yesterday and last night. We're about starved now." They were all saying the same, calling him my old father, my grandfather, "We want something to eat." My father said, "I've nothing to eat for you. There's nothing to eat." He Crosses His Legs said, "Nothing to eat! How about all those sheep? You've got lots of sheep all over under the trees. A man like you having so many sheep and saying he's got nothing to eat."

My father smiled and said, "If you're not lazy you can go ahead and help yourselves. I give you all those sheep. If you can eat them all just go ahead." They laughed and got off their horses, riding up under the trees, and took off their saddles.

There was a big crowd all around us. My father said to me, "Go over and round up all the sheep for them. Let them go to it." I rounded up the herd, and they got out and stood around it with their ropes. My mother walked up and pointed one out for them, and they roped that. Then she pointed out another. They roped four in all, two goats and two sheep. One was for Choclays Kinsman, one for Who Has Mules, one for Wounded Smith and one for He Crosses His Legs. They all had a bunch of people with them. They built four big fires around us and started butchering. My mother said to me, "Catch one." I caught one, and that was for ourselves and the many other people at our place. After that all the people who had sheep drove them over to the visiting-party. They were getting from two to four at a time out of a bunch. All the people who belonged on our side were giving sheep to the visiting-party, because so many of them had camped there. They were butchering here and there and all around where they'd camped.

My mother said, "Now we'll all help one another. One of you take the sheep out for us, and some of you go to the cornfield with my son." Who Has Mules had his son with him, and he said, "My son will go out with the sheep." He was a small boy at that time. Later he was called Smith's Son In Law. My mother said to the boy, "Take the sheep out for us, my son, my baby. Help us on that, and my son will take the men to the cornfield." They told three fellows to go to the farm. My mother said, "Get lots of corn and the grinding stone, and bring back all the dishes. We want to use them here. Be sure and bring lots of corn. We'll use some here and take some to the Nda. They'll use it over there." At the corn-field we tied the ends of the blankets together and filled them with corn and put them over the horses. Then we got the grinding stone and the dishes and buckets and went back. There the fellows started taking off the husks and cutting off the kernels. That was for corn-bread.

My mother told me to take a load to the Nda. I passed by the visiting-party, and there was meat all over the trees and inside the brush hogan. Some were still butchering, and flocks of sheep were still coming. The people were still giving them sheep. They were butchering all around the hogan. I went over to the Nda and dumped the corn right by the doorway where they were cooking. There it was just the same, meat all over in the big shade and meat all over outside. Every place I looked there was meat, and they were still butchering, and all around were flocks of sheep. The insides were all being thrown away, and piles of heads were everywhere. I looked for a while and then started back. I stopped by the visiting-party and looked, and every place I looked there was nothing but meat, meat hanging from the trees, and everyone was cooking. When I got back to our camp it was the same there too. All around the fires was the smoke of roasting meat. But here they were cooking the insides. The old man was sitting under a tree in the middle of a crowd. Choclays Kinsman was there and Who Has Mules and Wounded Smith. They were sitting right close together, and all around was a big crowd. Old Man Hat was talking, telling some kind of story. We were camped out in the open under a tree, and from this tree hung lots of fat. It could have been used for tortillas or fried-bread, but there wasn't a bit of flour, only cornmeal.

In the afternoon I thought I'd take out the herd. I was

herding a while, and when the sun was down I brought them back. It was cool then. About that time they started dancing the circle-dance. Some of the people at our place went over, some stayed. Then, when I came back with the herd and while the people were going over to the dance, an outfit started riding towards us from the Nda. That was Slim Man and his wife, the one who was a Red From The Waist Down, and another man. He was a Many Goats too, a clan brother of Slim Man's. He was from Bay In The Mountain. As soon as they rode up my mother looked up and said, "Oh, we've got nothing to eat for you, my son. The meat's all gone. There's just a little piece left. We had plenty, but they ate it all up. We haven't any more to eat." "Nothing more to eat?" said Slim Man. "How about those sheep over there? Are they no good eating? Every one looks good to me." Then my mother said to me, "Oh, my son, go and round up the sheep for your father. Let him get one for himself." I rounded them up, and he took over a rope, and while the sheep were running along, passing by him, he roped one, a four-year-old wether. He took it back and told this Many Goats to butcher it. The man tied up the legs and cut the throat and started butchering, and then Slim Man's outfit started cooking for themselves. All the other people had gone to the dance.

Slim Man said to me, "I'd like to see you dance tonight with the girls." But my mother said, "I don't like him to dance with the girls, because he hasn't anything to give away." Slim Man said, "Nothing to give away? He's got some cattle. You just go over and dance. You can dance for one of your cattle. For a man who has lots of stock like you to say, 'I've got nothing to dance for.' Go over and dance for one of your cattle." My mother said, "Don't you do that. Don't try to get out where they can catch you. Watch yourself. Don't let them catch you. Don't get out in front of the crowd." It was just getting dark. The rest of the people had all gone over. Old Man Hat didn't go, he was sitting there, and my mother didn't go either.

When Slim Man and his outfit were through eating they started over, and I went with them. They'd stopped dancing the circle-dance, and a big crowd, standing at one place, had just started singing. I went about among the crowds, over to the Nda and everywhere, running to different fires and looking all around. They built a big fire for the dance we called those-who-turn, and began dancing. Only five girls from the visiting-party and only six or seven from the Nda came out. They were dancing for a long time.

I was standing almost at the edge of the crowd when all at once a girl got hold of me. I tried to get away, but she hung on and started dragging me out of the crowd. She was strong, so then I just went out with her. I was ashamed to dance at first, but soon my shame had gone away, and from there on I went right ahead and danced with her. We used to have a lot of copper buttons. A man named Stingy Mexican used to make them. I had quite a long string, and I began giving her three at a time. Every time she wanted me to pay her I gave her three buttons, and every time I paid her I told her to let me go. But she kept hanging on to me, perhaps because she saw the buttons. I danced with her until they stopped the dance. I'd given over half my buttons away. She was a big girl. When they stopped dancing I paid her again, but she kept holding me. I told her to let me go. Then she said she wanted all the buttons. I said, "I haven't got any more." But she knew I still had some. She wanted them all and kept holding me. Finally I got away, but there were only a few buttons left.

I started right back to where we were camping and lay

down there and went to sleep. I woke up when it was almost daylight. As soon as I got up my mother missed the buttons. She said, "Well, look at that. What did you do with all the buttons? There's nothing but string around your neck. I told you you shouldn't dance. I know you've been dancing for those buttons." But I didn't say anything. About that time everybody got up. Slim Man was up too, and my mother said again, "He danced for all those buttons last night. Look at him. He's got nothing but string around his neck. He's given all the buttons away." Slim Man said, "Never mind about the buttons. There's nothing to the buttons. What do you want to talk about buttons for? You can get them any place. He didn't give any of his cattle away. He didn't lose one of his cattle. What do you want to talk about the buttons for?" My mother didn't say any more about it. Slim Man said to me, "Did you dance for your cattle too? I heard him say to that girl, 'I'll give you two head of cattle.' I heard him say that as I was passing by. Didn't you?" he said to me. But I didn't say anything. My mother was looking at me, maybe she wanted to say something, but she didn't, because Slim Man was there. He always knocked everything she said. That's why, I guess, she was afraid to say it.

That afternoon, after they were through treating the patient, Choclays Kinsman and Who Has Mules and their wives and some other people came over. They were all from the mountain. They said, "We'll eat lunch, and after we've eaten we'll all start back to our homes. We've been here quite a few days now, we've been away from our homes a good while, so we'd better be going back." Then after they'd eaten Choclays Kinsman and Who Has Mules and his boy who was herding for us and all the rest of their people left and went back to their homes. Lots of people left that day.

In the evening I went over to the Nda again. Some other

people at our place went over too, but my father and mother stayed at the camp. Even though many had left and gone home there was still a big crowd. I was running all around among the crowd again that night, walking up to different fires and back and forth to where they were cooking at the visiting-party's place. They sang for a while in front of the Nda, under the shade, and then they went back to the hogan of the visiting-party and started singing there. They sang again for quite a while, and then they built a big fire and started dancing.

This time I watched myself closely. I stood in the middle of the crowd, and after a while I went around and sat behind the woodpile. I was leaning over the wood, watching the dance, when, all at once, a girl held me. I don't know where she came from. I hadn't seen any of the girls walk out from the dance. There I was, lying and taking it easy, and she got hold of me. I said, "I don't want to dance. I haven't anything to give you." But she held on to me and began dragging me out, so I went with her and started dancing. After a while she stopped and wanted me to pay her. I gave her some of my buttons and told her to let me go. She let me go right away. I walked back to the woodpile, and just as I was going around behind it I got caught again. That was the same girl with whom I'd danced the night before. She was a big, strong girl. I tried to hold on to a log, but she pulled me right out. I paid her twice and told her to let me go. But she said, "No, I want to dance with you until they stop." Suddenly I got away, but just as I was going behind the group of singers she caught me again. But this time I was hanging onto a bush. Then I began to touch her legs, but she didn't move. Pretty soon I said to her, "Let's go out of the crowd for a walk." Right away she said, "All right."

It was dark behind the crowd. We went a long way to

where some ditches were running close together, where there was nobody around, and got down in a ditch, and there I gave her all my copper buttons. I asked her, "Have you got a man?" She said, "No." I said, "I bet you've got a man." She said, "No, I don't know what you mean." I said, "I know you've got a man." At last she said, "Yes, I had a man two years ago, but he left me, and now I haven't one." I asked her, "Where are you from?" She said, "I'm from on top of Black Mountain, from a place called Red Willow Spot. I came with my father and younger sister." A baby was crying over at the visiting-party's hogan, and when we were through she got up and ran away. I followed her, she was running ahead of me, but I was close to her all the way, and saw her go in and pick up a baby and nurse it. That was the one I'd heard crying. She'd said to me, "Come over to me after they're through with the dance." But I didn't go; when they stopped dancing I went home.

When I awoke the sun was up. My mother had brought back the horse she used for herding, and when I woke up she said, "Go get the others." I put the saddle on her horse and went after them, and when I brought them in we moved back to the cornfield. From there on we lived at our farm. Every time I took the herd to water I always went to where the visiting-party had camped. Sheep and goat heads were lying all around there. Pretty soon I couldn't go near that place any more. Everything had rotted.

We had a lot of corn, squash, pumpkins and melons too. The man who planted there, Blind Mexican, didn't show up all summer. He said he'd be back again sometime when the corn was ripe, but he never showed up. My mother said to me, "Dig a hole where we can bake some corn." I started digging and was working on that all day. The next day I dragged in some wood, and the day after, in the morning, I built a fire in the hole. While the fire was burning my mother and I began gathering up the corn. Half of it was dried, and half was green. The green corn we put in the hole at the end of the day. In the morning I opened it up, but the corn was only half done. But, anyway, we took it out and started husking. When we were through husking we laid it on the ground to dry, and everything was taken off the field. In about ten days, when the corn was good and dry, we stored it, and the squash and pumpkins too, and after that we started moving. We took the trail that goes to Valley Coming To The Edge. We went down that valley and on past Willows Coming Out to Lower Water. Quite away below that place we camped.

While we were living there I began to make myself a pair of moccasins. One day, while I was working on them, I heard a horse neigh down at the foot of the rocks. I went over to the edge of the cliff in my bare feet, and all of a sudden I heard a rattlesnake. It was coiled right where I was standing. I saw it just as it was about to go for me, and I gave one jump. It almost got me. Then it crawled away into a little pile of rocks. I went home and put on my father's old moccasins and then went back where the snake was and gathered up a lot of wood and piled it all around the rocks and built a fire. I had a big fire burning on the rocks and was watching there, but I didn't see the snake.

When I got home I told my father about it. I said, "A big rattlesnake got after me." He said, "What's the matter with you? Why didn't you go after him? You've got arms and legs, and the snake hasn't any. Why didn't you go after the snake and kill it?" I said, "I built a fire on it." My mother didn't like that. She said, "Why do you want to build a fire on the snake? You shouldn't build a fire on the snake. That's what you get for making string figures in the summertime." I used to work with this string all the time, making stars, one-star and two-stars and some called many-stars and seven-stars, and lightning and bows-and-arrows, and some called one-hogan and some called double-hogan, and some called two-coyotes-running-from-each-other, and a lot of other things. That's what I'd been doing in the summertime, and I always got caught at it. Whenever she saw me doing that in the summertime she'd scold me about it. But when the snake got after me I believed my mother; from then on I was afraid to play with the string in the summer.

After we'd lived at that place quite a few days we moved again down towards Among The Black Rocks. We had a winter camp there too. A hogan was there, and a sheep corral was up already. We renewed the hogan and the corral, and there we lived again. It was real cold by then, but no snow had fallen yet.

One day in the evening, after I'd come home with the herd and my father was back too from some place, my mother said, "Who Has Mules was here today. He said he'd like to eat some beef. I said to him, 'Come back again tomorrow morning. The old man will be home then, and I'll tell my son about it too.' That's what I told him, and he went home." She was telling us that, but the old man, my father, was lying there, he didn't say anything. I was lying there too, just listening to her talking. Pretty soon she said, "What's the matter with you two? Can't you talk any more? Why don't you speak? What do you think about it? If you don't want to have one of the cattle killed, why don't you say so? But I've already promised my cousin. I told him to come back tomorrow. I've promised him already that he can go and get the cattle. That's what I told him. I said, 'If you want to kill one go after them and bring them here, and we'll kill one, and we'll all have some beef.' That's what I told my cousin today."

My father said, "Well, we haven't anything to do with it. Why should we want to say anything about it? You've promised him already, and you've already given him a cow. Why should we talk about it? If you'd said you hadn't promised him, then we might have something to say, but you've promised him already that he can have one." My mother turned to me, "What do you think about it, my son?" I said, "You've given one to him already, so I've nothing to say about it." "Yes," she said, "he's coming again tomorrow. He'll be here, and I want you to say which one we should kill." My father said, "They're not here yet. If he really means to kill one, then he can go and get them. When he brings them back we'll see and decide which one we'll kill."

The next morning I went out with the herd. That day Who Has Mules went over to Choclays Kinsman, and they both went after the cattle. Late in the afternoon, when I got home with the herd, they'd killed a beef already and had both gone home. There was lots of meat all over on the trees. It was nice and fat. My mother said, "Who Has Mules took home a lot of meat, and so did Choclays Kinsman." We had meat for many days.

Several days after we killed the beef it snowed. After the snow my father started telling me about the snakes. He said, "You should talk to the snake. When you talk to a snake he'll know just what you're saying to him. He can hear you. If you talk to the snake the snake won't bother you. Maybe you'll step on a snake sometime when you're walking along, but the snake will know who you are, and even though you stepped on him he won't move, he won't try to do anything to you. So in the summertime, when all the snakes come out, the first one you see you want to talk to. In that way the snake will know you all the time. The same with the lightning. You must talk to the lightning too. When you first see the lightning and hear the thunder you should talk to them, and they will know who you are all during the summer. The same with the bear. When you go up on the mountain the first bear that you see, or even the track of one, you must talk to it, and they'll know you all the time, all during the summer. In that way they won't harm you; they won't bother you at all."

My mother had many prayers. When she made corn-mush —she made it every other day—she had sticks to stir it with, and when she thought the mush was done she'd take the sticks out and raise them. While she was holding them up she'd say a little prayer. She used to say, "We'll have something all the time. Our stocks and our hogan will be in good shape, and we'll live well all the time. We'll have lots of property and all kinds of beads and turquoise. And we'll have lots to eat all the time." That's the way she used to say her prayers. After we ate we all said our prayers too. We always gave thanks for our food and always prayed for more things to eat. We used to pray for everything.

12.

The death of the wife of Who Has Mules . . . In the spring they move and plant and shear again . . . He takes the wool to the store, and when he comes back they are so pleased and thankful.

THAT winter my father, Choclays Kinsman, bought a Zuni woman and her two children. She was getting to be quite an old woman, but she wasn't real old yet. For some reason or other she ran away and left her children. They heard that some people saw her going to Ganado, so he didn't go after her. He just kept the two children of hers, a girl and a boy. That made three slaves that he had, Choclay and these two. The girl was a big girl. She always herded the sheep. After I got to know her I used to go to her every other day when I went after the horses. I'd round the horses up quickly and then ride over where she was herding.

One day Choclays Kinsman's wife came to our place. She said, "We'd like to go to the Oraibi. From there we want to go and visit some of our relatives. We'll be gone for a few days, we don't know just how many, and we're leaving the two children at home. We're taking Choclay with us. The other two will stay home herding the sheep. While we're gone I want my younger brother to go over every once in a while, every day or two, to get wood and water for them, and to take care of them for us. We'll be very thankful if he does that." My father said, "Yes, he'll take care of those children." "We're figuring on going in two days," she said.

When the two days were up I went over. They were just

getting ready. They said, "We're about to leave." My father said, "She wants to visit her brothers and sisters, so we don't know how long we'll be gone. You must come every other day and take care of the children and the herd for us. Look after all our things. There's no water close by, so we've been using snow. It's quite a way to where we get it. There's a little on the shady side of that red mesa. But if you go on horseback you'll have some back with you in a hurry. You should get them some snow and wood. So watch around for us, and in that way we won't be worrying." His wife said, "Yes, my younger brother, that's what we want you to do. Please take care of all our things for us. Now that we know you'll be around all the time we won't worry about them." Then they got on their horses, and the old man said, "Now we're going. We'll camp on our way tonight, and the next day we'll be at the Oraibi. There we'll buy some food. When we're through trading with those people we'll leave all our things there and go on. So we just don't know how long we'll be gone, my baby. Take good care of our things. Take good care of the whole place for us." That's what he said to me, and they left.

When they'd gone I was alone with the girl. The boy was out with the herd, and we were both glad we'd been left at home alone. She said, "There's no more water. We've used it all up." I said, "Well, let's go and get some snow. You know where it is." Right away she said, "All right." When we got there I f—ed her first, and then we got some snow. At home we melted it and got some water, and she cooked some food, and after we ate I went out and chopped up a big pile of wood. About that time the sun was pretty well down, and the sheep were coming home. Then I started back and got home that evening.

From there on every two days I went over to those children. That was all I'd been doing for over ten days, and then they returned. I was there when they came back. They brought all kinds of food, corn, dried peaches, beans, different kinds of corn-bread and lots of dried deer meat. My father said, "When we got to the Oraibi we traded with them, and when we were through trading we left our stuff and went on to a place called Beaver. We visited the people there, and then went on to the foot of San Francisco Peak and visited some more. Tunes To His Voice was living there. Then we went up to San Francisco Peak and hunted around there. The deer were still fat. That's what I've been doing with those people, and after we returned from hunting we started home."

His wife had got a horse from her sister, and my father said, "I thought you wanted to give that horse to your younger brother." She said, "Never at all. You're telling a story. I never said that. I said, 'I wonder how my younger brother is getting along.'" "Well," he said, "that's what you said. You said, 'As soon as I get home I'll give this horse to my younger brother.'" She said, "No, indeed, I never said that. My younger brother has lots of horses. If he didn't have any, then I'd surely give him one. But he has lots of horses." That's what they said to each other, but I knew they were just joshing, so I didn't say anything about it. My older sister began giving me different kinds of foods and meat that they'd brought back, and soon I had a big bundle. When I got home with the big bundle on my back my mother was very glad and thankful. I said, "That's what I've been working for all this time." She said, "Yes, I know. It's very nice of you. If you hadn't gone over we wouldn't have all these foods."

One morning before breakfast a few days after, while I was putting the saddle on a horse, my father said, "Go over where the horses are and round them up. Drive them towards the water. Just let them go so they can get water; they know where it is." I got on the horse, and, all at once, as soon as I got on he stood straight up and then fell over backwards. I don't know how I fell, but I found myself lying between the horse's legs, right by his belly, and one of my legs was under him. It was close to the hogan, and my mother and father were both inside and must have heard something had happened. My mother came running out, and when she saw me she gave a scream and hollered, "The boy is under the horse!" The old man came out then, and both of them ran up to me. The horse was lying still, not moving at all. My father grabbed me, and my mother ran around and got hold of the horse's hind legs. She must have been a strong woman; she rolled the horse over all by herself. He never gave a kick. As soon as she turned him over my father pulled me out and took the stirrup off my foot, and the moment the horse was loose he got up and started bucking and ran away.

There was a little ache in my leg, and I was limping. While they were taking me back to the hogan my father kept saying, "Don't limp. Walk straight." My mother was angry. When we got inside she scolded him for that. "You always want the horses rounded up. That's all you think and talk about. Nothing will happen to the horses. Nothing will take them away from you. Why don't you leave them where they are. You're to blame that the horse fell on him." But he didn't say a word. After breakfast he went after the horse. A little way from the hogan he found the bridle-rings and sad-dle-blanket and the saddle all in pieces. He picked them all up and brought them home. When he found the horse the rope was still around his neck, and the bridle without the rings was still on him.

Quite a few days later they told me to go down to where

we'd stored our stuff and get some squash. I started off with one pack horse, going back along the way we'd moved. When I got out to our farm the sun was almost down. I uncovered one of the holes, and all the squash was rotten. Only three of them were good. I threw out the rest and covered the hole again, and about then it was dark, and so I built a fire and cooked a squash. In the morning I opened another, and that was all right. That was the pumpkins. I took out quite a few of those and cut them up. Then I covered the hole and started back. I had a big load on both horses. Way late in the evening I got home. They were both still awake, and as soon as I got back my mother came out and helped me. When we got the load off the horses she dragged it in the hogan. My fingers were so stiff and cold I couldn't hold anything. I just turned the horses loose and went in and started to warm myself. I was cold all over. As soon as the heat struck my fingers they began to get sore. My father said, "Don't get too close to the fire. You'll ruin yourself. Get back. Get away from the fire. Even though you're cold you'll be warm in a little while."

My mother put some pumpkins in a pot and started boiling them, and then she gave me some food. While I was eating she said, "Who Has Mules was here today. He said, 'My wife began to get sick three days ago. I got a singer for her, and he's singing now. I don't know what's wrong with her. I don't know how she got sick. She got sick all at once and was getting worse all the time, and now she's very ill.' That's what he said. He wanted us to know about it."

The next day my father said to me, "I want a horse. I want to take a ride over to that place. I want to see how they're getting along. So you go and get me a horse." I got a horse for him, and he rode over. He stayed there two days and two nights. When I got home with the sheep in the evening my mother said, "Your father came back today, but he's already gone over again. He said she keeps getting worse all the time. They've gone after another singer, named Dog Hater. There's a singer there, singing now, who's going on with his treatment. That's Curly Hair. So she just keeps on getting worse, and he's gone back already. He'll stay overnight again. He said he's coming back tomorrow and wants you to get a horse for him early in the morning. I want you to get two horses. I want to go over too, to see how she's getting along. Choclays Kinsman is at that place, and his wife also, and some other people. So I'd like to go over to see her."

In the morning I got the two horses, but my father didn't show up. I said to my mother, "Go on over and take that horse with you." "All right," she said, "I'll do that." Late in the evening she came home again. I was sitting inside the hogan. When I heard her I went out, and there she was, unsaddling her horse. She'd brought back the one my father had been using. We turned them loose, and she began telling me about it. "We don't know just what's wrong with her. She's very sick. She hasn't eaten anything for three days. We tried to get her to take something, but she wouldn't. She hardly seems to know a thing. Even at that they got another singer, that's Dog Hater, and he's going to sing and do a treatment also. And the other singer is there, singing and treating, but still she's just getting worse all the time. So I don't think there's any hope for her. Quite a few people are there. They get scared every time she goes a little unconscious, and the women begin to cry. I don't think she'll live." She was sitting there, talking about it, she was worried all night. Before we went to sleep she said, "Get another horse for me tomorrow morning. I want to go over again and see what they're doing."

In the morning she butchered a sheep and already had

the meat cut up when I came back. After we ate she took the meat and some grub along with her, and I took out the sheep. When I returned in the evening nobody was home. She stayed over there that night. The next morning I went out again with the herd and came back in the evening, and this time she was home. She said, "There's no hope. She's just lying there, not moving, only her heart is beating. Last night they star-gazed. The star-gazer said, 'The hogan, and the whole place around here, is all black. Nothing can be seen. That means death. There's no hope. Her time is coming close, though she'll live through the night and tomorrow all day, but the next night, sometime during the night, she'll be gone.' That's what the star-gazer said last night, and the people are crying."

The next day I took the herd to water. While I was at the water my father came over, and we started back with the herd to our home. I sat behind him on his horse, and he said, "There's no hope at all. I don't think she'll live any longer. She began to talk this morning, but no one could understand what she was saying." When we got home in the evening he said, "I came to get some sleep. I haven't slept for five nights. I'm about dead. But tomorrow you get me another horse, and I'll go over again. I don't think she'll still be alive, but, anyway, I want to go. So tomorrow morning you get me another horse."

I brought back another just as the sun came up, and after we ate he left, and I took out the sheep. When I returned in the evening he was already there. He said, "She died last night. They were just taking her away when I got there. I stayed until the two fellows came back from burying her, and then I began giving them a talk, telling them not to weep so hard, 'because she isn't the only one who has died. Death started from the time we were put on this earth. Everybody

223

is dying off all the time, right along. Many people are dying off by day and by night. We'll all be dead too, sometime. We'll all go. So try and forget about her.' That's the way I talked to them, and after that I left."

We lived on at that place, and we never did have any more snow. Only once we had a little, but from then on we didn't get any more. It was just cold all winter. While we were still living there Who Has Mules came to our place. As soon as he came in my mother started crying, and he was crying too. They cried for a long time. Then my father began to talk to him, he gave him a long talk, telling him not to think about her. "I know it's hard. That's the toughest thing that happens, when you lose a wife, or a child. They're about the same. But, even though it's hard for you, try and forget about it. As I said to you before, death is going on all the time. We'll be gone too, but we'll all meet each other again. So don't think about it. You're still young; you'll soon get another wife. While you're living try your best to take good care of yourself." That's what he was saying to him for a long time.

Who Has Mules said, "Yes, I'm in sorrow, but still I'm taking care of myself. I'm not thinking badly about myself, and I'm thinking about all my things. I'm not letting everything go. I'm still holding onto everything." Then he said, "That's why I'm going around among you, my clansmen. When I get lonely, when I can't stand the sorrow, I get on my horse and go and visit you, my clansman. Then, when I go around, I forget a little about it. So that's why I came here, and I'm very glad and thankful for your talk. That's what I came here for. I wanted you to talk to me, and now you have, and I'm so thankful for it." He stayed with us that day and night, and in the morning he went back to his home.

We were living right at the same place all the time, and spring was coming. In places that the sun struck things were getting green. Then my mother started talking about the farm. She said, "We'll move down again to the same place where we planted the corn. We planted there last spring and raised a lot of corn and some squash and pumpkins. We'll move back to the same place and plant some more, my son. So you think about it. We won't have to go and ask for seeds. We've got squash and pumpkin seeds, and we've still got some corn." That's what she said, but my father didn't say anything about it. It seemed to me he didn't care. But after a while he got up and said, "Well, we'll wait until it gets real warm. When the grass and other feed for the stocks get real green, then we'll move down. That's where I like to be, down in the valleys and out in the flats where we can see all around. Up here on the mountain we don't know where we are, it seems like, because we're always in the woods. We can't see far on account of the trees."

Quite a few days after, about the time the grass was getting green all over, they set a date, they said, "In three days we'll start moving down," and they told me to go and see how the cattle were getting along. I rode over to the cattle, but I didn't see any of them. I only saw their tracks. I was riding around there, hunting the cattle, when I saw Choclays Kinsman's herd. I thought, "I'll go over; maybe that's my older sister herding." I rode all around the sheep, but I didn't see anyone. I crossed a little ditch and looked around, and there, on the north side of the herd, I saw a dog lying under a tree. I knew this dog. It was a black dog and a good shepherd. I thought, "The herder must be there," so I started over. There was a clump of young trees there, and when I was close to them somebody got up and rode away, straight behind the trees. I knew that was Slim Man. He'd been with the girl. When I got there I asked her, "Who was that?" She said, "Slim Man." I asked her about it, and she said, "Yes, I was with him." She told me right out, and I'd thought I was the only one. I asked her about the cattle, and she said, "They're always around at Yellow Water." So I left and went to where the cattle were. Just as I rounded them up Slim Man came and helped me earmark the calves. After that he went away, and I just let the cattle go and started home.

At first they said, "We're going to move down to the valley in three days," but we didn't move until a few days after that. When we got down off the mountain, out to where our piece of land was, everything was greener there. The grass was higher too, and there was plenty of feed for the stock. We went out to where we'd planted all the things, and it was nice and damp. We were all glad and said, "We'll plant again, so we'll have some corn and other stuff."

We only camped there a few days and then moved down towards Anything Falls In, to Where The Gray Hill Comes Out. There we started shearing. Slim Man and his wife came. He brought a pair of shears. He said, "We'll help you first. After we're through here we'll all go and help Choclays Kinsman. Has he moved out yet?" I said, "No, not yet." "Well, he said he was coming out here soon. He'll be here any time. He said he'd move out here and start shearing right away."

We sheared for many days, but even so we didn't shear them all. We sheared only those with nice, thick wool and let the others go. We couldn't shear them, because there was too much wax in their wool. About the time we finished shearing Choclays Kinsman moved out to Anything Falls In, to the place called In The Wall Of Rocks; so when we were through Slim Man and his wife went over there. Before they left my father said, "Thank you very much for your help. Now you can take some wool. Take as much as you want. Just help yourself, my nephew." Slim Man said, "I'll take some. I'm very glad and thankful to you, my uncle." He packed up three blankets full as hard as he could pack.

A few days later my father said to me, "Go plant some corn in a little patch. It isn't time for planting yet, but, even at that, plant a little; we want to see how it will be. The pueblo people start planting from now on. So we'll see how it works." I took some corn and planted it in two places where the sun struck first in the morning. A week later he said to us, "Go to the cornfield and plant some corn now." We went over and were planting all day, but we didn't plant very much. When we got home in the evening my mother said, "Tomorrow I want you to go over to Old Man White Horse and tell them to come here and help us on planting. It's quite a big space that we have. If they come and help us it'll only take a day."

I went over to Old Man White Horse's place the next day and said to him, "I came here for help, my grandfather. I want my younger brothers to help me with planting. All of you can come and help us." He said, "Yes, we'll do that. All of your younger brothers and sisters will come. We haven't anything to do, so we'll go over and help you. There's another hogan over there. Go over to those people and tell them to help too. I don't think they've got anything to do. And when we get there kill a nice, fat mutton for us. That's what we like, nice, fat mutton. Feed us a lot when we get there." I got on my horse and rode to the other hogan, but nobody was home.

The next morning, just as I brought the horses back and we were getting ready to go to our farm, my father, Slim Man, came. He said, "We've been shearing for many days, and now everybody's tired. We're all tired, so today we took a day off. Everybody wants a rest today, so we're having Sunday. While everybody's resting I thought I'd come over and visit you people." My mother laughed and said, "We won't let you rest. We're just going to our farm to plant some corn, and I want you to help us. We don't want you to rest." Right away he said, "Yes, I will. I sure will help you. That's what I like to do, plant. That's different from shearing. I'll take a rest on it anyway." My mother said, "Yes, we'll have a good time planting, because some people are coming to help us. So we'll all go and take our sheep over too." Slim Man said to me, "Go ahead with your sheep. Get over there quickly and kill a nice fat one." My mother packed up all her stuff, dishes and grub, and while they were putting things on the horses I took the sheep to the farm.

When we got to the cornfield the other people were coming along after us. The whole outfit was coming on horseback. When they arrived some of them started butchering, some getting wood. Slim Man said, "Come on, let's start now. Let those women go ahead with their cooking." Some of them already had digging sticks; others began fixing some up, sharpening them. That's what we used to plant with. The corn I'd planted was up about four inches. They said, "We'll soon have corn; some has come out already." We were planting all that day until the sun was almost down. Then in the evening, when we were through, everyone went home, and we moved back to our camp too. Slim Man said, "In six days we'll take the wool to the store." My father said, "We'll be ready by that time. This was the only thing that held us back, but now we've finished it. We've got one job done. We won't have to bother with planting any longer, so now we'll just think about taking away our wool."

I herded for four days, and on the fifth my mother and I began packing up the wool. We were working on that all day. We had three blankets full packed good and tight. The next day we packed some more in small sacks. That evening my father said, "It's quite a job for you, just by yourself. When the pack begins to get loose on your way it'll be a job to straighten it. They're very heavy. We ought to get another boy to go with you, but we can't get anyone around here. Why don't you go along?" he said to my mother, "I'll be all right here at home." But she said, "No, no, indeed, I don't want to go. It'll be too much bother for me, too, and I don't want you to stay alone here at home." They were talking about it for a while, and then he said, "Well, I guess you'd better go alone. Just take one pack horse. I was thinking of your taking two, but it's too much for you. So just get two horses, one to ride and one for packing. And tomorrow, as soon as you're ready, as soon as you've put the wool on the horses, start off. Don't wait for those other people. Take the trail that goes by Where The Little Arroyos Stop. That's the better trail. When the people pass by here I'll tell them which way you went, and they'll catch up with you somewhere. Watch your pack horse all the time while you're going on your way tomorrow. Look at it every now and then and tighten up your load, so it won't fall off."

I brought back the horses in the morning, and we saddled them and put on the wool. We had everything good and tight, but there was no sign of the other people. My father said, "You can go ahead. Be sure and take the trail I want you to go on. The other goes through the woods. When you have a big pack on your horse you shouldn't go through the woods. So take the trail that goes across the flat." I got on my horse and started off, leading the pack horse. From the top of the hill I looked back, but no one was coming. I went right along, and a little after noon I got to Winds Cover The Water. The horses were all sweaty. I took the things off and let them cool and made a little lunch and ate. Nobody had shown up.

Just as I was going to saddle up the horses they came. The old man, my father, was riding in front. He said, "What are you trying to do? Are you going to start again?" I said, "Yes, I'm just starting to go. I've been waiting here for a long time." He said, "Don't hurry. Turn your horses loose and wait for us. We'll all start on together." He said to the others, "Unload your things and let your horses take a rest, and start cooking right away too." To the boys, he said, "Gather up some wood. Hurry up and build a fire. After lunch we'll start again. By that time the horses will be good and rested. Cook a lot," he said, "and we'll eat plenty, so we can keep on going the rest of the night. We won't be bothered with eating again. We won't eat tonight. We'll just stop some place and go right to bed. So cook a lot, and we'll eat plenty."

They built a big fire and started cooking, and I turned my horses loose. There was my father, Choclays Kinsman, and Choclay and the other boy he was raising. They each had a big load on their horses and were leading one pack horse. Then there was Slim Man and his wife, and they were leading one horse. So altogether there were six of us and nine horses.

After we ate we started packing up again, and it was a good thing they'd told me to wait. I couldn't lift the wool. After everybody had finished packing Slim Man helped me put the wool on the horses and tie it down. When we got to Peak At The Foot Of The Mountain it got dark. A little way from there we camped. My old father said, "We'll camp here, because from here on we have to go through the woods. Tomorrow we can go through the woods without any trouble." The next day about noon we got to Coyote Water. There we unpacked our stuff and took the horses to water and brought some back for ourselves in a jug. It was a hot day. We were lying around until late in the afternoon. When it began to get cool we packed again and started off. We almost got to Big Lake. When we were about to that place it got real dark, and so we camped.

The next morning we crossed the valley to Red Lake and went on and got to the store at Ganado by noon. As soon as we arrived the trader, Wearing Spectacles, came out and started shaking hands with us, saying, "Welcome, my sons-in-law." He was saying that and running around among us; he was so glad and thankful we'd come to his place. He was saying, "Thank you very much. I thank you all for coming to see me." The old man, my father, said, "Yes, we've come a long way. We camped at Coyote Water yesterday at noon, and there we had lunch. From there we went on and camped at Big Lake last night, and early in the morning we started without anything to eat. We haven't had anything to eat since yesterday noon. So we're all pretty hungry." "Oh, well, then," he said, "hurry and unload your horses and turn them loose. Let them rest. There's lots of feed for them up here a little way. Just take them up there, and they'll have plenty to eat. And there's water, water them first, and get some water for yourselves, too. And there's wood behind the building, plenty of it, so get some wood and build yourselves a fire anywhere around here where you can find shade, and I'll go in and get you something to eat. Come over to the store, and I'll let you have some buckets and you can get some water." He gave us a bucket and a dutch oven and a great, big pan full of flour. Salt and baking powder were already in it.

We had a big lunch there. After we'd eaten he told us to get in the shade. There was a shady place against the store. He said, "Stay there, because it's nice and cool." We took our stuff and got under the shade, and he came out to us again. He was a jolly fellow. As soon as he came out he started talking and laughing. He sat in front of us and said, "Any time now when you're ready you can take in the wool, and we'll start trading. I'll give you a good price for it. I'll treat you well. I know you've come from a long way. After you're through trading you can stay here tonight. You can spend a day or two or three or even four, because I like to have company all the time."

When we were through trading the old man, my father, said, "I guess we'll start home tomorrow morning, because we're all through trading. We've got what we want, so we'll go home in the morning. Even though you want us to stay a few days we don't like to loaf around here doing nothing. We're glad, and we'd like to stay with you another day, but we can't. We have lots of things to do at home, so we'll go in the morning. We don't want to eat up all your grub. If we did that, soon you wouldn't have any more store, because when we start we eat a lot, and we eat up the food fast. But, anyway, we're thankful to you for treating us nicely. You've given us lots of grub already. We don't want to stay here and do nothing but eat. Maybe some fellows would stay around just to eat, but we want to go home, because we've got lots to do." The trader said, "Well, I don't care about feeding you. I only care for friends, that's all. Even though I run out of grub I can get more, because it's not far from here to where I get it. But it's up to you. If you hurry home it's all right. I know you have many things to do."

The next morning he gave us some more food. We had the horses back that morning, but Slim Man said, "We'll start this afternoon when it gets cool. It's too hot to cross the valley. If we start late this afternoon we can cross the flat while it's nice and cool." The old man said, "All right, we'll do that. You boys take the horses back to where they were." So we took them back and hobbled them. It was a hot day.

In the afternoon we started off, driving the pack horses ahead of us. We kept going right behind them on the trail down to Snake Water and on to Red Lake and across the valley. At Big Lake it was just getting dark. We stopped there to water the horses and then went on. Way out in the flat that comes from Rock Corral we stopped and camped. In the morning we started on again. It was hot. There was no water all the way along, and we were thirsty. When we got to Coyote Water we took our things off the horses and watered them and took them quite a way to where there was feed and had our lunch. When the sun was well down, when it was cool, we started once more. At Winds Cover The Water we watered the horses, and the sun was down. The old man, my father, said, "What shall we do? Shall we camp here, or shall we go on?" Slim Man said, "We'll go on. We don't want to lie around here. We're about home now, so we'd better go on." Out in the flat, a little beyond Where The Little Arroyos Stop, they branched off, and I went on by myself. I got home way late in the night.

I took the things off the horses and turned them loose. About that time they made a light in the hogan. When I went in my father was making a fire. He was sitting close to it and starting it up. My mother went out, and we both took the things inside. After we'd taken everything in I went out again and chopped some wood and built a big fire. My mother was so thankful for all the stuff. She said to my father, "You'd better poke the fire. Have the fire burning quickly; our son must be tired and hungry. So you keep poking the fire." He said, "Yes, the fire's going. It'll soon be all burned up, so you'd better hurry with your cooking. Cook something for him. Hurry up."

My mother was sitting there with all the grub scattered around her, taking things out of the sacks, and she was so thankful. "Thank you very much, my son. This is what we wanted, my baby." She opened another sack, and there she pulled out a robe. "What a nice robe," she said. "This is a pretty robe." She reached in the sack again and pulled out another. "Another one! This is pretty too." I had the prettiest one down at the bottom. She pulled that one out and said, "Oh, this is prettier than those two." My father said, "What are you talking about. They're all pretty. There's not just one that's pretty, they're all pretty robes. That's what we want. We're scarce on robes. Now we've got pretty ones. That's what you call having something." Then she opened another sack. I had a roll of leather in that one. When she got that out my father almost got up. "That's what I want," he said. "That's what I was wishing for for a long time. That beats all the other things. We can put that on our saddles, and we'll have it for many years." They were spreading the things out and looking at them by the fire, holding them close to the fire where there was light.

After they'd looked at everything they took the cheapest robes, and my father said, "We're both old now, so we don't care for anything that's pretty. It won't look good on us." He picked up the fancy one and threw it over to me. "We'll have these two robes, and you can have the fancy one, because you're young. It'll look good on you." I sat there and looked at the robe. My mother said, "Pick up that robe. Don't just look at it. What's the matter with you? Pick it up. It's given to you." Then I picked it up. I wanted that robe very much. That's why I bought it. I wanted them to take the black ones. While I was coming on my way I was wishing for it, thinking, "I wish they'd both pick up the black one and give the fancy one to me." And there they did. I was so very glad about it. I said, "I'm very thankful for this robe." My father said to my mother, "Don't bother with those things. Put them away and go on with your cooking. You'll see them tomorrow." "Well, then," she said to me, "you go and bring in some meat." I went out and brought some in and began cutting it up. While I was doing that I began to tell about my trip.

My mother was searching around in a sack for some salt and got out the tobacco I'd brought for my father. She unwrapped that little package—there was one sack and a plug of chewing tobacco—and threw them over to my father. When he saw the tobacco drop on his lap he almost fell over backwards. He was so very thankful for it. Right away he opened the sack and rolled himself a cigarette. I just went ahead with my story. When he'd lighted the cigarette he said, "Come over here and sit by me and tell me about your trip. Let her do the cooking." My mother said, "That's all you want. You always want to hear some kind of story. And you're a big storyteller too. He's helping me here on the meat." He said, "Do it yourself. Go ahead and cook some lunch. I want him to tell me about his trip." I went over to him and told all about my trip, about going over and about when we got there, about what Wearing Spectacles had said and how he'd joshed with the fellows, about the lunch he gave us and how he'd fed our horses in his pasture, about selling our wool and about all the trading that we did, and then about starting back.

He said, "That's fine. I'm glad to hear about the trip you've had. What kind of a man are you talking about? Is he half Navaho? How is it that he talks just the way we do?" I said, "I don't know anything about him, but they say he's a real Mexican, so I don't know where he picked up all our language." "Well," he said, "I wonder where he picked it up." I said, "He wanted all the wool that's left. He said to us, 'Be sure and bring all the wool to me again sometime.' " "Well," my father said, "whenever they go again they'll let us know, and you can take the wool that's left."

He was sitting there, smoking, talking about Wearing Spectacles and the things I'd brought. He asked me about the groceries, about the flour. There was a big, tall tree outside our hogan. I pointed to that tree and said, "The flour is stacked about as high as the tree outside." He was surprised. "What a big stack of flour," he said. Then he asked about the dry goods. I said, "A whole lot of dry goods are stacked up on the shelves. The shelves are full of groceries and dry goods. And there are lots of robes of all different colors and designs, and a big stack of leather of two colors and different sizes."

He said, "That's what I want you to see. That's what I want you to acquire and have. When I talk to you of things like that, I know sometimes you look and act as if you didn't want me to talk to you. When I talk to you it seems to me you hate me for it. Every morning I always tell you to get up and not lie in bed, sleeping all the time. I always wake you early in the morning and tell you to go out and race. That's what I want you to race for. If you race for it you'll soon get all these different things. You must be lively all the time. Do all the tasks yourself. Don't hold yourself back.

What I really mean is, don't be lazy." He talked to me a long while, but what he said was all about how I should live, how I should take care of my things and how I should take care of myself when I grew up to be a man. He talked to me about many things. While he was talking my mother said, "Leave him alone now. Let him go to sleep and rest. He wants to rest, he's tired. So let your little one go to sleep and take a rest." He said to me, "Don't listen to her. She wants you to go hungry and starve. That's what she's leading you to." But he only talked a little while longer, and then he stopped, and we went to bed. I went right to sleep.

13.

He loses a horse and a girl, but is consoled . . . The old man begins to go down . . . Why Slim Man never came around any more . . . "I'm full of sorrow for the days of my youth" . . . His father speaks to him of property and life, and teaches him some songs.

I WAS herding a few days, and then my father said, "We'll round up the horses and see how many of the young stallions need cutting. They scatter all the mares, so we'll go over and cut them." My mother took out the herd, and we went over and rounded up the horses. There was a corral at the place we call Tsowahi Mountain. We drove them in there, and he went in and tried to rope one of the young stallions, but he missed him. He fixed his rope again, and while the horses were passing by he started to rope another. Just then one of them stepped on a stick. It was quite a long stick, and the stick raised up and ran into the horse's groin about a forearm's length. The horse began kicking and bucking, and there was my father, standing and looking at the horse dragging the stick around. "Alas," he said, "what has happened?" Then the horse stopped a little, and he put the rope on it and grabbed the stick and pulled it out. As soon as he pulled it out the blood came pouring from the horse's belly. The horse jumped around, and while it was jumping the blood was gushing out, and the horse was neighing. In a little while he quieted down, and suddenly he dropped and rolled over and stretched himself and died.

That was my horse. As soon as I saw he was dead I gave a great cry. I cried out as loud as I could, and my father was standing there, looking at him. Then he walked up to me and put his arm around my neck and held me against his breast as hard as he could, saying, "Don't cry, my baby, don't cry. You mustn't cry. Quiet down now, my baby, you mustn't cry for a horse. Nor the sheep, you mustn't cry for the sheep either. So stop crying now, my baby." But I wouldn't listen to him. He was holding me, trying to quiet me, but I couldn't stop crying.

That was the horse I liked best. My father never rode that horse. It was built so nicely, and it was tame and lively. I never used a whip on him, and I never kicked him. As soon as I got on him he wanted to go. He'd be raising himself up and wanting to go as soon as I got on him, and if I held him back he'd start to go sidewise. That's why I liked this horse best. That's why I was so sorry for it.

He kept saying, "Don't cry, my baby, stop crying, my baby." But I couldn't help it. Then he pointed to a mare. This mare we used to call Grey Horse. He said, "You can have Grey Horse's little one. That's yours now. You can break that horse, and soon you'll have him tame, and he'll be just the same. Tame him and make him lively. You know how to make a horse lively. So now you quiet down, my baby." I quieted down then, and he was wiping my tears. There he paid me for the stick. The stick killed my horse, but the stick didn't pay me; he paid me for the stick. We'd intended to cut the young stallions, but instead we turned them out and let them go towards the water and started home.

When we got home my mother was sitting by the fire and cooking. As soon as I got off my horse I walked up to her and said, "Mother, Spotted Nose died." She stopped what she was doing and turned around to me slowly and said, "Is it true Spotted Nose has died? How did he die?" I said, "He ran against a stick, and the stick stuck into his belly. He didn't live long after that." When I said this right away she started crying. She almost made me cry again, but I held myself back. My father got off his horse and walked up to us. He said to my mother, "Don't cry. You know very well you mustn't cry for the horses, so you stop now. He was crying too. He cried when his horse was dead. I had a hard time stopping him, until I gave him another horse, and then he stopped. So you mustn't cry now, my children. I've given one back to you already. That was my fault. I was going to rope a horse, and while they were passing me he ran against a stick. But I've given one back to you already, so don't cry for the horse." Then my mother quieted down and was just weeping. She said, "The baby's horse died. I'm very sorry, because that was the only good horse the baby had. The baby had only one horse, and that's dead now."

My father was sitting there, not saying anything for a while. Then he began to talk to me about the horses. He said, "You've been crying for only one horse. That isn't the only one you're going to have. You've got mares, and one of these mares has hundreds and hundreds of horses in her. They're all that way, all the mares. So why should you cry for only one horse?" He picked up a handful of dust. "There's the number of horses you're going to have. From the time you grow up until you die of old age you'll have that many horses," he said, as he threw the dust in front of me. "Just keep to your work. Take care of all your things and all your stocks, and in a little while you'll have many horses and sheep. You'll get lots of property from them, and soon you'll have silver belts and silver bridles, beads and turquoise of all kinds. So you must take care of everything." He said to my mother, "You know all about it, since the time I picked you up. Before I married you you'd been with lots of men, but not one of them that I know of treated you the way I'm treating you now. You never did have any horses, or cattle, or sheep, or any kind of property. You never even got enough to eat. But since I married you you've been eating different kinds of food, and now you have horses, sheep and cattle, and besides them you've got some property."

Several days after that I went over to the farm. The corn was about a foot high, but there were a great many weeds all over the field. I couldn't see a piece of ground, it was so covered with different weeds. I hoed a little in a few places and then went home. When I got home I told my father and mother about it. My mother said, "That'll spoil our corn. We'd better start hoeing. If we don't hoe up the weeds it'll ruin our corn. You'd better go and ask your younger brothers to help you. Tell Old Man White Horse and your grandmother, so they can come with all their children and help us again. And go over to your father and tell Choclay to help you too. In that way we'll save our corn. Go and tell them while we still have grub. We've still got plenty of grub, enough for them, so you'd better go and tell them to come and help us." My father was lying there; he didn't say anything. But then he was old, he left everything to us.

I got me a horse and rode down to my grandfather's place, Old Man White Horse. I said, "I've come for help again, my grandfather." He said, "On what?" I said, "On hoeing. I went to our cornfield this morning, and there were a lot of different weeds all over the field, and they're so thick. That's where I want help. I'd like to have all my younger brothers help me on that, and you too, my grandfather." He said, "All right, we'll be there. How many hoes have you got?" "I have only two. Maybe you've got some. If you have bring them along." "Yes, we've got some here, and we've got some more at Rock Stump. The boys will go over and get them. And there's Has Done It living over there. He's got some hoes too. I think he'll let us have them. He ought to, because he's your in-law." He was just joshing. He just said that to me, because I always called Has Done It, my uncle. That's what they say if you call a fellow, uncle. I said, "I'll take a ride over to my father's place. Maybe I'll get someone over there to help me too." He said, "Yes, do that. Go around and tell them to help us. Gather the men, so we'll be through hoeing perhaps in one day. We'll be there tomorrow morning. Kill a good, fat mutton for us again. We want lots to eat. That's the only thing we want."

When I got to my father's place, Slim Man was still there, and I told them to help me with hoeing. The old man, my father, said, "Yes, they'll be over. The other two are not strong, so I think perhaps only Choclay will come." They said just the same to me, "Be sure and kill a nice, fat mutton for us tomorrow morning. We won't help you unless you kill a nice, fat mutton." Then I started home. I'd gone quite a way when they asked me about the hoes. I said, "I haven't any. I've only got two." They said, "Why didn't you buy some? A lot of them were hanging up in Wearing Spectacles's place. You should have bought some of those."

Before I went away my father said, "Choclay and the other boy went after the horses early this morning, and they haven't shown up yet. We're waiting for them to come back. They've both been herding, but they didn't show up, so the girl took out the herd. Did you see the herd down at the water?" I said, "No, there were no sheep around the water." Right away I began to think about the girl. He said, "She took the herd out in that direction." Slim Man said again, "Be sure and kill a good, fat mutton for us tomorrow morning. Kill a three-year-old wether, and a good-sized one." My sister said, "What do you want with a three-year-old wether? You can't eat it. They're nothing but fat now. There's no meat on them. If he did kill one it would be of no use. It would spoil on him. Nobody will eat the fat." She said this while she was laughing. She used to laugh at everything. She used to be laughing all the time. Slim Man said, "I said it because he's got lots of sheep. He doesn't know what to do with them." Slim Man and my sister, Choclays Kinsman's wife, were calling each other cousin and laughing and joshing.

Then I left and started after the girl. I rode up to Anything Falls In, and at the water there I saw the sheep lying on the hill under the trees. She'd driven them up under the trees where there was shade, and there she was sitting. She'd built a fire and was boiling milk, and she had some corn-bread. As I rode up she took the milk off the fire and broke the corn-bread in pieces and dropped them in the milk and started eating. She looked strange. She always used to look up at me and smile, but she wasn't paying any attention to me. When I got off my horse she was looking angry, but I just went up and sat by her and started eating with her. She used to be smiling whenever she saw me, but instead she was hanging her head and wouldn't look up.

She said, "Where are you going?" I said, "I just came over to see you." "What did you want to see me for?" "You know. What we always have when we get to see each other." "Yes, it was that way. It used to be that way, but not now." I said, "Why?" "You said something about me. You both have been making fun of me." I said, "I don't know what you mean. With whom have I been making fun of you?" "Don't ask me that. You know it yourself." I thought, "She must mean me and Slim Man. He must have said something to her about me." I began asking her about that. "How did you hear about me? What did I say of you? And what did I do to you? How did I make fun of you? Tell me just that part. That's all I want to know, because I don't know anything myself. I never made fun of you. I never said anything bad about you. So, please, tell me what I said." But she said, "You know all about it, so why do you want to ask? And I don't want you to touch me any more. I don't like you any more, so you'd better get on your horse and go." But I kept asking her what I'd said, but she wouldn't tell, she just kept saying, "I don't want you to bother me any more. I mean it." I said, "I'm not thinking that way about you. I was the first one to marry you, and I was going to live with you. I was going to take you to my home. Even though I saw you with that fellow I never said anything to you about it. I just let it go. So why do you want to act that way to me?" She said, "Don't talk to me. Go away. I mean it. I don't want you to touch me anymore. I don't like you."

I reached down in my pocket—I had a dollar and a half—and tried to give her that, but she pushed me away, saying, "What do I want with that? I have nothing to do with that. I told you to keep away from me. I mean it. So you go on, get away. If you don't go away, if you don't leave me alone, I'll tell on you." When she said that she almost killed me. I was all choked up, I could hardly get my breath, and my heart began beating. She scared me with that. I began begging her, saying, "Please don't tell on me. Please, you mustn't tell on me. If you tell on me we'll both be in shame." I begged her for a long time. At last she said, "Now you go away and don't bother with me any more from here on. If you go right now I won't tell. I told you long ago to go on and get away, but you kept getting after me, and that's why I said

I'd tell on you. But I mean it, if you don't go away and leave me alone I'll surely tell on you. If you go now and leave me, then I won't." Then I left. I got on my horse and rode away.

I was so sorry for her. While I was riding along back to my home I was thinking about her, thinking how she used to smile and laugh and talk to me, and how she used to act. I was thinking about that and almost cried. But after a while I thought, "Oh, well, I'll just let her go. She's not the only woman there will be for me. I'll get another girl better than her. She's a slave anyhow. I don't want to marry a slave. I'll get a better girl." When I got home the sheep were there, and after I told about my trip I took them out and herded until the sun was down.

The next morning we moved to the cornfield, and I got some water and gathered some wood for my mother to cook with. While we were cooking the people from down below arrived, Old Man White Horse and his outfit. He brought four boys and two women. After a while Slim Man and his wife and Choclay and the girl who didn't want me any more came also. She'd come to help cook. About that time the sheep arrived at the farm, so right away my mother killed one, and while the women were cooking we put handles on the hoes. After we'd eaten we went out in the field and started hoeing. We hoed all that forenoon, and they made fun of me about the few places where I'd hoed up the weeds the day before.

At noon we heard them calling us to come over and get some lunch. So then we went back, and everything was cooked. While we were eating they started making fun of me again. They said, "That's the way a lazy man does. That's the way to discover a lazy man. Now we know who's lazy. We all know now that one fellow is lazy in this crowd.

Only one man here with us is lazy. The rest are all good and strong and lively, all willing to work, all wanting something to do. They don't just want to play around with their hoes. But we know now there's one fellow right here with us who's lazy. All he wants is to play around with his hoe." They were laughing, and I was so ashamed. When I looked at the girl a few times she was laughing too. But I just made believe I didn't care what they were saying.

After lunch we all went out in the cornfield again and hoed until late in the afternoon. Then they wanted to go home; so we all stopped hoeing, and my mother said, "Thank you very much for helping us hoe up the weeds. You've done a great deal for us. If you folks hadn't come the weeds would still be in the corn. But now you've almost finished. That little patch there, we'll work on that ourselves. I'm very thankful to you all," she said. Slim Man had gone back, and my mother caught a wether goat and gave it to those two women. That was for all of them, all those seven people. They were one whole outfit. They were giving thanks to my mother while they were about to butcher. I started out with the sheep towards our place while my mother was packing up the grub and dishes. They were still there when I left.

We didn't do anything after that. There was nothing doing, nothing going on. I was just herding day after day. The wool was still lying around. My father said, "Let the wool lie there. We can't take it to any of the stores. It's too hot now, and there's no water around by this time. Water is scarce now. So we don't want to be bothered with the wool. We'll wait until it cools off, or until we have rain." I went to the cornfield every once in a while and kept hoeing wherever I saw the weeds come out. I carried the hoe around over the field, and there wasn't a weed anywhere.

246

We stayed at our farm all summer, but this time we didn't get as much corn, and it didn't grow as high. But anyway we had a little. There weren't any squash or pumpkins, they'd all dried up. We didn't have much rain that summer. When the corn was ripe we began husking it, and after that we laid it out to dry. When we had all the corn laid out in the sunlight my mother and father said, "We'll take the wool to the store. We'll pack it up and take it to Keams Canyon. From there we'll go and visit the people. So you must make a corral around the corn. Fix it up well, and put up scarecrows all around, so that nothing will get at it. Then, when you're out with the sheep, you won't be worried."

The next day we packed up the wool, and the day after that I went out and got the horses for them, and they started off, leading one pack horse. After they'd gone I took out the sheep. That was all I was doing for eight days, herding sheep and tending to the horses.

One day, when I was driving the horses to the water, I saw a woman riding along on horseback. She was the one we called Woman Who Flips Her Cards. She used to snap her cards down when she played, so that's what they named her after. I went around the hill and rode up in front of her. She was going after water. As soon as I met her I reached out for the bridle and held it. She said, "What do you mean by that?" I said, "I want you to ride away with me." "I'm after some water," she said, "because there's no water at my home." I said, "It won't take us long. We'll be over there in the wash. Nobody'll see us there." So we went down in the wash, and I got off my horse, and she got down off hers. As soon as she got off she sat down, and as soon as she sat down I went up to her. We both liked it very much. This woman had a husband, and she said, "You're better than my husband." I said, "You mustn't tell on me, because if you do your husband might get after me and kill me." She said, "I won't tell on you, because I know, sure enough, my husband would get after you." I reached down in my pocket and got out two dollars and gave them to her. She liked it and was thankful.

They returned on the ninth day and brought a lot of food, some from the store, flour, coffee, sugar, and other little stuff, and some that they got from the Hopi. My mother said, "Your younger brother went to the Hopi for us and got us some food." They'd brought some dried peaches, but they weren't thoroughly dry, so she put them out in the sunlight. And they brought back seven strands of red beads and a robe. They said, "We paid some money for these beads, but we still owe the people twenty head of sheep. They'll be here any time." The robe was given to them by the same people. They were Red From The Waist Down. My mother got a lot of calico cloth from them, and calico dresses of different colors already made. She had one of them on when she came home. That was her first calico dress. Before that she had dresses made of white muslin.

One day, when she was still wearing white muslin dresses, my father and his younger brother, Choclays Kinsman, were sitting in the hogan. She got up and was going to walk out, and while she was walking in the middle of the hogan, just passing the fire, the string around her waist broke, and the skirt slipped to her feet. There was nothing underneath. Just about then I was coming back with the sheep, and I heard her cussing and swearing to herself. When I came inside she was sitting close to the fire. She said, "The string around my waist broke. I was so ashamed that I didn't have anything on me before these men." My father said, "What's wrong with you? There's nothing wrong with you. That's nothing. We all look about the same. That's what you get when you're not watching yourself." She said, "I've been watching myself closely, but the string broke anyway. I don't know how it broke." The two men were sitting there with their heads down, not looking up. My mother was bashful, and they were too.

It was, perhaps, two or three days after they got home that my father, Choclays Kinsman, came to our place. Old Man Hat was lying in bed, hardly able to move he was so tired and sore. He said, "I'm sore all over and kind of sick." His brother sat down beside him and said, "What's the matter with you? You don't look as if you were well." My father said, "Yes, I'm sick. I took a long trip. We just got back the other day. That made me kind of sick." His brother said, "Why don't you let him go to the store and take over the wool. He's big enough now for that distant journey, and he's young. He wouldn't mind it even if he took a trip longer than that. You should have let him go with one of my boys. Choclay was home doing nothing part of the time. Why didn't you call for help? Why do you want to go that far? You know you can't stand it. You're too old now to be taking a trip that far. So that's what you've become sick from. You must have strained yourself lifting the wool." But he said, "I wanted to visit some of the people over there. I was anxious to see them. That's why I took the trip. But perhaps I have strained myself. I can't tell, I can't say, because I don't know. Maybe something is bothering me."

After the old man left I fixed up a hole and stored the corn. After I'd put all the corn away they said, "We'll move down to Many Streams." But we passed that place and went a little further over a hill. We lived there quite a few days and then moved again way below to another hogan. There we lived a long time. Close by was a little rocky hill, and behind the hill was a nice level place for a long distance. I had the horses out in that flat, and from the top of the hill I could see them all far off in the valley. It sure was a nice place. There was plenty of grass and other different kinds of feed and plenty of water. We lived at this one place over three months, but nothing happened, nothing was going on, and we never heard of anything. We were all alone, and I was herding all the time and tending to the horses. The old man was lying around; he wasn't able to do anything. He used to go and round up the horses sometimes, but he wasn't able to do that any more.

There was nobody to talk to him. Slim Man always used to come around, but he'd quit coming, because once, when he came to our place, he wanted a buckskin from my father. My father had some good-sized buckskins. Slim Man asked for one, but instead the old man turned around and pulled out his buckskin leggings and gave those to his nephew. Slim Man just looked at them. He never touched them or said anything. He just got up and walked out. After he left the old man said, "That's a nice way to act. He asked for a buckskin, and I gave him my best leggings, already dyed. That's worth more than a whole buckskin undyed. That's the way I'm thinking about it. My buckskin leggings are worth more than a whole buckskin. And he didn't even touch them. I thought he'd give me thanks, but he didn't say anything. He just got up and walked out and went away." A few days after Slim Man said, "I'll never help him again from here on. I was the only one who took good care of him. I did a lot for him. Even though he's got brothers and sisters and nephews and nieces none of them come around and help him. I was the only one taking good care of him. But not now, because I asked him for a buckskin, I wanted a whole buckskin, and he threw his old leggings to me."

That's why Slim Man quit coming to our place. He quit everything. He never helped the old man any more. It wasn't altogether that he put off helping him; he was only thinking that way about him. Whenever I went to his place and wanted help he always helped me. He helped me with anything, but not the old man. When he needed help Slim Man wouldn't help him at all. When the old man got sick he never came to our place. There were some singings and treatments for him when he was sick, but Slim Man never came and helped with those doings. Even though he never helped he was there after the old man died, and when they separated the stocks he got a bunch of horses and some cattle. That was all, no sheep. Even though he didn't help he got some of the stock, because everybody said to him, "Take care of your son." They meant me.

From that little rocky hill we moved to Flowing Through Rocks, and from then on he began to be sick. My mother said to him, "You've got enough sheep, horses and cattle, and besides that you've got property. We ought to put up some kind of doings for you. What do you want to use it for? I thought you wanted to use the sheep, horses and cattle for something like that. We ought to get a singer to do something on you." But he said, "How will we put up some kind of doings? There isn't anybody around to help us. If somebody were around then, perhaps, we could put up some kind of doing. But like this, when we're all alone, we can't do anything. So let the things that are bothering me kill me. I know I'm not the only one who's going to die. Many people are dying off all the time. So I'll be gone anyway."

Then he said, "I think I know what's bothering me. I know two things are bothering me. The Feather Rite is bothering me, and another thing is the Enemy Rite. However, I don't think anybody will put up an Nda for me. But I want to get a singer who knows about the Feather Rite. I want the Feather Rite to be done on me. But not here. It will be over at the place called Where The Mexican Fixed The Spring. I know the Feather Rite is bothering me, because once years ago when I was hunting with another fellow we shot a deer. The deer was lying on the ground, and when I got close to it it jumped up and ran against me. I was so frightened. I went between the horns, I was lying over the horns, and he started to run with me. The other fellow happened to come along and grabbed the deer's legs. There I was saved. We threw the deer down and killed it. So I'm sure the Feather Rite is bothering me through that. And the Enemy Rite is bothering me too, because years ago a bunch of us killed a Mexican, and I took his overcoat and held it where there was blood. I didn't know my fingers had blood on them, and I ate with that blood on my fingers. So I know the Enemy Rite is bothering me too." That's what he always said. Even before he took sick he always mentioned those two things. Whenever he had a little headache, or an aching some place he always said, "The Enemy Rite and Feather Rite are bothering me."

He said, "I'm thinking about myself, and I'm full of sorrow thinking about the days of my youth. I used to have many good times. I used to travel around on this earth through many good-looking mountains, through many different good-looking trees. I've traveled around out in the flats, going through the good-looking hills, crossing the valleys through lots of different good-looking weeds and grasses of all kinds, drinking of nice-looking streams of water and nice-looking springs. When I was young I went to lots of places, and now I've got so old I can't do anything, and I'm suffering. So I'm full of sorrow for myself."

After that he turned around to me and said, "Now it's up to you. You know well enough now. You know what's happening and what's going on every day and night. You know I'm too old to do anything more for you. You know I'm going down every day. So you must look after all the stock, cattle, horses and sheep, and the little property we have. You must try your best to take care of all the stock, so that when I'm gone you'll have something to live on. If you take care of them you'll have sheep and cattle to live on and horses to travel around with. That whole thing will give you clothing of all kinds and all kinds of food. By taking care of all things you'll soon be a man who has everything. And you know your mother is getting old too. Soon she too will be going down. She may live for some years yet, she may die of old age, or she may get sick and die any time. You know we both will be gone sometime, and so you must look after all the things. Try to raise more, so that after we're both gone you'll be fixed all right.

"I'm telling you this, because I don't want you to be poor. You must patch up your moccasins, the soles and tops, and your clothing. You must patch up all your clothing, because everything is scarce, everything is so expensive. You mustn't throw your clothing away as soon as it gets torn. Even though it has many patches, wear it, and do your work in your patched-up clothing. By doing that there'll be a whole lot of saving. In that way you'll get ahead. If you throw your clothing away as soon as it gets torn there'll be a lot of waste. The same with your saddle and the whole outfit of a horse. You must patch up your saddles and bridles, saddle-blankets, ropes and whips. You mustn't try to get new ones every time they're broken. Even if you have one or two new outfits of clothing keep them until you want to go somewhere, and then get them out. But put them away as soon as you get back, and put on your old clothing again and start in with your work.

"You must look after your stocks. You must look for good grazing and good water. You should ask the people where to find water and good grazing for them. As long as you take them around where there's good feed and water you'll have good-looking sheep, horses and cattle. You must look ahead for yourself and your stock. And about yourself. You must not lie, you must not steal, you must not try to cheat anybody, and you must not talk about women in a crowd. If you talk about women in front of anybody you'll surely get a name, and you'll be sorry when you get a bad name from a woman."

But I'd already told lots of lies, and I'd been around with women. But I kept it all to myself. Whenever they asked me if I'd been with a woman I always said no. Even though they'd noticed me I always denied it. So I'd told them a lie lots of times. I didn't steal or cheat anybody, but I kept on telling lies. That's the way I was. However, from there on I held onto their words, but still I didn't put my lies away.

He said, "Now you must go right ahead with all you've learned from me. You know about almost everything. As I said to you before, you must take good care of your stock. When you have stock you won't go poor, you won't starve. You may go hungry for half a day, or maybe all day, but you'll have something on hand, something that can be eaten the same day. You may not have any other kind of food, but you'll have meat on hand, and you'll be saved by that. You won't starve to death when you run out of food, for you'll have meat. When you get hungry for some kind of food just trade off your meat. In that way you'll be fixed well all the time."

Two days after he'd spoken to me, that morning, he asked about the horses. "How many horses have we got? Do you know anything about it? Did you ever count them?" I said,

"Yes, we've got sixty-two horses altogether, but I don't think many of them will have colts. Only about ten or fifteen maybe will have young ones. Then it may run up to seventy or more, close to eighty. But I don't think we'll have twenty colts." He said, "That's all I want to know. I don't think I'll get to see one hundred horses, because I'm going down all the time. I don't think I'll live that long. I'm sure it'll run to over a hundred, but I won't get to see them. That's the way I feel about it."

Three days later, while my mother was herding the sheep, she found four big arrowheads. Two were just like black glass; you could see through them. They were the same size, about six or seven inches long. The other two were yellow and striped. They were great big ones, twelve to fourteen inches long. At the point, for about two inches, they were narrow and round. And she found two round stones. One had a hole through it. The old man said, "That's what the singers use. When they want to say their prayers they'll get those stones out and hold them in their hands. While they're holding them they'll say their prayers. They're what you call Big Bead. That's what they say in their songs. When they're singing you'll hear them say, Big Bead, and that's what they mean." My mother said, "I found them where the people of the ruins had their houses. The two yellow ones were lying on top of the ground. The others were in the earth. I saw one of the black ones sticking up, so I dug it out, and there I found the others."

Nothing was done about it. We just put them away. But afterwards I found out that if anybody picks up something like that they always have something done for it. But we didn't have anything done about them. We never had any kind of doing at our place. When he was well, from as far back as I can remember, we never had any kind of singing or treatment for him or my mother, and I was never treated either. Not even just a little thing like what we call the Ghost Rite Blackening, or the Enemy Ritual Blackening. And we never had a Blessing Rite, nor did we ever have a singer who knew the Blessing Rite pray for us. I don't know why we never had any doings at our place. I always thought he must not believe in any kind of singing or treatment.

About five days later we moved to the place called Baby Rock. After we'd lived there a few days my father said, "We'll move again to Where The Mexican Fixed The Spring." My mother said, "We ought to turn around and move back on Black Mountain." But he said, "No, I'd like to go to Where The Mexican Fixed The Spring. That's where many of my relatives are. That's why I'd like to go there." So we started again down in the valley to where there was lots of greasewood. He was getting weaker and weaker.

One morning, about three days after we'd moved among the greasewood, he spoke to me and said, "My boy, I'm getting worse and worse. I think I won't live much longer, so you must learn some songs and prayers about the horses and sheep, and about the jewelry and the farms. If you learn some songs and prayers about these things you'll be all right later on when you get to be a man. Even if you learn only one song of each of them you'll be fixed all right as long as you live. And you'll live a long time and get old, if you learn some of the songs to make one live long. You'll be like me, as old as I am."

That afternoon, while I was herding not very far from where we were living, he came to me and said, "You go home and gather up a lot of wood for tonight. I'll take care of the sheep." I went back, and before dark I'd gathered together a big pile of greasewood. When I'd finished I went inside and fixed my bed. My place was on the north side of the hogan.

In the evening he brought the herd back, and as soon as he came inside he lay on his bed. My mother was lying down; she was about to go to sleep, and I was tired and sleepy too. He was lying against his big pillow and said, "Get up and make a fire. Bring in more wood." I got up and made a fire and brought in more wood and then lay down again.

He got up and said, "Get up, my boy, you mustn't lie." So I got up, and he said, "You haven't learned anything from me, and I'm going down all the time. You ought to learn something about the stocks, how to handle them. You ought to learn some songs and prayers about them, because if you don't know anything, if you don't know any songs, you won't have healthy stocks. As soon as the cold weather comes they'll get some kind of disease. Maybe they'll catch cold, maybe they'll get some kind of soreness, maybe they'll get bugs, or they may freeze to death. If you know some songs about them you'll have a good herd all the time. You'll be raising them year after year and get many lambs. The same with the horses. In the springtime you'll have colts, and they'll be looking fine. If you don't know any songs you'll soon lose all the stock. So you'd better start in right now and learn something, because you won't get a song from anyone else. You don't know any of the people of your clan, you don't know any of your clansmen, you just know your fathers, but I know they won't teach you anything. I know they don't want you to learn anything about these things. So you'd better go ahead and try it right now."

Then he started with the songs. He sang six and told me to repeat them. I repeated them, and he said, "Repeat them again." I repeated every one and he said, "Repeat once more." So I repeated every one again. Then he said, "That's right. Every one is correct. The rest can be counted." So I just counted the others, and there were twenty-eight altogether.

After we'd put these songs away he started on another set. They were twelve in number. They were the same as the others, but with just a little different tune. "All these are called Driving Songs. When you're out with the herd you sing these songs, and while you're singing you take out your corn pollen and give it to the sheep." When we were through with the second set he started on another. They were twenty-eight. I learned four and just counted the rest again. They were all exactly alike in tune and words, but altogether different from the others.

When we were through it was morning. He said, "Now you've learned some songs about the stocks. I know you'll have good-looking stocks all the time. And you'll have strong stocks. None of them will be weak. They won't die off on you. They won't get any kind of disease. That's as far as I want you to learn from me. The rest of your fathers know all about these songs. There are more songs, but the other fathers of yours will teach you those. I know they will, when you ask them. A fellow shouldn't be stingy about the songs. So try and ask them. Don't be afraid to tell them you want to learn some songs about the stocks. If they're unkind to you they won't let you learn any; if they're kind enough, I'm pretty sure they'll teach you some."

That was all. That's as far as I learned some songs about the horses and sheep from him. That was the only time he sang songs for me, just that once, and no more. I never learned any from him again. He had a great many that he used on all different things, but I didn't get to learn any of them. If he'd lived longer I'd have learned more about the other things, but I never got the chance. That day, while I was out herding, I practiced and repeated all the songs I'd learned and got them fixed in my mind.

14. *The end of Old Man Hat.*

THE day after a man named Wearing Ear Rings came to our place. A boy, his nephew, brought him over to us. The man was blind. He was Bitahni's older brother, and a younger brother of my mother's. The boy went right back to his home, and the old man stayed with us there at that place for two days. Then we started to move again. We put him on one of the tame horses, and my mother tied some dishes and jugs over the saddle. In one of the jugs she had boiled blood mixed with meat and corn-mush. She said to him, "Don't try to lead the horse, just let him alone. He'll know where to go," and she said to me, "Take him and drive the horses with him." So I started off, driving the horses with this man. We went quite a way to where there was lots of grass, and I said to him, "Stay here with the horses. I'm going back and help with the herd." He said, "I'll be all right."

I went back to the herd, and as we were driving the sheep down to where he was we looked for him, but he wasn't anywhere around. We could only see the horses, all scattered out. I went over where I'd left him and started tracking him. There was a lot of wild cherry brush, about as high as cedar trees, and he must have let the horse go, maybe he kicked the horse or whipped it; he'd been riding all around in this brush. In the middle of a thick bunch was a little bare spot, and there I found him. He'd been riding around in that little space trying to get out, but he couldn't, because the brush was thick and close together. So then, I guess, he gave up trying and stopped his horse right in the middle of the bare spot. When I got there he was sitting on the horse and chewing away on the boiled blood. He must have been hungry and reached around and found something to eat in the jug. There he was, having his lunch.

I said, "What are you trying to do? Are you trying to run away from us? I told you to stay with the horses." I took hold of the bridle and led the horse out of the brush. He didn't say a word. I started trotting the horse and said to him, "Now whip the horse and kick all you want to." We trotted all the way back to where the horses were. When we got there my mother scolded him for that. "What did you run away for? You ought to know better than that. You know you can't see anything. You should have stayed right at one place. You know very well we'll take care of you. Now don't try to run away again." I rounded up the horses and started off with him once more. We went a little way, and I told him to stay there. As soon as I left him he began kicking and whipping his horse, letting it trot around with him and chasing the horses all over. I went up and told him to stop. I said, "You're chasing the horses in all different directions." But he never said a word.

He was doing that all the way to Sloping Meadow. When we got there that evening my mother said to me, "It's too much trouble. He makes too much work for us. Tomorrow you take him back to his home. We've got too much to do. We can't look after him all the time. So you must take him back to his home tomorrow." She said to him, "You ought to know better than that. You should stay with the horses. They were going on the trail, taking their time. But instead of riding behind them you make your horse go. You've been chasing them around so they don't know which direction they're going. We've had a hard time trying to stop you from doing that. You won't do what we tell you to. We've got all kinds of things to do, and you make more work for us. And the old man there's not able to do anything. We have to look after him, and I can't do much. My son is the only one who's taking care of us and the other things. He can't be bothered with you all the time. So I guess you'd better go back to your sister's place." He said, "It's all right with me. I was thinking and wanting to stay with you a few days, but I guess I'll go back tomorrow." "Yes," said my mother, "you'd better go back tomorrow, because you make too much work for us. We're tending to the herds and horses and to our things and to ourselves, so we can't bother with you all the time. You might fall in the fire, or in a ditch, or an arroyo, and that would be bad for you. So you must go right back to where you were before."

The next morning I saddled a horse and got him on it and started off. He didn't live very far from where we were camped. There was a point, and behind this point was his sister's place. That's where he was staying. While I was leading the horse with him he began to kick and whip it and tried to make it go. He nearly ran over me several times. I told him not to let the horse go, but he didn't mind me. He'd stop a while and then start in again. Finally I got him back to his sister's place. As soon as I got him there I started back to our camp with the horse. I was glad that I had him out of my way, and all of us felt just the same.

I herded the rest of that day and all the next day. The day after some horses got away from us, and I was looking for them. I was hunting them all that day and rounding them up. My father was herding. He wasn't out far from where we'd located; he was just watching the sheep around close to camp. When I came back in the evening he was just coming in. He said, "While I was looking after the sheep a bunch of them passed above me on the rocks. Just as they passed by they started running. When they started running I cussed them.

I said, 'Evil spirits, where are you going?' and one of them spoke up and said, 'Over there.' That's what one of the sheep said to me. They were running back towards the place from which we drove them." My mother said, "I wonder why the sheep said that? We ought to turn around and go back to our place. Maybe the sheep don't want us to move on. They say the sheep know everything about what's going to happen to them or to us. Something ought to be done for that." But he said, "Oh, there's nothing to it. Nothing will happen. We'd better just move on." So he put that away, and nothing was done about it. Today, when anything happens like that, when a fellow hears something, or sees something, or has bad dreams, they always get a singer to do something about it, to straighten things out. But he didn't seem to believe anything at all, and so nothing was done.

Then, in about two days, we moved to a place called Cottonwood Row. We stayed there three days and then started again down the little canyon to a place called Little Canyon Meadow. In this canyon there were lots of poisonous weeds. The day after we moved there I was herding the sheep in these weeds and walking around in them. That evening, after I returned with the herd, I began to scratch myself. First I scratched my fingers, and in a little while I was scratching my arms. Then I began scratching my legs, and soon I was scratching myself all over. The next morning my whole body was swollen up. That was because I'd been walking in those poisonous weeds.

That morning we went on to Where The Mexican Fixed The Spring. Some people were living there. There was Old Man Little Yellow, who was a Poles Sprung Out In Water, and a man named Anger. He was a Bitter Water. He was Old Man Little Yellow's son-in-law. Then there was Old Man Blue Goat, my father's nephew, and another man named

Always Spitting, who was an older brother of Blue Goat. There were also two of Old Man Blue Goat's nephews. They were my father's grandsons and sons of the old woman, my father's niece. She lived there and her daughter and granddaughter. They were Many Goats. Those were the people my father wanted to have put up a Feather Chant for him. That's why we moved there.

We camped a little way from where these people lived, and the next morning I went over to their place with my father. Before we started to go and visit them he got out his red beads and put them around my neck. They were the ones he got from Keams Canyon. When we got inside the hogan the old woman and her granddaughter were sitting there. Old Man Little Yellow was sitting there too, and so was Blue Goat. Anger and Always Spitting were out some place. Soon after the other woman came in. When we entered the hogan my father walked up to the old woman and sat down beside her, and she put her arms around his shoulders and began to cry, saying, "Alas, my son, alas." They held each other quite a while, and the others did the same. Everyone walked up and put his arms around him.

They put two sheep pelts on the ground for us, and we sat down, and my father began to tell about the trips we'd made and all about himself. After he'd told everything he said, "I came here because I want you people to help me out. I'd like to have a Feather Chant performed on me." When he was through talking about it the woman said, "Yes, we're willing to help anyone. We'll all help you, because we know all about the different chants. Lots of times we've had different chants right here at our place. So we'll surely put up a chant for you. We have two boys who are both willing to do something for anybody. They're always glad to help." Old Man Little Yellow said, "They'll surely help you out, but I'm not able to do anything either, because I'm too old. That's why I can't get around quickly. But the boys and the others will do all the work. They like to do something of that kind. They always like to have a chant at any time." We stayed at these people's place all day until evening, and then we started back. As soon as we got home I lay down and went to sleep. I guess they told all about this to each other.

In the morning I got the horses we'd been using, and my father said, "Get on one of the horses and ride around. See if you can find some good grazing. If you find good grass somewhere for the horses take them over there." So that day I went out riding among the sand hills and on top of Lines Of Thin Rocks. There I found some feed for the horses. When I came back I said, "I found nice green grass on top of Lines Of Thin Rocks." "That's what I thought," he said. "Everything gets green first here in this flat. Up on Black Mountain and around the foot of the mountain the grass hasn't started getting green yet. But around here, I know, the grass and other things are getting green." While we were staying at this place I had the horses there, where the good grass was, and from there on I just tended to the herd. Once in a while I'd go to see about the horses.

One evening, about five days later, my mother came back from those people's place. That's where my father was. She stayed over there with him every day, and in the evening she returned to where we were living. This evening she came back and said, "They're going to put up a chant. They've got everything ready. They've got enough baskets, enough of everything, so they're going to give a chant for your father. They're going to get a singer named One Birth After Another. He's the one who knows the Feather Rite."

The old man was getting worse all the time, but still he just kept quiet about himself. By the looks of him he was very sick, but still he kept quiet. In the morning I brought in two horses for her, and she went over to that place and brought back the girl to help her pack. They were just beginning to pack up the horses as I went out with the sheep. When I came back in the evening everything had been taken to the other place. I went over there with my herd and put it in a little cliff and then went over where they were going to hold the chant. My father was lying there in this hogan, and there was the singer's medicine-outfit, but he hadn't come yet. Old Man Little Yellow's son had gone to Carriso Mountain for medicine the singer wanted. He was away until the evening of the next day. When he came back he brought some medicine with him, and that night the singer arrived. They told me to take his horse to where there was grass, so I unsaddled it for him and took it away and hobbled it. That night they told him what was wrong with my father, and after my father had told all about himself the singer said, "Well, then, we'll build a big fire four times for you, and you can take the medicine while you're sweating." While they were still talking about it I went to sleep.

Every morning while they were singing and treating my father I went out with the herd, and every morning they killed two sheep, and in the evening as soon as I came back I went to bed. People were coming in every day. In the evening after the fourth fire my father, Choclays Kinsman, arrived, just as I got back with the sheep. He said, "I didn't know a singing was going on until yesterday. When they told me about it, right away I thought, 'I'll go to that singing.' That's why I started off this morning from my home, and now I've got here."

When they were through with the fire, after they'd built a big fire four mornings, they started in with their sand-painting for four days more. It was a nine nights chant. The first day they started their sand-painting, when I came back with the herd in the evening, another man was sitting by the singer. He hadn't been there that morning when I left. Today we call him Undresses Again, but at that time they used to call him Red Woman's Grandson. He was a Red Clay, a nephew of One Birth After Another. He was learning the Feather Rite.

The night after that, while Anger was on his way back to his home, as he was passing the sheep corral, he heard something. He stopped and looked; he saw the sheep looking at something; he gazed all around, and there he saw somebody in the middle of the sheep, and that was his wife and this man, named Red Woman's Grandson. He didn't say anything about it until the next day. I'd been herding all day again, and when I came back in the evening with the sheep I heard them talking about something, and it was that. There was a big crowd in the hogan. More people had come. They were all strangers to me. Anger was sitting on the east side of the fire, talking. He said, "I put up this chant. I talked about it and put it up. I went around and gathered up the necessary things. I got everything ready. That's how the sing started. I didn't want anything like this to be done to me. But this one fellow has hurt me very much. I don't know where I stand. I can't go any further with the chant. Even though it's toward the end it's got to be stopped right now, unless you do something for me." That's what he was saying when I came in, and I was wondering what he was talking about. There was a big crowd in the hogan. I looked around; nobody was looking up; they all had their heads down, smoking away while he was talking.

I went over to my father, and he said, "Raise me up." I raised him, and he sat up and started talking. He said, "I know all there is to know about such things. I know more

266

about it than all of you people. I know just how it starts and how it happens, because I've been all through it. Lots of times the same thing has happened to me, but I tried never to think about it. I always put it out of my mind, because, when I think of it, it's nothing to me, there's nothing to it. We're all doing just the same to one another. All of you people who are here now are all wishing for another man's wife, even though you have a wife of your own. I know every one of you has been around with another man's wife. Nothing can be done about it. It's always that way, with no end to it. And so I think there's no use talking about it. So we'll drop it and put it away. I just want all of you to help me out. That's all I want. Perhaps, after these doings are over, we'll talk about it, but we won't get anything out of it. It'll be just talk. So we'll put it away, and I want all of you to stay and help me, until the doings are over." Then he lay down again.

Anger said, "Well, I want him to go right now. I don't want him to stay around here. I want him to get out of my sight right now, because if he stays around here all during the singing I might do something to him. So I want him to leave." The singer said, "You just keep your mouth shut. You think you're doing all this, but I am. I'm trying my best to help the patient. I don't want any bad talk in front of me. You want us to go and leave right now, but I won't, and I don't want him to go either, not until we're through with the singing, and then we'll go." Anger was just getting ready to say something else, but my father, Choclays Kinsman, spoke up and said, "That's all right, my son-in-law, just be quiet about it. We'll talk about it for you after this doing is over. If you want to stay with your wife don't talk too much, and if you don't want to stay with her you can go right now and leave her. You don't want to talk too much about it. So just be quiet, until after the doing is over, and then we'll see about it for you." He didn't say another word. He just got up and walked out. I guess he went home. He didn't show up again.

In the morning—it was the last day—I tied up four sheep to be butchered. While they were butchering I went out with the herd and was herding all day. When I returned in the evening I saw more people, more men and more women. Many of them were Red House, and some were Standing House, and a lot were Many Goats. It was a big crowd that evening. As soon as it got real dark they started singing. Red Woman's Grandson was beating the basket. He was the leader. The singer was lying down, taking it easy. Towards midnight I got tired sitting up and went to sleep.

The next morning the doing was over, and everybody started leaving for his home. Before I left with the herd I went inside the hogan, and Choclays Kinsman was saying to my father, "I guess I'll be going back, my older brother. I think you'll be all right, but we'll see how you feel in two or three days. However, I believe you'll be all right, so I think I'll start back for home this morning. You just keep still and take good care of yourself. Don't try to go anywhere, because you might hurt yourself again. Just lie in your bed and be quiet." My father said, "I don't know. I'm going down all the time. I'm getting worse. That's the way I feel about myself. I'm so weak. There's something moving all around my body. When it begins to move it hurts me so badly. When it moves back and forth on my back, up to my neck and down to my hips, I suffer, and it makes me so weak. That's the thing that's bothering me the worst." His younger brother said, "I'll come again in two or three days. In the meanwhile my nephew will stay here with you to watch and take care of you." That was Slim Man's younger brother, his real brother, the one who was killed by Red Woman. He was her clan brother, but still she killed him.

Old Man Hat said, "I don't think I'll get well. I don't think I'll live long. That's how I feel about myself, because of the way I look now. I look at myself, and there's nothing on me, no flesh on me any more, nothing but skin and bones. That's why I don't think I'll live long. I think I'll die any time. So you'd better come and see me in two or three days. Maybe I'll still be living. If I live that long you may have a chance to see me again." Then he said, "I'm so thankful you came, and I'm so glad my nephew will be around here with me. Be sure and come and see me again. About eating, you know I can't eat anything that's hard, only things that are soft, something I can swallow. But I don't take much, only two or three swallows. But I drink plenty of water." Choclays Kinsman said, "Even though you're that way, my older brother, you'd better keep eating all the time. By doing that it'll give you strength. If you don't you'll surely get weak. Even though you're so weak now and not able to eat, try to eat and swallow something. Somehow or other you might get over your illness. If you quit eating food, then you'll sure be gone." That's what he said, and then he left, and I went out with the herd.

When I came back in the evening there was no one around. Everyone had gone. He said to me, "Press down on my back." I walked up and sat by him and began pressing down on his back with my hands, pressing down back and forth from his hips up to the back of his neck. He said, "Keep pressing on me all night." I was working on him all night long. Early in the morning I took a little sleep and then went out with the herd. In the evening, after only a little sleep again, I started pressing on his back. I kept it up all night. I knew he was going down fast that morning, he was so weak. While my mother started pressing down on him I went out with the herd.

269

That night he was rolling all over his bed. He said to me, "Go get me Anger. Tell him I want him. I want him to do something on me. I want him to treat me in some way. If he asks, 'What does he want me for?' don't tell him I want him to treat me. Just say I want him over here. Just tell him I'd like to see him. I'm suffering from pain, a pain that goes all around my body. It's beginning to get worse right now. So you go over and tell him I'd like to see him." I went over to his place, and just as I was going in the hogan, just as I got to the doorway, his wife came out. I went inside, and there he was, sitting by himself. I said, "They want you over where we're staying." He said, "Who wants me?" I said, "My father would like to see you." "Why does he want to see me?" "I don't know what he wants you for. He just said he'd like to see you. That's all he said." He didn't say a word. He took out his tobacco, rolled a cigarette and lit it and started smoking. When he was through he said, "All right, let's go."

We went back together. My mother raised him up, and while she sat behind him, holding him up, he said, "I sent word over to you, my son-in-law, because I want you to do some kind of treatment on me. Help me out, even though I've hurt you. I was the one who hurt your feelings, because I came here and wanted you to put up a chant for me. You put it up, and while the singing was going on a fellow got after your wife, and she belongs to my clan. So, in that way, I hurt your feelings. But, even at that, I want you to help me with some one of your treatments. I'm suffering from pain right now, so please help me."

He didn't say anything. He was sitting by the fire, hanging his head, for quite a while. Then he said to me, "You go over to my place—I guess maybe that old woman's back—and get me my medicine-outfit." I went over and brought it back to him, and he said to my father, "I'll sing over you with the Red Ant Song." So that's what he started on. I sat up part of the night and watched him singing and treating the old man, and then I went to sleep and slept the rest of the night. In the morning, just as I woke up, he finished his singing and treatment. He sat back away from him and said, "I don't know what's bothering you. I can't say; I'm unable to find it. But I know I can't do anything for you, and I don't think anybody could. I think the pain that's in you is from a witch. Somebody bewitched you. You're too far gone right now, so you belong to him. That's why I don't think anybody could do anything for you."

My mother said to me, "You go over to your mother's place and get the boy, your younger brother. Tell your mother you need help on herding. Go over to their place this morning." I said, "It's too late. I want to take the herd out right now. I'll go over and get the boy tomorrow morning." She said, "No, I want you to go right now. Let the herd go. Maybe somebody will take it out for us. You go and get the horses and take a ride over to their place, because there's too much work here for us; we need help. I want you to do things around here while your younger brother is herding. So you'd better go for him this morning." I said, "All right." When I brought the horses back I saddled one and started over to this woman's place. She was Bitahni's Sister. They were the people to whom I took the blind man. They'd moved out of the canyon to a place called Scattered Boulders.

When I got to their place the woman, my aunt, was at home, and the blind old man, her brother, was a little way from the hogan. He was trying to walk, but he couldn't; he just stood up and sat down again. I said to my aunt, "I came for my younger brother. My mother sent me over, and she says to you, 'My younger sister, please let your boy come over to help us for a few days.' So that's what I came here for. I'd like to take my younger brother back with me. I want him to help me with the herding, because we've got so much to do at home. My father is getting worse all the time. He's very weak now and says he's suffering from pain. So I'd like to be with him all the time. That's why we'd like to have the boy help us." She said, "Yes, you can take him. He has nothing to do around here. He does nothing but play all the time. He's out now with the children, playing way down below. So you can take him. Go over where they're playing."

I got on my horse and rode over and said to him, "Come on, sit behind me." He got up on the horse, and I went back with him to his home. His mother said, "Your mother wants you to help her with herding, so you go over and herd for her." He didn't say anything, and so we started back. It was late in the afternoon. I didn't have a thing to eat there, because there wasn't anything.

When we got home my mother said, "Choclays Kinsman came again this morning. He arrived just about at noon, and I gave him something to eat. As soon as he'd eaten he got on his horse and went to get a singer, named Supernatural Power." This man was living at Water Flowing Out, far away from our place. Late in the afternoon of the next day my father came back with the singer's outfit, and that evening the man came. They wanted him to do star-gazing first. He went out and star-gazed, and when he was through he came back inside. He said, "I saw you sitting on a bearskin. The head of the bear was towards the east, and you were sitting on the skin, facing the east too. And this whole place was all black. That means no hope. You've killed yourself with your own witchcraft. You tried to bewitch someone, but you witched yourself instead. That's what you're killing yourself with, so there's no hope. Nobody will cure you." That's what he said

272

when he came back inside. Anger said, "That's the way it looked to me. Last night I was treating him all night, and I said to him, 'Nothing can be done for you.' That's the way I found it to be."

My father said, "So there was all darkness around here." The star-gazer said, "Yes, the whole place here is all black." The old man said, "Well, if it's that way, then nothing can be done. Don't try to do anything on me any more, because there's no use. I know very well I'll die." Again the star-gazer said, "I saw you sitting on a bearskin facing the east. You tried to bewitch someone, but your witchcraft came right back into you. That's what you're killing yourself with." The old man said, "No, I'm no witch. Everybody claims I am, but I'm not. But I know somebody is killing me with his witchcraft. When I was young I got into a quarrel with a witch, and he tried to kill me. But I got him and told him to take all his witchery out of me. So he took out what he'd shot into me, and from there on I lived well for a long time. My younger brother is sitting there right now, he knows all about it." He meant Choclays Kinsman. "I think he didn't take all of his shots out of me, and that's what's killing me now. I can't get him again, because he's dead, so I'm a goner too."

They were talking about it all night. They didn't do anything but sit and talk. Supernatural Power said, "I really saw you, and I really mean you have bewitched yourself. Even though you say, no, I saw you. So there's no hope, unless you beg me to save you. But you say you're not a witch, but I know you are, and you're killing yourself with your own witchery. If you'd only say it was true, then I'd help you. If you don't tell about yourself you'll surely die. There's still a chance, if only you say you bewitched yourself. If you just say, 'I've bewitched myself,' then I'll help you. I can get your witchery out for you." But he kept saying, no, so they quit talking about it.

The next morning they began more treatments, but they didn't do him any good. I don't know how many days he lived after that; I didn't know anything all that time, because I didn't get enough sleep for many nights. That got me kind of crazy. I was so tired I never thought of anything, just him. He was getting worse every day and night. When he was about to die he said, "Don't worry about me. It's all right with me, because I'm old now. If I hadn't taken this sickness I wouldn't have lived long anyway. So you don't have to worry so much about me. I'm not the only one who's going to die. I've seen lots of my grandfathers, and they've all died, and my grandmothers too, and many aunts and uncles and nephews and nieces have died, and my father and mother died, and many of my brothers and sisters. Lots of people I've known have died. So I'm going too. I'm not going to live forever anyway. I'll get to see all I've known when I die. So you don't have to worry so much about me. But worry about yourselves. Take good care of yourselves while you're living, until the end of your lives. We're all coming and will get to the end. We all know we won't live forever. So you must take good care of yourselves."

Then he said to Choclays Kinsman, "My younger brother, you go over and get me another singer, the one we call Plucked Whiskers. Get him for me. If he doesn't cure me it's all right. I want him to do something on me with the Witch Rite. So you go over and get him. And give him a horse." Choclays Kinsman put up a horse of his own besides, so that made two they were going to give him.

Early in the morning I brought in the horses and saddled one for him. Everything was ready to be eaten, and after we all ate he went off for this man. I took out the herd and was herding all day, and in the evening when I came back he was back too. He'd brought the singer with him. The old man was about to die. The singer started singing and waving his eagle feathers over him, and my mother said, "Don't just wave those feathers. I didn't send for you for that. Get out that bad thing that's in him. Try to suck it out. Save him for me." But he said, "No, I don't like to do that. He's pretty far gone. If I cut him it'll be the end. I don't want to do him any harm. I don't want to hurt him. He's hurt enough now." My mother kept begging him to take out the "bean" that was in him, but he kept on saying, no. So he didn't, and nothing was done for him; everybody was just crying all night, and this man, Plucked Whiskers, was crying too.

He said to my father, Choclays Kinsman, "It's all right, my uncle, everybody's dying off. Every creature on this earth is dying. Even the mountains are caving down. He was like Blanca Peak, or like Mount Taylor, or like Carriso Mountain, or the La Plata Range, like Gobernador Knob or San Francisco Peak. He was like one of the mountains. He had everything and knew everything, and everyone knew him, and everybody named him. So don't be worrying about him. We'll all be gone. We want to take care of and look after ourselves. While we're still alive we should help and take care of each other. When we die that's the end of it. Nothing can be done about death. We've all got to die. When we die we're gone forever. No one will bring us back. So there's no use worrying so much about it."

He was lying still, just breathing a little all that night, and just as morning came, just as you saw a little white and blue sky coming over the mountain, he passed away. He died that morning and all his relatives and friends began to cry. As soon as he died they told me to go and round up the horses, and while his relatives and friends were holding him and crying I

275

started out, and while I was running I was crying too. I caught my father's racehorse and rounded up the others and drove them back. Everybody had left him and come outside.

We used to have a blue horse. It was the best horse in the bunch. I put a rope around that horse's neck and led him over to the hogan where my father was and put the saddle and bridle on him. Some of his relatives were still inside, fixing him up. They put new moccasins on his feet and cut a great big buckskin of his in half and put it around him for leggings. They dressed him in all his clothes and put on two bunches of beads that he had.

When he was dressed one of his nephews and I went in and got him. Our hair was untied, and we were covered with ashes. We put him on the horse and all his things beside him. There were two big bundles of stuff, and then we started off. The other fellow was leading the horse, and I was by my father, holding him, so he wouldn't fall off. We went to a little cliff and put him in a hole under the rocks and built a wall around him and covered him with rocks and all the poles we could find, and over that we put some dirt. We fixed him so nothing would bother him. After that we destroyed all his things and faced the horse to the north and killed it.

Then we started back, running and jumping over the bushes, so no evil spirit would catch up with us. When we got home we set fire to the hogan in which he died, and after that his brother, Choclays Kinsman, came up with a rifle and shot the racehorse. We were standing by him, and he said to us, "Face the horse to the north." We went over and faced it north, and then he shot another. We went over and faced that one to the north again, and he turned around and shot another one, and we faced that one to the north. As he was turning to shoot again a fellow came up and grabbed his rifle and begged him not to kill any more.

A little way from home they had a pail of water ready for us to wash in. It was mixed with the leaves of a tree struck by lightning. We washed the ashes off ourselves over there and then went back in the other hogan. There was a place for us two, right beside each other, on the north side. Everybody else was on the south side. When we got inside we put our clothes back on, and while we were dressing the others started cooking. It was almost noon. All this time we hadn't eaten anything. They'd said, "Nobody should eat until everything has been fixed up."

When the food was cooked we started eating. We had ours apart from the other people. They said to us, "You two have to eat separately, not with the others, and you shouldn't leave anything in the dish. You must eat up everything. If you want more they'll put some in your dish, just enough for you to eat. And you mustn't touch anything, nor bother anything. You mustn't bother the fire. And nobody should walk in front of you, or go near you. You two mustn't separate. Whenever one wants to go out to take a leak, you should both go. Even though the other doesn't need to, you both should go. You have to stay right by each other, so nothing will go between you. None of you should go between them," they said. "When any of you go out you shouldn't go towards the north, nor look towards the north. As soon as you go out turn around towards the south. You should only be on the south side of the hogan, and none of you should look around. You might see something. If you look around you might see evil spirits, and that'll be bad for you. You'll get sick from it and die. You mustn't say, 'evil spirits,' and you mustn't say, 'grave,' and you shouldn't face toward where the hogan was burned. You have to do these things and not say things like that for four days. During the four days you must all be quiet. Don't do anything, or say anything out loud. You must all go easy on everything."

Three days after he was buried they got some soap-weed and hauled some water. That was for us and the others too, but ours was separate. Early the next morning we all got up and washed ourselves all over. When we were through the two of us washed our clothes and hung them up to dry. It was before the sun was up. Then the other fellow and I took our corn pollen and went out towards where we'd buried the body. Quite a way from the hogan we stopped and put some pollen in our mouths and some on top of our heads, and some we sprinkled about, naming the body and saying, "You've gone away from us now by yourself." Those were the only words we said, and then we turned around and started home.

Inside the hogan we gave the corn pollen to the fellow sitting by the doorway, and then all the people began taking some and saying their prayers, saying, "We'll live long, and we'll live good lives. We'll be on the good path, on the happy path all the rest of our lives." After that they talked to us, telling us how to take care of ourselves, and how to take care of the others. "In that way," they said, "you'll live a long and good life. And some day the same thing will happen to you. When you die you'll be fixed just the same way."

15.

They divide the old man's goods and move away . . . The bear that killed a horse . . . They move back to Anything Falls In, and he looks up an old friend . . . Comedy at Oraibi . . . He is suspected of killing the people's cattle.

AFTER we were through with all these doings we rounded up the horses and saddled them and put on all our stuff and moved away to a place called Salt Water. When we got to that place all the sheep and horses were there, and there was a crowd, all my father's relatives and a lot of people from different places, talking about how they'd divide the things up. My father's brother, Choclays Kinsman, got on his horse and rode over where the sheep were, and everybody moved there after him. He said, "I'll give sheep to every one of you. Some will get twenty head, some fifty, and some of you will get a hundred. In that way every one of you will get some sheep. I'll do the same with the horses. I'll give each of you a horse or two. I don't want any sheep or horses for myself, because I've got enough. But it's up to you, my relatives and friends, if you want to give me a sheep or a horse it'll be all right. I'll be thankful for it. But before I start giving them out to you I want my boy to have his first. We'll all help separate my boy's sheep and horses, and then I'll start giving you some."

They separated the sheep for us, and my mother and I had a little over five hundred head. And they separated fourteen horses of mine. My father came up to me and said, "Get two more out of that bunch. Any two you like." So I went over and got me a young mare and a three-year-old stallion. I didn't get any of his sheep. He'd had close to nine hundred head, but his clan relatives got them all. They got all his cattle too. But the cattle were up on Black Mountain, so all the people who were related to him went up there and rounded them up and gave one or two heads to each other. There was only one steer in the bunch, and my father's brother kept that for himself.

When they were through giving out the sheep and horses to each other we moved away from there towards the San Juan. That was my mother and I and the little boy, my younger clan brother, who'd been herding for us. He was about seven or eight years of age. He could do everything you told him to, so we didn't have to worry about him when he was out with the sheep.

We lived there a long time. One day, around in June or July, a fellow came to our place. It was a real hot day. He said to us, "I'm trading some stuff for sheep, but we haven't any more things left, only this silver belt. We had a lot of jewelry with us and robes and shawls and a lot of other little things, but we've traded it all. This is all that's left, just this silver belt." He gave it to my mother and said, "This belt is worth eighty head of sheep. It's really worth a hundred, but I'll put the price down for you. I'd like to get eighty sheep for my belt." There was a crowd around, some saying, "Too much. You're losing your sheep for nothing." But some said, "It's worth it, because silver belts are scarce. You can't get one anywhere. If you take it you know you've got something worth while. You'll have that silver belt all your life." So my mother and I took it and sorted out eighty head of sheep, and the man turned them in with his bunch and left.

One day, some time after that, my mother said to me, "You've got an older clan brother living about sixteen miles from here close by the river. His name is Bushy Hair." She told me what he looked like, and about his age and size. "You go up there and visit him," she said. "You'll find him living there." So I saddled my horse and started off. About noon I got to a place and saw a man sitting in the hogan. I wondered if that was the man I'd come to visit. I went up and shook hands with him, and while he was holding my hand he asked me a lot of questions. Pretty soon he found out we were in the same clan, and he said, "You're my brother." He was about fifty years old. He asked me, "How did you get to know I lived here?" I said, "My mother told me all about you and your home." He began asking me a lot of questions again, and I started telling him where we'd started from and where we'd located until we got down there by the San Juan. I told him how my father got sick and how he died and everything. He said, "I knew your father a long time. I know he was a good and kind man. He used to have a lot of stuff."

He made me a long speech about life while they were preparing the food for me. He had a lot of children. When everything was cooked and ready we started eating, and while we were eating he was still talking to me about different things and different ways. When we were through he asked me, "When are you going back?" I said, "I want to go back today, because I've got a little brother herding sheep. I'm kind of worried about him." He said, "I thought you'd visit me. Why don't you stay for a day and overnight and go back tomorrow?" But I said, "I have to get back today, because there's lots for me to do at home. My mother is alone, and my little brother is herding, so I'm worrying about them. I've got to get back as soon as I can." Then he turned around and got hold of a sack and dragged it over to himself. He untied it and put in his hand and pulled out a buffalo skin. It was quite a big one and had a lot of hair on it. I'd never seen a buffalo skin before. They were scarce. Only the people who were rich had them. He handed it to me, and I was sure glad and thankful to get it. It made me proud. I said, "You're a kind man, a kind brother of mine. I didn't think you'd do this for me."

After that I started back. When I got home my mother said, "Where did you get the buffalo skin?" I said, "My brother gave it to me." "Your brother gave it to you?" I said, "Yes, my brother gave it to me." "Oh," she said, "that was nice of him, giving you a buffalo skin. Now you've got something worth while. You can have it a long time," and she told me how to use it and how to take care of it. "Have it clean all the time," she said, "because that buffalo skin is worth a lot. You must take good care of it. Don't throw it around to get dirty. If you throw it around and don't take care of it, if you let it lie around, it won't last long. If you take good care of it and put it away where nothing can happen to it you'll have it a long time."

Quite a few days afterwards my mother said, "We'll move again up on Carriso Mountain. It's too hot here now for us and the sheep. On the mountain it's cool, and lots of our relatives are living up there. So we'll move and get acquainted with some of them." We started off and moved way on top of the mountain to where a lot of people were living. When we got there my mother went to the different hogans and got to know a few of our relatives.

One day a fellow came to our place and said, "I want help. Last night a bear killed my horse. So I want to get that bear and kill him." Then he left; he was going around to all the hogans. I went after my horse and put the saddle on him and got my rifle and went over to his place. A crowd was there already. The man pointed to a canyon on the north side of the mountain and said, "This bear killed my horse down in that canyon." He said to the crowd, "Some of you go on the west side of the canyon and some on the east. The rest of us will go right in. In that way we'll get him. As soon as any of you see the bear go right ahead and shoot him. Watch closely. Have your rifles and pistols loaded and ready, for sometimes the bear gets behind a rock, or a tree, or a dead log lying on the ground, any place he can find to hide himself, like a little ditch, or a bush. Or he'll get in the water, even into a little hole, or stream. Sometimes he gets in there and watches for a person, and sometimes he gets up in a tree, so that you can hardly see him. So you must watch out closely for yourselves. Now you can go," he said. "Go around by twos, and keep close together. Don't leave one another. I want three fellows to go into the canyon. The rest of you go on top. I want the three fellows to have their rifles and pistols filled with cartridges, and they should have knives and hatchets."

Then we started. Three fellows went into the canyon on foot, and the rest of us went around the top on horseback. Three of us went way around to where a big black rock was standing. We tied our horses under the rock and climbed on top, and from there we could see plainly all around. We could see the three men walking down in the canyon, moving along slowly, close together. About halfway they stopped and looked at one another and pointed across the canyon, making all kinds of motions. Then they turned and climbed a little way up the west side, and there they stood and aimed across the canyon and shot, one after the other. Soon the bear cried out, growling so that we could hear him way up on the canyon, but we couldn't see him, we only saw the small cottonwood and oak trees moving. We heard him holler for quite awhile, and then there was no more noise. The three men went over, and when they found the bear was dead they hollered to us, saying, "The bear is dead! Come down and look at him." Everybody started down.

When we got there we asked them, "Where's the bear?" They pointed across to a bush, "The bear is lying in that bush," they said. We went over, and the man who'd gathered the people together said, "All of you, now, shoot this bear, as many times as you want to, because he's a thief. He's killed lots of horses, cattle and sheep. That's why I want every one of you to give him a shot." They started shooting the bear, and soon the smoke was almost like a cloud. That's what we did. We all gave the bear a shot, and after that one fellow started butchering him. The rest of us just stood and watched. But he only opened the belly and got the gall off the liver. "This is all I want," he said.

In the fall we moved to the foot of the mountain where some of the people had farms. A lot of our relatives had farms at Water Flowing Out, and we located close by them, because we wanted to get some corn and other stuff. We stopped and lived by Small Curly Hair's grandmother and her children. They had a good farm and lots of different stuff.

While we were living there we heard that some Utes from way up in Utah had camped on the north bank of the San Juan. They'd come to trade. They had lots of buffalo skins, buckskins and lion skins. My mother gave me two small rugs and said, "Go over and see what they've got. Maybe you'll get a buffalo skin for them." When I got to the place where the Utes were camping they said, "These Utes are here for trading. They want single and double saddle-blankets and good-sized rugs." I said to them, "I'd like to get a buffalo skin." They laid out a bunch, and I pointed to one and said, "I'd like to have this." They said, "Your blankets are not worth it. You've got pretty small blankets. This is a good-sized skin, and we want a good-sized blanket for it." Some were cut in half, and they said, "You can have two of these." They'd both been used, but still they were almost new and good-sized. The Utes were just about to start off again for some other place. I thought to myself, "I wish I had a lot of blankets with me. If I did I could get more buffalo skins, buckskins and lion skins." But then I didn't have anything at all, so I just started back while they were packing their horses.

In the fall, when it was getting colder and colder all the time and everything was put away, corn and stuff like that, my mother said, "My boy, we'll move back to Black Mountain, because there isn't any feed here for our stock." That's what she said, even though there was lots of it. Right away I said, "All right, mother, I've been thinking that way all the time. I'm always wishing I were over at Black Mountain." And I was, too, because I had two women over there. I was so lonesome where we were. I said, "I want to go right away, because I've got cattle there. I want to see them. I didn't make any ear-marks last fall, and this spring they've had more calves. I want to round them all up and make an ear-mark. I'm sorry for my cattle. I'm wondering how and where they are." While my little brother and I were packing the horses she went around to the hogans, saying good-by to all our relatives, telling them we were leaving. When we had everything ready she came back, and we started to move from there way across the valley to the foot of the mountain at Anything Falls In.

One day after we got there I said to my mother, "I'd like to go around among my relatives. I haven't seen them for a long time, so I'd like to visit them and see them and shake hands with them." She said, "All right." But I just said this to my mother. I didn't want to ride around all over among my relatives. I just wanted to find out where my women were. So then I started off and got to a hogan where some of my relatives were living. They were glad to see me, and I was glad to see them too. We shook hands, and they asked me if I'd come back to live with them. I said, "Yes, I've moved back." They made me something to eat, and after I ate I left. I found out at that place that the woman called Woman Who Flips Her Cards was living close by, so I went to her place and found her sitting in the hogan. I went up and shook hands with her, and she sure was glad to see me. She said, "Where've you been hiding yourself?" "Oh," I said, "I was around here all the time." "I never saw you. You must have been way off some place." "Yes, I've been way around the San Juan River and Carriso Mountain. Now we're back. We've come back here to live again." She started cooking something for me, but I said, "I must go. I want to go around and see my relatives. I had enough of eating awhile back."

While I was outside standing by my horse she came up and held my hand and put her arm around my shoulders and said, "Tomorrow, about what time will you be coming through here?" And I said, "Tomorrow, sometime before noon, I'll be going back, and I'll pass by here." We made a date then, and I told her to meet me on the canyon. There was a little canyon about four miles from where she lived. Right off she said, "All right. Even if my husband is home I'll go over, and we'll meet each other there." "All right," I said, "when I'm coming back I'll look for you."

Then I started on for where some more of my relatives were living. These were two old women who used to feed me when I was a baby. They were getting old. I stayed at their place overnight, and in the morning I got my horse and put the saddle on him and tied him to a post and then went back inside the hogan. The two old women said, "My, you're in a hurry. You ought to stay with us today and tonight." I said, "No, my mothers. Yes, I'm in a hurry; I'd like to go up on Black Mountain and round up my cattle, because last year I never did round them up and ear-mark them. So that's why I'm in a hurry. I want to get up on the mountain today sometime, and tomorrow morning I'll be ready to round them up." They said, "Well, it's all right, you can go now. It's true you have your cattle on the mountain." We talked awhile longer, and then I started out. "Wait awhile," one of them said to me. She dragged a sack full of things over to herself and untied it and pulled out a buckskin and gave it to me. It was a good-sized skin. I went out then and got on my horse and started home. I rode along all morning, and about noon I got to the canyon where I was going to meet that woman. When I got on top I looked around, and there she was, sitting under a tree.

We sure had a good time. After that we sat there, talking to each other, and I told her all about the trips I'd made. By that time it was evening. I didn't know it was that late. I said, "I want to go. It's getting too late for me. And your husband might miss you now." I tried to leave, but she was holding me and said, "My husband left this morning for Black Mountain. He won't be back until tomorrow, perhaps. I want you to stay with me all night tonight at home." "I can't," I said, "I could, but I've got to get back today. And you can't tell, your husband may be back tomorrow, or he may be back tonight. If he finds us, or if he finds me there, we'll sure get something we won't like. So I'm afraid to stay around here." I begged her, saying, "Please, let me go. I want to go, so that we won't get caught." She let me loose then, and I gave her the buckskin I got from my mothers.

While I was standing by my horse she came up to me again and put her arms around my shoulders and kissed me. "Now," she said, "you can go. I want you to keep this up. We'll keep this up all the time, every time we meet each other. Even if you get a wife I want you to come and meet me somewhere, because I'm yours and you're mine, and I think a lot of you, more than of my husband. That's why I want you to come, whenever you want to." I said, "All right, I will," and then I got on my horse and started home. When I'd gone a little way she said, "Wait awhile." I rode back, and she said, "We ought to stay together overnight." She begged me again, and I said, "I'd like to, but I'm afraid. Your husband might come back tonight, or he might even be back now. So I just can't. And about the buckskin, you must put it some place where he can't see it. Hide it away." "No, no," she said, "I won't let him see this buckskin until later on. After we sell our wool I'll take it out and say, 'I bought this buckskin from the trader.' So don't think I'll let him see it. And now, don't worry about me or yourself." Then she let me go, and I went home.

I got back in the evening and unsaddled my horse and turned him loose. My mother was sitting in the hogan. She asked me, "Where have you been? You must have had a good time yesterday all day and last night with your relatives." I laughed and said, "Yes, mother, I had lots of fun with my relatives all day yesterday and last night and up until noon." I didn't say anything about the buckskin. I just told her about the trips I'd made among my relatives. That was all, and we went to bed.

The next day we started moving up on Black Mountain to where we used to live at Willows Coming Out. We located there, and I started off after my cattle, to see if they were still around. I was hunting and rounding them up for many days, but still I didn't get to see them all. They were hard to find. Some were down in the canyons, down in the gulches, and some way on top of the mountain. I just took what I found and let the rest go.

It was late in the fall. The snow was on the ground. I said to my mother, "I want to go to the Oraibi's place where we used to trade before." She said, "All right, that'll be fine. We haven't any corn, nothing more to eat except meat." In the morning we caught four sheep and four goats, and while my little brother went out with the herd we started butchering. We cut up all the meat that day, and early next morning I put it on the horses and started off. I went along all day, leading one pack horse. I never stopped. The sun went down, but I kept going until I got there, late in the night.

Everybody must have been sleeping. Everything was quiet. Only the dogs were barking. I went to where I used to stop and tied my horses and unpacked them, and then I went up the hill to where they lived. There was no sign of anyone. I went up the ladder to where I always used to stay, but nobody was around. I thought they must be down below. I bent over the hole through the floor and said, "Where is everybody? Is everybody sleeping?" and a woman, who used to know me well, heard me and recognized my voice. She could speak a little Navaho. She got up and said, "Oh, who is there? Is that you, my friend?" I said, "Yes." She dressed herself, and everybody got up and dressed and came to where I was. She asked me, "Where are your horses?" I said, "Out there where I always tie them." "Have you got some meat?" she asked, and I said, "Yes." She said to her children, "Oh, let's go down there with him and bring up all that stuff for him." So they went down, and after I un-saddled my horses we carried the meat and saddles up the hill to their place. Right away they started cooking me some lunch, and the two boys went out again and took my horses to where there was feed for them. When everything was cooked I ate, and after I'd had enough we went to bed. It was about midnight.

In the morning, after we got up, they started cooking all different kinds of food, and we started eating. While we were eating they all began to talk. I sat there, eating away, I couldn't say anything. After awhile a man came in from another house. I shook hands with him, and he said, "Well, my friend, you came again, and we're all glad to see you." This man knew our language. I asked him, "What are all these people talking about?" He said, "Why?" "Well, be-cause I just don't know, because I can't understand them. I thought to myself, 'I wish I knew their language. If I did I could talk with them.' " He turned to the crowd and said something. They all looked at one another and laughed and began to talk with him. While they were talking they looked and pointed their lips at me, or pointed at me with their fingers.

The man said to me, "All these people here are glad to see you again, and they're thanking you for bringing them more meat. They all say, 'We're very glad to see him. We haven't seen him since three years ago. He hasn't been around for three years, and now he's grown to be a man. At first when he came he used to be a small boy. From then on he came here many times. He's almost been raised among us. That's the way we're thinking about him, because the first time he came he was only a little boy, and every time he came he was getting bigger and bigger, and now he's a man.

That's what we've been saying among ourselves, talking about him like that.' "

I laughed, and they all laughed, and then I told the fellow all about my trips. I said, "The old man I used to come here with, my father, is dead. He's not living now, and so I'm just with my mother and a little boy. The boy is my younger brother. We moved all around, up to the San Juan and around Carriso Mountain, and now we're at our old place on Black Mountain. That's where I'm from." They said to me, "You should come every once in a while. That's what we want you to do. You're our best friend, better than any of the other Navaho. When you lived here on Black Mountain you always came and brought us meat. We had meat all the time. You were mainly the one who brought us some. We sure missed you for three years, and we missed the mutton. We had a hard time getting meat all these three years, and now, today, we're having lots of it. So please come and bring us meat whenever you want to." They asked me, "When are you going back?" I said, "I'll stay here all day, and to-morrow morning I'll start home." They said, "We're glad you're going to stay with us today and tonight. You've never stayed over a day with us before, but now you want to stay, and we're very glad. We'll start to do the cooking for you now, so you can take home with you some ready-cooked food, and so you won't get hungry on your way."

The women who were there said something, and they were all laughing again. The fellow who spoke our language turned to me and said, "That woman over there said she's wondering if you have a wife. She says you're her son, and she'd like to see her daughter-in-law." They laughed; they were all laughing. I didn't think she'd say that to me. I didn't think she'd say I was her son, but she called me, "My son." They talked some more and kept laughing, and I said, "No,

I haven't a wife yet." The woman said, "Well, my son, if you haven't got a wife, we'll get you one right here. We'll get you one of these Oraibi girls, so then I'll have a daughter-in-law." I said, "It'll be too hard for me, because it's a long way from where I live. It'll be too much work, going back and forth. You know it's a long distance to Black Mountain. I don't think I can stand all the trips I'm going to have to make." They laughed again, and I said, "I want to go outside and take a walk."

All at once, while I was going around to different places, I heard a lot of people laughing and shouting up above me. I climbed up a ladder to where all the noise was going on, and there was an old Navaho and his wife, and a whole lot of Oraibi men and women standing around and talking. While I was wondering what had happened I looked down, and there was an Oraibi running towards us. His hair was untied, and as soon as he got on top where we were he ran up to the old man and grabbed his blanket and started dragging him around, saying, "You picked up my wife's c–." The old Navaho said, "No, my friend, I didn't pick it up. Search me, see if I've got it on me anywhere. You'll find I didn't pick it up, because I haven't got it."

I asked a fellow, "What happened? What are they quarreling about?" He said, "An Oraibi woman and this Navaho were climbing up the ladder, and about halfway up he lifted her dress and grabbed her between the legs, and everybody saw him doing it. That's why they all screamed and hollered and made all this noise. That's why the Oraibi is after him. The woman is his wife, and he wants the Navaho's blanket. He wants him to give him the blanket for doing that."

People were coming up all around us, and as soon as they got on top they all started laughing. They made so much noise you couldn't hear a thing. The Navaho kept begging the fellow to let him loose, "Because," he said, "I never picked it up. She's got it herself. You just go over and let her give it to you. So you leave me alone, because I haven't got it. If I'd picked it up and had it with me I'd sure give it to you, but I haven't got it, and you know I haven't, because you've searched me. Now you just go over to your wife and tell her you want it. She'll surely give it to you."

After a while the Oraibi gave up and turned him loose. Maybe he knew the fellow didn't have it. The Navaho's wife was sure mad. She said to her husband, "Why are you doing these things? Can that thing help you, by just touching it? If you want it, why don't you cut the whole thing out and swallow it?" My, but she was mad at him. Everybody went away while she was still talking, but the old man didn't say a thing.

I went back where I was staying, and there was quite a crowd inside the house. They'd opened the meat and cut it up, and everybody had a piece beside him. I began to trade with them, and they each gave me a dish full of corn and after that dried peaches. One woman had a small bowl and wanted to give me that one full of peaches. But it was pretty small. I said, "You've got a small bowl, and I want as much as I got from the others." She was after me, begging me for the meat, but I didn't let her have it. After a while she borrowed a bowl from another woman and put in some dried peaches and handed it to me. Then I took the peaches and gave her some meat.

The people I was staying with took two whole mutton, and after everybody had left the woman went into another room and got a large basket and filled it with corn and poured it on a blanket. She filled the basket sixteen times. That was for the two mutton. Towards evening they all came in again from the different houses with corn-bread and cornmeal. They said, "This is for your lunch on the way back." In the morning they helped me take out my stuff and pack it, and then I started home. I stopped on the way and camped overnight and got back the next day. My mother was very thankful I'd brought all that food. She said, "Now we've got enough for all winter."

Quite a few days after I said to my mother, "I want to go where the cattle are and drive them home. I want to kill one." "All right," she said, "that's nice. We'll have some beef." I got my horse and went to different places on the mountain, but I couldn't see a thing, the brush and trees were so thick and close together. At last I found a bunch and started to chase them down to my home. While I was driving them along one and two at a time began going out of the bunch and turning back. But I just let them go and kept behind the others. When I got to the edge of the woods I had only four left, and soon two of those turned around and ran back. I was still pretty far from my home. I went on driving the last two, and when they tried to go back I just shot them. I couldn't drive them any further.

I got home and said, "I killed two head out there." My mother got up and said, "Did you really kill two?" "Yes, mother, I killed two of them," I said. "Oh, who's going to eat all that meat?" I said, "Oh, we'll have meat all winter." Then we both picked up a knife and sharpened them and went to where the cows were lying. They were both nice and fat. We butchered and cut them up and put the meat on the trees. It was dark then, in the evening, and we went back home. We took back just a little piece and left the rest on the trees. In the morning I went out and started bringing it in. I piled it up inside the hogan, and after that we cut it up in pieces and left it outside to dry. The trees outside our hogan were decorated with meat. My mother said, "You ought to have killed just one. We've got too much. We can't eat it up ourselves." I said, "Well, mother, we'll have meat a long time, for all winter. We won't kill any sheep."

While the meat was still on the trees a man came to our place. He said, "Where did you get all the meat?" My mother said, "Oh, it's my son. He killed two head of cattle." After he left he must have told the other people about it. A few days later another fellow came. He said to me, "A fellow told me you killed someone else's cow." I said, "No, these two belonged to me." "Well, why do you want to have so much meat on hand? You're all alone with your mother and little brother, only the three of you." "Well, because I was mad at them. I'd been chasing them around all day and was tired, so I was mad, and that's why I killed them." He said, "The other fellow has gone after his cattle. If he misses one or two he'll think one of these was his, or both of them."

Not long after that two more fellows came. They were sent over to ask about the cattle. They said, "The people living on Black Mountain and down at the foot of the mountain say these cattle that you killed weren't yours at all. They must have belonged to somebody else. Now you tell us the truth about them." I said, "These two cattle that I killed were both mine. You two just go back and tell all those people they were mine." I told them the same thing. "I killed them because I was mad at them, because I'd had a hard time getting them and chasing them all day. That's why I killed them. After I killed them I said to my mother, 'We'll have meat now for all winter, and so we won't kill any more sheep.' That's the way I killed two head of cattle, and they both belong to me." Before they left I took them to the corral where the two heads were still lying and showed them the ear-marks. "Now," I said, "you know they were mine, so you two go back and tell the other people they must not bother me any more."

About the middle of winter the little boy, my brother, ran away. Maybe he was tired and didn't want to herd the sheep. He used to ride a horse while herding, but every time he went out he always fell asleep. He'd go to sleep on the horse, and the horse would go around with him while he was sleeping. I don't understand why he never fell off. He used to disobey us. We tried to get him to do things right lots of times, but we couldn't. My mother used to talk to him, but he wouldn't pay any attention. He didn't care to have her talk to him.

One day she gave him a good talking to again. She said, "It's dangerous to ride a horse while you're sleeping, even though the horse is tame and gentle. You can't tell about horses. You might fall off and get caught in the stirrup, and even though the horse is tame it'll run away with you and tear you to pieces." She said a lot of things to him that morning. While she was still talking he got up and walked out. We waited for him to come back, but he didn't show up. After a while my mother said, "Where's the boy? Go call him and look for him." I went out and called him, but he wasn't around. I saw his tracks and tracked him for a long way, and then I thought, "He must have run away and gone back to his home." That was the last we saw of him.

16. *His mother marries him off.*

WE stayed there all winter, and early in the spring we moved to Hill Across. Slim Man was living there, and a lot of other relative of ours. A few days after we located there my mother went around to visit them. When she returned she brought a double saddle-blanket back with her. She handed it to me and said, "I got you a saddle-blanket." "Where did you get it, mother?" I asked her. "I got it from a woman I never knew before. This was the first time I'd ever met her. When I started home she gave me this saddle-blanket and said, 'We'll be friends from now on.'" I said, "I wonder what she wants for it. Maybe she wants some sheep." My mother said, "I don't know what she wants. Maybe that's it."

One day, not long after that, I said to my mother, "I'd like to go to the store." "All right," she said, "that'll be fine, we'll get some grub. We've only got a little left." We sheared some sheep and got some wool and packed it up. While I was out after the horses she went around to the hogans where our relatives were living, and she went over where that woman lived, from whom we got the saddle-blanket. The woman said, "I'd like to go to the store; we haven't any grub either. But I've got no way to go. I haven't got a horse." When my mother came home she said, "The two fathers of yours want to go also." She meant Slim Man and Choclays Kinsman. "But they want you to wait until two days from now. Tomorrow and the day after they'll be shearing their sheep. And that woman does too, but she's got no way to go, so I want you to lend her a horse."

When the two days were up a boy came to our place early in the morning and said he wanted to borrow a horse. I got the horses and let him have one, and that morning I packed my wool and started off. I was going to Slim Man's place, but they'd already left. About the time I caught up with them the woman and her son came along too. While we were riding along toward evening, all at once, I missed my whip. "I've lost my whip," I said. "It must have dropped back a little way." I started to look for it, but soon it got dark, and so I got off my horse and went quite a way on foot before I found it. When I got back to where my horse was tied the woman and her son were waiting for me. The other two had gone. We tried to catch up with them, but it got too dark, and we couldn't go any further. Then I looked around and said, "I think we'll camp here. This is a good place. There's lots of grass for the horses."

I took the horses a little way and hobbled them and then came back to where we'd camped. The woman already had the sheep pelts down for our bedding. She said to me, "There's your place. You sleep there. I've got a place fixed for you already." It was right close by her. I sat down on the pelt, and she gave me her lunch. "Here's some lunch. If you want to eat, take some of that." I opened the sack and started eating, and when I was through she put the things away again. Then I took off my moccasins and clothes and went to bed. As soon as I lay over I fell asleep. About midnight I woke up, and there was a blanket over me. She'd covered me with a blanket and was lying right close by, but I didn't say or do anything to her. I just rolled over and went to sleep again.

When I woke up in the morning she was sleeping beside me with her arm around my breast. But I didn't say anything; I just pushed her hand away and thought, "We'll start early."

I got up and put on my clothes and moccasins and went after the horses, and when I brought them back we started off again early in the morning without anything to eat. I was kind of bashful. Soon the sun was up, and about then we caught up with the other two fellows down in the canyon where the store was.

In those years the traders used to give the customers something to eat and lend them dishes, so after we camped we went to the store and got a panful of flour and coffee and sugar and all the other things and took them back to where our camp was and started cooking. After we were through eating we took back the dishes and started trading. The white man was glad and happy, because we'd brought him lots of wool. We sold our wool, pelts, skins and blankets, and bought flour, coffee, sugar, baking-powder, salt and all the other little things. The woman who came with us bought all kinds of stuff, grub, calico, robes and a hat for her son, but I don't know how much her blanket was worth.

A woman in the store came up to me and said, "I arrived yesterday and camped here last night. I'm way from Black Mountain too." I knew this woman well, and she knew me. She used to live quite a way from our place at Willows Coming Out. She asked me, "Who's that woman? Is that your wife?" I said, "No, she just came along with us." Then she turned to the trader and bought fifty cents' worth of sugar. She handed it to me and said, "I bought this for you, because I know you well. You can remember me by that."

After that we started off and rode all day without stopping. We camped overnight at Cow's Water, but I didn't go near the woman. I fixed a place for myself and went to bed. Early the next morning we started again and kept riding along, and in the afternoon we got back to our homes.

My mother was always going out and visiting our relatives,

and every time she'd go to where this woman lived. She wanted to get her for me. But I never thought of her. I didn't care for her at all. One day, when she went over there, she saw the woman weaving a nice blanket. She had all different kinds of colored yarn which she'd bought at the store, and that's what she was using. It had a lot of pretty designs. My mother saw the blanket and thought it was very nice, and she found out the woman was a good weaver. The woman said to my mother, "That's how I weave. I always weave like this, and I know all kinds of designs. When I finish with a blanket I go and sell it to the trader, and I get a whole lot for it. My blankets are worth more than other women's. I had a husband, but he didn't care for this kind of blanket, so I just let him go. I didn't like him at all, and so I let him go, and now I'm alone, just with my children. I'd like to get another man who can help me along, but I can't get one anywhere. I've looked all over, but I can't find one at all." My mother said, "I like your weaving, your work. You're a good weaver and a nice woman. I wish you'd make me a rug, but I haven't any yarn like that that you have." The woman said, "If you had some I'd surely make you a rug. If you want me to weave one for you just go and get some yarn like mine. You can get it at the store."

Sometime after that she went over there again and began talking with the woman. "I'd like to get you to stay with me. I'm thinking if you'd like to have my son. I'd like to know right now. If you like my son I want you to stay with him. If you do, from there on we'll help each other, and we'll live together. I know all your works and all your weavings. I know you're a good worker and a good weaver. I've been looking for a woman like you, who knows about weaving, but I can't find one. That's what I'm thinking. What do you think about that?"

The woman said, "It's all right with me, but I don't think your son cares about me. If he wants me, if he likes me, I'd sure like to have him, because I know he's a good fellow. That's the kind of man I'm looking for. I liked him the first time I saw him. I thought to myself, 'I wish I had him.' I've wanted him all this time, but I just can't get him, because he never comes around. I was going to ask him the time we went to the store, but I was afraid to talk to him. That one night when we camped out, when we slept together, I was going to ask him if he liked me, but I didn't say anything, and he never said anything either. If he'd said something to me at that time I'd have said something too, but we didn't talk to each other. So that's why I thought, 'Maybe he doesn't like me.'"

My mother said, "Well, what do you think about it? If you say, all right, I'll surely let you have my son." The woman laughed and said, "Well, it's up to him. If he likes me I'd like to have him." Then my mother told her all about me, that I was alone and a single man. She said, "My son is a good worker. He never goes out for nothing, and he doesn't know anything about gambling, and he never goes around to the singings. He only knows about the sheep, horses and cattle. And he takes good care of himself. He's not like these other men, who don't know anything."

She was away all day, over there with this woman. She said to her, "I want you to stay with my son. Now you go around among your relatives and tell them what I said." But the woman said, "My relatives won't say anything about it. It's up to me. I want him very much. And my mother there, she doesn't care, she won't say anything. So now you just go home and bring your son over here." "Well," my mother said, "that's nice. I'll give you two horses and one bull." The woman said, "All right, I'm satisfied." Then my mother set a date, she said, "I'll be here in a couple of days."

Around evening I came back, and she was home too. She was just beginning to cook some food. After we were through eating she put everything away, and we were sitting by the fire talking. All at once she said, "My son, I was over there where that woman lives. I've been staying with her all day. I think she's a good woman. I know she's a good weaver, and she knows a lot of things besides. I asked her if she wanted you, and she said all right. She said she's been wishing for you all this time, and I said to her, 'We'll be together. So I want you to stay with my son.' I promised her two horses and one bull, and she was satisfied with that, and so I said, 'I'll be here with my son in two days.' What do you think about it?" But I didn't say anything. She said, "I think it'll be nice, having this woman here with us, because she's a good worker and a good weaver, and she's got three children. She'll help us a lot. So I want you to stay with her." I thought, "What's the matter with my mother? She must be crazy, telling that woman all those things without letting me know." But I didn't say a word. She was talking to herself for a long time, but I didn't bother her at all.

When she was through talking I said, "Well, mother, you don't know what you're talking about. You must be getting crazy. You must be a little off, because that woman, whom you want me to have, that woman, I think, is older than I am, and she already has children. And I know she's got a husband too. I've never seen her husband, but I know she's got one." "No, my son, I know what I'm talking about. I asked her a lot of questions, and I asked about her husband. She said, 'I haven't got a husband. I had one, but I didn't like him, and so I let him go. And now I'm all alone, just with my children and my mother.' Now, my son, don't say anything, just go and take this woman, because I know they'll help us a lot. You know I'm getting old. I can't do all the work around the home. I can't stand it all. And you're just by yourself, doing all these tasks, and need a lot of help, and so do I. That's why I want you to stay with her. They'll be here with us and help us on the sheep and on weaving and on everything around here of which we've got so much to do, just by ourselves. You know there's too much work for us alone." I didn't say anv more, but she talked on for a long time.

After breakfast the next morning we turned out the sheep, and I went herding. That day my mother went among our relatives and told them what she wanted. They all said, "That's nice. We'll have a wedding. We'll all be there." But my father, Slim Man, didn't like this woman for me, because, he thought, she had a husband. He said to my mother, "You'll get your son in trouble." She said, "No, I don't think so, because the woman said she hasn't got a man. Her husband left her for good. So I don't think there'll be any trouble." He said, "It's up to you, but I'll be there too."

When I got home with the herd my mother said, "All our relatives are going over with us to the woman's place. They're all glad to know you're going to get a wife. Your father is coming this evening. He was the only one who didn't like her, but afterwards he said, 'It's all right. I can't say anything, because you've already set a date.' " When he came that evening he began to talk to me about a lot of things. He said, "I've been with lots of women. They're all different. Some of them are good, some are not. We don't know what kind of a woman she is. Maybe she's all right. Maybe not. But we'll soon find out." That's what he said and a whole lot of other things besides. He stayed until midnight, talking to me, and then went back to his home, and we went to bed.

The two days were up that next day, and in the evening we started over for where the woman lived. But our relatives didn't come. They didn't show up. Only my father and his wife, they were the only ones who came, and so only four of us went over. We didn't take the two horses. While we were on the way my father said, "If they give us mush it'll be all right. If they just give us some lunch it'll be all right too." When we got there he said, "Well, that's our place, I guess, where that fire is, south of the hogan." There we found a little shade made of cedar branches. It looked like a corral. We went inside, and the two women went on the north side and sat on a sheep pelt there, and Slim Man sat on a pelt on the south side. They said to me, "There's a place for you. There are two sheep pelts lying here close together. You sit on the left side, and the woman will be on your right."

We were just by ourselves, sitting there, talking to each other. My father said, "Well, we're here now, and we're all alone. If we want to have a wedding in the right way we should have a whole lot of our relatives with us, but here we are all alone. It looks like we're on our way to some place and just camping out. That's the way I feel about it." He talked for a long time. "We'll let this go and see how the woman is. Maybe she'll be all right later on. We'll soon find out. It's up to her. If she's not a good woman, we'll let her go."

Quite a while after we heard a noise outside, and there she was. She had a basket in her hand, and two of her sons were with her. They came in with a lot of tortillas and two rib-roasts and two front quarters, already cooked, and coffee and other food. They set it down by my father, and then the younger boy brought in some water in a cup. She set the basket in front of me and sat down beside me. She was all dressed up. Everything on her was new, and the basket was a brand new one too. It had never been used before. My father said, "Are you going to give us that basket or not?" She said, "Sure I'm going to give it to you. That's why I brought it in." Then he said, "Have any of you got corn pollen? I haven't any with me. I forgot to bring it. I left it home." He asked me, but I said, "I haven't any." My mother didn't have any either, but the woman had some tied onto her belt. She took it off and handed it to my father. He said, "This is a funny way to have a wedding. If you had a father or an uncle he'd have had the corn pollen with him, and he'd have put it on the mush and around the edge of the basket, but I guess I've got to do it myself." He got up and put the pollen over the mush in the basket, and when he was through he said, "Now you both wash your hands." She poured some water on my fingers, and when I was through washing I poured some for her. Then we ate of the mush from the four sides of the basket and from the middle. After that my father got up and turned the basket around and said, "Now you can go ahead and eat all you want." After we'd had enough we gave the basket to my mother, and she ate some, and then we all started on the food. My mother said, "We'll leave this basket here, so you both can use it all the time." I thought she'd give the basket to my father, but she said, "We'll leave it here with these two and let them use it for themselves." Slim Man said, "Everything looks funny to me. I feel funny about it."

After we were through eating he said to the woman, "We didn't know each other before, we never met, but now, to-night, we've met, and we know each other now. We're all thankful to you for giving us this meal, for all the different kinds of food we've eaten. Everything was nice. It all tasted fine, and we all had enough. We appreciate it and thank you a lot. Now, from here on, you two will stay together. You both know how to take care of things, how to do things, how to take care of yourselves." He said to the woman, "You're old enough. You already have children. You already know how to take care of them, and you know how to weave and all the other things. You know about living, so I can't say much to you." He turned to me and said, "Now, you're a man, you know how to tend to the sheep, horses and cattle, and how to take care of your home. And you know about taking care of your property, and every other little thing. You know all about work of different kinds, so I can't say much to you about it. Only one thing you don't know, how to live with a woman. But you'll soon find out, and from then on you'll know how to take care of a woman and children. I can't say much to either one of you. You already know everything. So I'll quit, and if there are any other people here, I'll let them talk. This will be all for me."

After he was through they said to one another, "Well, now, we'll go home." My mother and Slim Man's wife took the meat and all the other food that was left and went. I stayed there overnight. Early in the morning I got up, and after I ate some breakfast I started home. When I got there I went ahead and tended to my work. I didn't go back to that place. But I had to let the old bull go; I gave her the bull and two horses.

Quite a few days after, it was around the middle of spring, I said to my mother, "We'll move down to Anything Falls In, and there we'll shear our sheep, because there's lots of grazing around that place." She said, "All right, we'll do that." When we packed up to move the woman rode over to our place and took the herd, and I took the horses, and we started off. Her mother and children followed along right after us, and when we got to that place they settled down about a mile away. As soon as we got there she turned around and went to where her mother and children had located.

I went to her place the next day and stayed overnight. That evening she said to me, "Two men came yesterday. They're both staying over with my mother. One is my stepfather, and the other is a brother of mine. The one man is lame, and my brother is crippled. He crawls on the ground like some kind of animal. The crippled man is a singer. He knows all kinds of different chants." While she was telling me this I heard a noise, and the crippled man came crawling in. He crawled up and sat right close beside me. I was surprised to see him. His legs were short and thin, and his feet and toes were real small and thin too, and his fingers were all twisted up. He shook hands with me and called me brother. He said, "I'm glad to meet you. I've never met you before, but now we've met each other, and I'm glad to meet you. I heard you're my brother-in-law. I was pleased to hear that. I never knew you before. I just knew your brother over at Keams Canyon, and that brother of yours is my brother-in-law too. And now, you here, you're my brother-in-law. That's what I heard, and I was pleased to hear that."

The next morning I got up early and started home. I always went and tended to my work, because I had a lot of things to do. She never said anything to me. We had a lot of work, lots of things to do all by ourselves, but she never came to our place. My mother used to say, "I wonder why my daughter-in-law doesn't come here? She ought to stay with us and help us along. We've got lots of work, and we need help. She knows we've got lots to do, but I wonder why she doesn't come around." That's the way I was thinking too, but I never said anything to her about it.

When I got home I started shearing sheep. I sheared until noontime and then turned them out and herded the rest of the day. When I brought my herd back again towards evening I saw a horse standing there at home. I was wondering whom that horse belonged to, and I thought to myself, "Maybe some of our relatives have come." I put the sheep in the corral and went over, and there was a clan grandfather of mine, sitting in the hogan. My mother was cooking some lunch. Soon everything was ready, and we started eating.

When we were through my mother put the dishes and everything away, and my grandfather started telling about his trips and about the place where he was living. He told about all kinds of things for a long while. Then he said to me, "Well, my grandson, I heard you got a wife. I was glad to hear that. But when I heard you got a woman I know, as soon as I heard that, I didn't like it, because I know this woman has a husband, and you know she's got children, and you're single, and you're just a young boy yet. You ought to have better sense than that. You ought to know that that woman is older than you are, and that she's already got children. So, my grandson, I felt very badly about it."

Then he said, "Now, my grandson, you know a lot about your sheep, horses and cattle and all about your property, and you think a whole lot of it all. If this woman is a bad woman she'll soon get you in trouble and make you forget all about your things. That's why I felt very badly about you. And now everybody knows you're married to this woman, and later they'll call you Lame Man's Son-in-Law, or maybe they'll call you Crawling Man's Brother-In-Law. There you'll get a name you won't like. When you hear everybody calling you by a name after these two fellows you'll feel very badly about it, you won't like it, and you'll feel ashamed too. Now everbody calls you by a name that you got from your mother. Your name goes by your mother's name, and everybody knows it. They all say, Abaa's Son. You've got a good name after your mother, and now they'll change it. That why I don't like you to have that woman, because I'm ashamed about that. I know very well they'll soon call you by either one of these two names. Maybe they'll name you after both.

"Maybe it's not your fault. Maybe it's your mother's fault." He pointed to my mother. She was there with us while he was making all this speech to me. "Now there's your mother, named Abaa," he said, "and you go by her name." I said, "Well, my grandfather, it wasn't my fault. It was my mother's fault. I don't know why she got this woman for me. I never thought about her, and I never wanted her. But my mother went over to her place many times, and at last, when she came home, she said to me, 'I've got you a woman now, and I want you to live with her.' I didn't say anything about it. I went over, even though I didn't care for her, because I didn't like to turn my mother down. That's why this thing happened." My mother said, "Well, everything is done. We were all alone here, no one to talk to about these things, no relatives around, you were all way off, far away from us, so that's why I went ahead and got this woman for my son."

I stayed at my home that night, and in the morning, as soon as we'd had our breakfast, my mother and I started shearing. In the afternoon I went out to round up the horses and came back towards evening. My grandfather was still there, and that night he started talking to me again about the same thing. The next day he wanted to go home. He said, "I want some wool to take home with me, even just a little will be all right." I packed two blankets full of wool for him that morning, but he stayed around until late in the afternoon. Then he said, "Now, my grandson, I guess I'll leave for home while it's cool." I put the wool on his horse for him and tied it down, and then I led the horse into a little ditch. There he got on, from the bank of the ditch, and rode away.

In the evening I went over to where the woman lived. Nobody was around. Everything was gone. There was nothing. I thought to myself, "I wonder what's happened? Maybe I got left. Maybe I've been pushed out." I stayed around awhile, not knowing where to go, and soon it got dark. All at once I heard somebody cough, right close by on the west side of the hogan where her mother was staying. I went over and looked around, and there was a fellow sitting. When I walked up to him he leaned over against his saddle. I looked around, but there was nobody else; he was all alone. I thought, "I wonder what this fellow is doing here?" I asked him, "Where are you from?" "Oh," he said, "I'm from way off, from Black Mountain, where there's a place called Black Mountain Sitting Up. That's where I'm from." "Where are you going?" "Oh, I'm just going around here to different places, just to visit around. Where are you from?" I said, "I'm from down below here. I live a little way down here. That's where I'm from." That was all we said to each other. I stayed a few minutes, but neither of us said any more.

I thought, "Maybe he's the one they've been talking about. Maybe this is the fellow whose wife I got." I got kind of scared there, and so I just walked away. While I was going back the dogs heard me and began to bark and run at me, but I turned and said, "Shh!" and they quieted down. They knew me right away. Just then I saw something black. It looked like a person standing or walking. I stopped and looked at that black spot, and then I saw it moving towards me. It came right up to me, and it was she. She asked me, "When did you come?" I said, "I came just as the sun was going down." "Where did you stay all this time?" "I was staying around here." "Oh, go on," she said, "you weren't here a while ago. I was here, and there wasn't anybody around." "Sure," I said to her, "I've been here all this time. I was just going to start back home, but I saw you coming, and so I stopped and sat down here." She didn't say any more, but she asked me, "Did you have something to eat before you started from home?" I said, "Yes, I had enough." She went in the hogan and brought out some sheep pelts and blankets. She laid the pelts out on the ground and the blankets over them; she had all my bedding fixed, pillows and everything, and then we went to bed.

I couldn't make up my mind to ask her about the man. After a while I said, "There's a person sitting over here. Who is it?" She said, "Oh, go on, you're just saying that. There isn't anybody around. Is there really someone over there?" "Sure," I said, "I know somebody's over there." "Who is it? A man or a woman?" "It's a man." Again she said, "Oh, go on, you're just saying it. Were you over there with him? Do you know that fellow?" "No, I don't know him." "Did he say where he's from?" "Yes, he said he's from way off, from Black Mountain Sitting Up." "Where did he say he was going?" "He's not going anywhere. He said he just came here." Then her heart began to beat. I could hear it, and I noticed then and thought to myself, "That's her husband, who's come after her." She tried to talk, but she could hardly get her breath.

That was the last night for me. We had a good time for a little while, and then I went to sleep. When I woke up it was morning. She was still sleeping. My blanket was way underneath, so I let it go and started home.

A woman and two children came to our place one day. One of the children was her granddaughter. The woman knew all about my wife. She said, "She's just like a dog. I've known her a long time. She began going around with men when she was a little girl. She went with Navaho, Whites, Mexicans, Hopi and all the others. That's the kind of woman she is." She told me all about her. When I heard these things I was so sorry for myself and so ashamed. I felt very badly. Even though I'd left her I didn't want to hear about her, I didn't care to listen. But she kept on talking, first about the woman and then about her husband. "Sure enough, that was her husband. Before she married him he never had a wife at all. He used to go among the horses. So when they found him with the horses they gave him a name. His name is Horse's Ass. You've been with Horse's Ass's Wife." When I heard this it almost killed me. The rest I hadn't paid any attention to, though I felt badly about it, but this last was the worst.

After a few days I went out to round up the horses. About the time the sun was down, as I was driving them towards the flat, I saw a hogan where a grandfather of mine was living. He belonged to my clan, and his wife was a Many Goats. I rode over to their place and tied my horse to a little stump and went inside. He was sitting in the hogan, and his wife was there too. I went up and shook hands and sat down beside him. He turned and looked at me for a long time, then he said, "Why don't you throw those ragged pants of yours away?" He grabbed a piece that was hanging down and tore it off. "A man like you having these kinds of clothes. You ought to throw these dirty, ragged things away. Why don't you buy nice clothes for yourself? You have lots of sheep, lots of horses and cattle. You ought to get new clothes. Trade off some of your sheep, horses or cattle for some good clothing. Why do you want to have on these dirty, ragged things? No wonder your wife is leaving you. I was out, and as I was coming back I met her on the way to Keams Canyon. I asked her, 'Why are you leaving?' and she said, 'Because I'm left for good. My husband left me. He doesn't like me any more, so that's why I'm leaving for Keams Canyon.' I said, 'No, I want to see about it first. When I get home I'll go to my grandson's place and talk to him and tell him that he shouldn't leave his wife. So you stop and camp here. I mean it, I'm going to his place, and I'll send him over here. He'll be here tonight with you.' That's what I told your wife, my grandson." He talked to me a long time, and at last he said, "You must go over and try to get her back. She's a good-looking woman. You can't get one like her anywhere. And I know you can't get another any more." But I never said a word. I'd found out all the bad things about her, so I never said anything. I just let him go ahead and talk.

From there I went to where my father, Slim Man, lived and told him all that had happened and all I'd heard about her. "And now I'm single again. I've left her for good. I don't care to see or hear about her any more." He talked to me then about lots of things and about women. "That's right, you're safe now. You won't get in trouble from here on. I'm glad you left her for good. Now we'll let that go. We'll quit talking about her and talk about our cattle. Well, my son, when do you want to go and round up the cattle?" I said, "I can't say just when, because we're still shearing. Perhaps after we get through. But I've got to take my wool to the store. Perhaps after that we'll go and round them up." He said, "We'll shear all our sheep, and when we're through we'll put the wool away and tend to our cattle. When we come back from there then, after that, we'll sell our wool. So I want you to set a date." "Well, I think in about two days." "That's fine. I'll have to be quick with my shearing. Perhaps by that time I'll be through. We'll bring some cattle back with us. I want to kill one. My moccasin soles are worn, and all my hobbles are torn and worn out too. That's why I want to kill one, for meat and for the hide."

That night, when I came back from my father's place, I told my mother what he'd said to me, that in two days we were going on Black Mountain to round up the cattle, and that he wanted to kill one. She said, "That'll be all right. That's nice. We'll have some beef. He'll give us some meat, and he'll cut us off a piece of hide for our moccasin soles and for hobbles." Then she began to tell me about the woman who was staying with us. She said, "This woman said she'll leave her granddaughter here with us." She was a pretty girl about eleven years of age, but I didn't let her say much about it. "I don't care to hear about those things," I said. "The girl is too young, and she might be worse than the other one. So I don't like to hear about it." She quit talking about it then and let it go. She must have told the woman what I said, because the next day they started home. My mother gave them two blankets full of wool and a mutton.

When the two days were up I went to my father's place. He was there with one of his boys, and the three of us started off early in the morning. About halfway up the mountain Slim Man turned to us and said, "Come on. Hurry up and whip your horses. We'll run them a little way." I thought to myself, "I wonder why he wants to run them up the mountain?" We whipped our horses, and all at once his horse shied with him. When it shied he whipped it and cussed it, saying, "Horse's Ass!" And right there was the woman I'd left, and the man, her husband, was there too, and that was his name. My father had said it to his horse, that was the way he'd cussed it, but he'd named that man. They were living in a little shade close by the trail. I'd thought they were way off some place, but there they were. We passed them and went on, and when we got to the top of the mountain my father began to laugh at what he'd done. "I said it because I don't like the man," he said.

We went along, walking our horses, and Slim Man said, "I only got eight head of cattle when your father died, so we'll kill one belonging to Who Has Mules. He got most of them. I told him at that time I wanted ten, but he only gave me eight, so we'll kill one of his." From there on we began hunting the cattle, and by evening we had quite a bunch. We chased them in a canyon, and Slim Man said, "Now we'll kill one, because we haven't anything to eat. We've got nothing but coffee and a coffee-pot." I roped a yearling and wound the rope around a tree and choked it while he got a rock and hit it on the forehead. Then we killed it and started butchering, and the boy started building a great big fire. After we had all the meat cut up we cooked some and had lunch, and then we went to bed. The next day we rounded up some more, but we didn't see them all. Late in the afternoon, when we were through cutting them and making ear-marks, we packed the meat on our horses and started home. The next day I packed up my wool and took it to the store.

17.

He visits relatives and collects several gifts, including an old gun . . . He is admired and envied for his good clothes and accused of picking up a string of turquoise . . . He lies with Slim Man's wife to his regret . . . They steal peaches from the Oraibi.

ONE day, after I'd come back from the store, I thought I'd go and visit Plucked Whiskers. His clan was Red House. He was living on the other side of Carriso Mountain at Round Red Rock. I started off one morning and passed Baby Rock and Big Oak and went on crossing the valley until I got to the top of Red Mesa. Right at the edge of the mesa was a spring called Spring At The Edge, where Under Death was living. His clan was Standing House. He had a family there, and I stayed with them overnight. The next morning I went on to Abahadi's place at Water Flowing Out. He called me nephew, and I called him my uncle. He said to me, "I'm glad you came. We'll make a sweat-house and take a rest." There was a sweat-house up already, so we just gathered some rocks and built a fire on them, and when they were hot we put them inside. We were in the sweat-house all afternoon until evening. He said to me, "To-morrow you can have one of my horses and ride over to Plucked Whiskers's place." I stayed around there the next morning waiting for the horse, and about noon they brought it in, and I started off again, on to White Rocks Sitting

Around. From there I climbed up over the mountain and cut straight across the valley.

He was living up on a red mesa, and when I got to his place I tied my horse outside and went in, and there he was, sitting in the hogan. As soon as he saw me he got up and made a place for me, and I sat down beside him. He put his arms around me and called me my son, and I put my arms around him. He said to his children, "This is your older brother, because he's my son." A little boy was standing by his father, and he said to the boy, "This is your brother, because he's my son." The little boy was jealous and said, "Why didn't you tell us you had a son? I thought I was the only one." "No, my son, sure enough, that's your brother, so you shake hands with him." The boy stood there awhile, he didn't want to at first, but his father said, "Go ahead and shake hands with your older brother." Then he came up and shook hands with me. Another son of his went out and took the saddle off my horse and led him away to where there was grass. It was evening then. That night we told all kinds of stories to each other, and when we got too sleepy we went to bed.

After we ate the next morning he asked me, "When are you going home, my son?" I said, "I'm figuring on going back this morning, because I've got so much to do. I can't leave my home for long. So I think I'll start back this morning." "Well, my son," he said, "I'm very glad you came and visited us. I'm thankful to you for coming. That's the way to do. Come again any time you want to. I'm always anxious to see you." He turned around and pulled out a sack full of things and took out a great big buckskin and a double saddle-blanket. It was a fancy blanket woven with Germantown yarn. He laid the buckskin and the saddle-blanket on my lap, and then he pulled out a rifle and laid that on my lap too. It was in a buckskin sack, and there was a pouch with caps, and a cow's horn with powder. After that he gave me the ramrod. I was so surprised. I pulled the rifle out of the bag and asked him, "How do you work this gun?" So he showed me how to load it. He said, "You should be careful with it. As soon as you put in the cap you mustn't throw it around, because it's dangerous then." He showed me different ways of loading it. He said, "If you want to shoot a rabbit, or something small, put in just a little powder. If you want to shoot something big, like a deer, you must put a whole lot of powder in it, so it'll have lots of power. It's an old, old gun, but it still shoots straight. You can kill anything with it. If you handle it carefully, and if you take good care of it, you'll have it a long time." But I was afraid to use it.

He said, "Now, my son, that's all I have." I said, "Thank you very much, my father. I'll go back home now." I went out and tied the things in back of my saddle and put the belt with the pouch and the cow's horn over my shoulder. It looked as though I was going to start trouble. The belt was all decorated with bullets and caps and powder. Then I got on my horse and laid the rifle across my lap and started off. By the time I got on top of the mountain I was tired of carrying that gun, but I didn't know what to do with it, and so I just kept holding it there in front of me on my lap and started down and got back to Abahadi's place that evening.

Early the next morning I dressed myself and went over to another hogan, where Bitahni Woman was living. She was an older clan sister of mine. She was just getting up as I entered. "Oh," she said, "here's my younger brother. I didn't know you were around. I'm so very glad to see you. I was thinking about you the other day. I heard you'd passed by. I didn't know you were still here. Where did you go? Are you going somewhere? Or are you coming back from some place?" She was saying all this while she was holding me with both arms. Then she let me go, and I said, "Yes, I passed by here. I went to a fellow's place. That's where I'm coming back from, and I'll start back for home this afternoon." "Oh," she said, "you're not in that hurry, are you? What are you so in a hurry about?" I said, "I'm hurrying because I've got so much to do at home, and there's nobody to help my mother. She's all alone, so I want to get back as soon as I can." She made a fire and cooked some food, and when everything was done we started eating.

After we ate she turned around and pulled out a sack and untied it and took out a double saddle-blanket. It was a brand new one with fancy designs. She gave me that and said, "This is the only thing I have." I gave her many thanks and then went back to the other hogan. There the people stood looking at this saddle-blanket, saying, "What a nice saddle-blanket that is. She's been weaving it. You've got a nice saddle-blanket. It has pretty designs."

My uncle asked me, "When are you going back?" I said, "I'll start back sometime this afternoon." "Well, then, we'll go to the sweat-house again," and he sent his boys over to gather some rocks and build a fire. We were in the sweat-house until about noon, and then went back to his home. My uncle said to his wife, "Cook something for us. My nephew's going home this afternoon. After he eats he'll start back." Right away his wife started cooking. After lunch he gave me two good-sized buckskins. I had quite a lot then, two saddle-blankets and three buckskins. Still that wasn't much, but this old gun, that made me a big load. When I got home at Anything Falls In I unsaddled my horse and took the things inside. My mother was so surprised. She was saying thanks to the people and asked me, "Why didn't you go to other relatives of ours?" I said, "Those things were enough for me. If

319

I'd gone to another hogan or two I'd have gotten some more, but my saddle strings wouldn't have been long enough."

I was tired and wanted to take a rest, so I lay down and went to sleep. When I woke up I thought, "I'll go over to my father's place." They were just coming back from the sweat-house when I got there. He said to me, "You ought to have come long ago. You'd have been in the sweat-house with us." I said, "I didn't see the smoke. If I'd known it, or seen the smoke from the sweat-house, I'd have come, but I didn't know it. That's why I'm late." We went inside the hogan, and he asked me, "Where did you go, my son? I heard you'd gone some place." I said, "I went over onto the other side of Carriso Mountain. I've been gone three days and just came back this morning." "What did you go over there for?" I said, "I just went around and visited my relatives." "Did you bring anything back with you?" "Yes, I brought some things back with me." "What did you bring?" I mentioned the things, and he said, "That's nice, my son. All those things that you brought back are worth a lot. They're hard to get. Buckskins and saddle-blankets are hard to get, because they're scarce. I'm glad to hear you went around and visited your relatives, and I'm glad to know you brought some things back from them. That's the way to do, my son. You must go around among your relatives and visit them every once in a while."

I stayed at his place, talking with him until about evening, and then went back home. My mother had the food all ready for me, and I started eating. While I was eating she said, "I heard they're going to have an Nda down at Water Under The Rocks. They're going to take the decorated-stick to Cheek. Yesterday a fellow came back from there and said, 'In nine days from now they're going to start the dance.' That was yesterday that he said that. So it's eight days now."

I was thinking about it and made up my mind I'd go. The next day I thought, "I'll have somebody make me some arrows." I had arrows, but they were old, only my bow was still new. I took some feathers and a buckskin and went to the man named Mexican Blanket. He knew how to make bows and arrows. I said, "I'll give you this buckskin for making me some arrows. I'd like to have them done before the Nda begins. Could you have them done before then?" He said, "Yes. Tomorrow I'll go to the foot of the mountain where I'll cut some sticks, and the next day I'll have them all drying." He got out the feathers and counted them three by three. "It's enough for twenty," he said. I said, "I want arrowheads on every one of them." "Sure, I've got some arrowheads already made. I can have the arrows done in about four or five days." "I want them all fixed up good," I said, "so I can take them along with me to the dance," and he said, "Yes, sure, I'll make nice arrows for you."

I already had an arrow-sack, but it was old, all the hair was worn off, so I decided to make a new one. I'd never made one before, but, anyhow, I thought I'd try. I got out a big lion skin and buried it in the ground, and when it was good and damp I put the old one on top and drew a line all around it. My mother said, "You ought to take the skin to a fellow who knows how to make them." But I said, "I've already cut it out, and I'm already starting to sew it." "You mustn't sew all the way around," she said. "A man shouldn't sew all around the whole quiver. You must stop when you get to the nose, because a man shouldn't sew across the nose. Only a woman can do that." I said, "You can sew it for me, mother, across the nose." "All right, maybe I can. I can't see the holes very well, but I'll try it anyway." She went out with the sheep and was herding all day, and when I got to the nose I stopped sewing and started working on a bow-sack. About sundown she came back with the herd and sewed the patch into the arrow-sack across the nose for me. The next day I worked on them all day, decorating them with ribbons and beads.

The day before the dance was to start Mexican Blanket brought the arrows. They were nice, and all of them looked just alike. He had nice arrowheads on them, good and sharp, and some poison from the middle to the tip, and some kind of blood all over them. They were so nice, and all of even length. I thanked him very much. When I put them in the quiver over my shoulder, my mother said, "Oh, that's pretty! You made that arrow-sack so pretty. Now you mustn't lose it. You must keep it and have it safe all the time. If you don't take good care of it some kind of worm will get at it and eat off the fur. Oh, that's so pretty, with all the decoration." I hung it up and walked around it, looking at it, and it sure did look fine.

The next day I got my horse and put my new saddle-blanket on him and buffalo skin, and my new saddle and silver bridle. After that I went inside and dressed myself in all my new clothes. I put on my straw hat and silver belt and the best beads I had around my neck, and in my hair I had a bunch of owl feathers. Then I got on my horse and rode to Slim Man's place. He used to have nice, big ponies. I said to him, "I'd like to use one of your horses." "Yes, sure," he said, "you can rope one. Whichever you like." I knew every one of them, and I roped one that was the best of all. A lot of fellows were there, borrowing horses from him. They all said I looked strange to them, because I was all dressed up. They said, "You look nice with that bow and arrows and that hat of yours." We used to get these hats from the Apache. Then we started off for where they were going to have the Nda. There was a big crowd at that place, and they all looked at me too. I was kind of bashful, and so I turned around and rode down in the wash and took the saddle off my horse and tied him to a tree. I wanted him to cool off. And I took off my bow and arrows and hung them on a tree, and I took off my old hat and hung that up too.

When I got back to where they were having the dance I went inside the hogan where the patient was. They were decorating the stick in there, and some singers were singing. After they were through puttings things on the stick they brought in some food, and we started eating. They said, "Everybody hurry. As soon as we've eaten we'll start off, because it's a long way to go. We'll start early and take our time, so the horses won't be tired when we get there." When everyone was through eating they said, "Get ready now. Get your horses ready, and get on them. As soon as this man takes out the decorated-stick we'll go at once." I went to where I'd tied my horse and saddled him, and I put my bow and arrows over my shoulder and put on my hat. About then everybody moved away. The fellow who had the stick went ahead, and the rest of the crowd was behind him. When I joined the crowd they all began to look at me. I was so bashful. But after awhile I didn't mind it any more.

I was riding on the north side of the crowd, so as not to get in the dust, when a fellow rode up to me. He was my brother, my father's clan brother's boy. He rode up to me and said, "Don't ruin my things. Take good care of my bow and arrows for me, and take good care of my hat and take care of my horse. Take care of all my things. If you ruin them you can't have them any more." He joshed at me that way, because he was my brother. When he said this the whole crowd laughed. They must have told him to ride up and tell me that. But I didn't say anything; I just thought, "He's an evil spirit." This fellow didn't have anything at all; he was poor.

We went along, crossing flats and arroyos and going over hills. When we got to Hollow In The Rock everybody stopped, and they said, "Take the saddles off your horses and let them cool off." While we were resting some fellows picked up my bow and arrows and were looking at them, saying, "What pretty arrows you've got, and what a pretty quiver. And what a pretty bow you have and bow-sack." In a little while the whole crowd came up to me. They were looking at my bow and arrows and sacks, and some were carrying around my hat, saying, "What a nice hat you have." They got out all my things, turning over my saddle and looking at it, spreading out my buffalo skin and saddle-blanket and passing them around to one another and talking about them, and some of them were laughing. A man named Slow came up and said to them, "That's what you call a man's property. I know he's a man. And that quiver has a name. It's got a name, and the arrows themselves have a name, and so has the bow. They all have names. Some of you don't know anything about it, so you mustn't laugh. A man who has things like that has all kinds of stuff. I know that fellow. He's got property. He's got stock. So you musn't laugh at him, you evil spirits, you, laughing about him."

After that the crowd scattered, and we started again. It was almost sundown when we got to Cheek. The fellow to whom we gave the decorated-stick was Wounded Smith. His clan was Red Clay. He used to make bits; that's why they called him Smith. We gave him the decorated-stick, and he sang a little song, and after that he took off all the yarn and passed it around to the women. Then, after we'd taken the saddles off our horses, we all ate, and when everybody'd had enough they started beating the drum and singing. Wounded Smith said to me, "You dance tonight, my cousin. I want you to dance all night." But I didn't say anything. When it got dark I went away from the crowd and spread my saddle-blanket and buffalo skin and went to sleep.

When I woke up in the morning the people were just coming out with some grub, and after we had breakfast we went to the hogan and stood in a bunch by the doorway, singing there for quite a while. They threw some things out of the smokehole, and afterwards some fellows brought out some stuff and gave it to us. One fellow gave me a robe and about nine yards of calico. Then they took the drum inside, and we got on our horses and started back. Some of the fellows rode as hard as they could, but I took my time along with some others. We got back where they were having the Nda a little after noon. I let my horse rest there a while and cool off and had some lunch, and then started home. I lived quite a distance from there.

When I got home in the evening I said to my mother, "I got this robe and calico. A fellow gave it to me. What shall I give him?" "Oh," she said, "you can give him anything. It's up to you. You've got some things. Just think about it yourself." I said, "I'll give him my gun. It's just about enough for this robe and calico." "Oh, you don't want to give a man that old gun," she said. "Aren't you ashamed? You know it isn't worth anything at all." But I said, "Mother, you don't know anything about guns. You think it's old, and it is old, but guns are worth a lot. You can't get a gun anywhere. So I want to give it away." Again she said, "You ought to be ashamed. Everybody will see you giving that old gun to the man." I said, "Well, mother, I'll take it along anyway." She turned around and looked at me and said, "Take one of your saddle-blankets and wrap it around the gun, and then you can take it."

I tied up my horse and stayed at home that night. I didn't go to the second-night's-dance. While it was still real dark the

325

next morning I started back and took the gun with me. I got there just as the visiting-party arrived, coming along out in the flat. The fellows from the dance rode out and met them, and there they all came, as fast as they could, and rode around the hogan. Then they stopped, and everything was quiet.

A fellow was talking where the visiting-party was camped, and I went over, wondering what was the matter. They were talking about a fellow who'd lost a strand of turquoise. He may have lost it while they were chasing one another around the hogan. They were asking for the turquoise, but nobody'd seen it, so they told the whole crowd to go look for it. They got on their horses and went back, right close together in line, as far as where they'd started chasing one another, but they didn't find it. After that they brought the visiting-party some grub, and when they were through eating they went to the hogan and started singing. Then all the people on our side went in with some things, and I went in too, taking my gun. When we came out I gave it to the fellow who'd given me the robe and the calico. From there on they started treating the patient until about noon, and then everybody had some more to eat.

Right on top of that a fellow came up to me and said, "The people who are camping over there want you to come over." I said, "Why?" He said, "A fellow saw you pick up the turquoise while you were riding along. You had your gun-rod in your hand, and you picked it up with that, while you were riding. That's why they want you." I wasn't alone, I was with five other men, and we all went over. There they started asking me about it. A fellow was standing there, his clan was Reed People, and they pointed to him and said, "That fellow saw you pick it up with your gun-rod while you were riding along." And that fellow was a nephew of mine, and his clan was close to my father's. I asked him, "Where did you see me pick it up?" He said, "Yes, my uncle, I saw you pick it up with your gun-rod while you were riding along." I said, "I never thought of anything like that until we got here. Then we heard the turquoise was lost. I came with these fellows." The five men said, "We came with him, and we didn't see him pick up anything at all. He never went away from us. We were with him all the time. That fellow's a liar. He doesn't know what he's saying, because he's a little off." He was that way all right, but the other people believed him.

I was riding a good-sized horse, and I said to the people, "Get a gun-rod for me and put a strand of turquoise on the ground and see if I can pick it up." They laid a strand on the ground, and as I rode by I tried to pick it up with the gun-rod, but I couldn't; I just pushed it around. I missed it several times, because I could only just reach it. Then they let me go, but they were still talking about it when we left.

We went quite a way from that place and took the saddles and bridles off our horses and let them eat grass. While we were lying around there, late in the afternoon, they called for me again. They said, "Sure enough, you picked up that turquoise. This man here says he saw you, and we all know he's not lying. We all believe him, so you just hand it over. It's no use your saying you didn't get it." I said, "I never knew anything about the turquoise, and I didn't pick it up anywhere." They said, "Don't say no. Don't say you didn't pick it up." But I said, "I haven't got it." "If you give it up," they said, "we'll give you a buckskin and a woven dress and a silver belt. If you give up the turquoise we'll give you all that." I said, "Where could I get it? If I found it I'd give it up right away. I'd give it back to a man for nothing. I wouldn't want to be paid for it if I had it. So now I haven't got it." But they didn't believe me. Everybody was saying, "He picked it up. He's got it and won't get it out. Maybe he'll get it out in some years from now, but he won't get it out soon. He's hidden it some place." The five fellows were helping me, and we kept saying, "We haven't seen the turquoise." They were talking about it from there on until after the dance. They tried to find it in many different ways and were after me about it.

The next day the Nda was over, and I went home. I told my mother all about it. I said, "I had trouble yesterday all day. A fellow claimed he saw me picking up a strand of turquoise that a man lost." She knew this fellow who claimed I'd picked it up, and she was mad at him. "They ought to know better. Everybody knows he's crazy. They know very well he's a little off. He doesn't know what he's talking about. But still, you say, they all believed him. They must be crazy too."

A few days later I heard my father, Slim Man, was having a singer to sing over him for one night. I said to my mother, "I'd like to go to that singing." Right away she said, "Yes, sure, you'd better go over." I said, "I wonder where he's having it? He has two places." He had three wives at that time; two of them were Red From The Waist Down and one was Red Clay. My mother said, "It's at the Red Clay's place." I went over that evening, and there was the singer named Hairy Face. He knew the Wind Chant, and that was the chant he was giving there. My father said to me, "You ought to have been here this morning to help us. But you'll help tonight, bringing in wood and getting water for the cook." I said, "All right. I didn't know you were holding the chant. If I'd known it yesterday, or this morning, I'd have come and helped you. I got to know of it just a little while ago." "Well," he said, "that's all right, my son. You help around tonight, help get more water and wood, and help make a fire."

Late in the evening they started singing. The singer said to us, "Don't go out after I start, not until I say you can. From then on you can go back and forth." He started singing, and everybody helped him. After he'd sung a long time he said, "Now you can go, whenever you want to." I went to the hogan where they were cooking and stayed a little while, and then I started back. About halfway between the two hogans somebody came toward me. That was my father's wife. I stepped out of the trail, but when I tried to go by her she grabbed me and took away the handkerchief that was tied around my head. I told her to give it back to me, but she said, "No, I haven't got your handkerchief. If you don't believe me, search me." I searched her, but she didn't have it with her. I don't know where she'd put it. All of a sudden she grabbed me, and as soon as she grabbed me she sat down. I didn't say anything; I just lay on top of her. But afterwards I was afraid and sorry. I wanted to go back where they were singing, but I changed my mind and stayed outside all night.

Two or three days later I met her again. I was rounding up my horses, and when she saw me she came up and grabbed the beads around my neck. She said, "I want your beads." She was holding me, and I was saying, "Let me go. We'll surely get caught. If I give you the beads, where will you keep them? Where will you put them?" She said, "I'll have them with me. I've been thinking about you all the time. Your father already has two wives, and I'm the third. I don't care to go with him, because he has two wives already. That's why I want you. I want to go with you, and now I won't let you go. I'll take you back to my home, and you'll have to stay with me." I begged her not to hold me, but she kept hanging onto the beads. I said, "I won't give them to you, because you've got no place to put them. I'll give you the beads all right, but I'll give them to your brother." At last she let me go. I had a hard time getting away from her.

I always used to go to my father's place, but I was afraid to go over now. I just stayed around at home, and every time I saw him coming I'd start to go out for something. I always tried to have something to do outside while he was at our home. I was so sorry. My mother must have heard about it some way. One day she said to me, "You were found out. The same morning your father had that chant he found his wife sleeping. Even though it was daylight she was still sleeping, and by that your father found out you'd been with her. But she never did admit it. How about you?" I said, "No, I don't know anything about it. I didn't go near her."

In the fall Slim Man came to our place and said, "I'd like to go to Man's Water, to Tunes To His Voice's place. I want you to go with me. They're going to put up a Night Chant. I got word, and they want me over there for help. So we'll go and help those people. We'll start from here in about seven days." I said, "All right, I'd like to go."

When the seven days were up we started off. As we were going along we got to a place where a fellow had a lot of nice, good-sized horses. He loaned me one that was a race-horse, and I put my saddle on him, and then we went on. It was a long distance to ride. We'd been riding all day, and about evening we got to Big Flat House. There we stopped for the night. We turned our horses loose and hobbled them and made a fire and cooked some coffee. After lunch we put our things away and fixed a place to sleep. I went around and gathered some wood for morning, and after that I took off my moccasins and went to bed. My father was out some place, taking a walk, I guess, and didn't come back until it was real dark. Then he spread some saddle-blankets on the ground and went to bed. But he began talking about things, telling me stories.

We were talking for a long time, and then he said, "That

night, when I had that chant over me, you came, and I told you to help the cooks. I told you to get them some wood and water and help around. But that night I missed you. You went out, and a little later the girl went out after you, and you never came back inside, and she didn't come back either. You were both out somewhere. I know it, because you were away all night. I was suspicious of you two. Now you must tell me the truth. No one's around. Just we two are here, so you mustn't be bashful. If you like that girl, and if she likes you, just let me know right now, and you can go with her. In that way there won't be any trouble between us." I said, "No, I never went around with her. I was out there at the cooking for a while, and then I went over where my horse was tied. I laid a saddle-blanket on the ground and thought, 'I'll take a little rest,' but I went to sleep. As soon as I woke up I thought, 'I'll just go back home.' So I did."

He kept asking me, trying to make me say yes, trying to make me admit it, but I kept saying, "I didn't go near her." He didn't believe me at all. He said, "Don't say you never touched that girl, because I know you've been with her. I know it very well, and I tracked you too. I know where you were lying. I know you worked on her. I know it by your tracks. So, now, you mustn't deny it. Just say right out that you did it, and I won't say anything to you about it, and I won't do anything. There won't be any trouble for you." He kept saying that to me all night. "And everybody thinks about you that way. It's not only I. They all say, 'That fellow, Abaa's Son, goes around to all the hogans. He's had everybody's wife. We think we've got a wife, but they all belong to him. We're just taking care of his wives for him.' That's what they're saying about you. So it's bad for you. Soon you'll be in trouble. Now you'd better be quick about it and get yourself a wife. Or, if you want this girl of mine, you can take her. Then you won't get in trouble."

He was saying all kinds of things to me all night. Toward the end I said, "It's no use for me to get married, because I've got so much to do for myself and my mother, and I've got to tend to my sheep, horses and cattle. So I don't want to monkey with a woman. It's nothing to me. They're good for nothing. That's the way I'm thinking about them. If I get a woman she'll be holding me tight, and everything I've got now will all have disappeared, and I won't ever know where it's gone to. So I'd like to be alone. I like to be single. Then I can go anywhere I want to. And I don't want to leave my mother, and I don't want to leave all my stock. That's the way I am. So don't talk to me about it, and don't think I was around with your wife. You think so, but I wasn't. Don't think I got after your wife, my father. I wouldn't treat you like that. You've always been kind to me. Why should I bother you that way? I wouldn't treat you cruelly. So just put it off, my father. Don't think about it. You want me to tell the truth, so I'm telling you the truth now. I never did such a thing. I wouldn't want to bother you behind your back."

In the morning we got our horses and ate lunch and started off. It was a long way to travel. In the afternoon we passed the Hopi village and then the Oraibi, and it was almost sundown before we got to that place called Man's Water, where they were holding the Night Chant. There was a big crowd. My father said, "We've been riding for two days, and we're tired. You sent us word, and that's why we came, even though it's a long distance. So here we are." They said to us, "Go over where they're cooking."

Tunes To His Voice was sitting over there. He was the one who was holding the sing. His daughter was the patient. When he saw us coming he got up and spread some sheep pelts way back in the shade. We went in and sat down and shook hands with him, and he gave us many thanks for coming and visiting them. My father said, "I had so much to do at home, but I let everything go, because I got word from you, and that's why we're here." "Yes, I sent word," said Tunes To His Voice. "I knew you'd come, and I'm glad you have, and glad we're meeting each other again. A whole lot of people are here, but it looks like there's nobody around to help me. I'm the only one going among these crowds, telling them what to do. I'm glad you've come. You can help me show them what to do, getting water for the cooks and hauling wood. We want a lot of wood for the last night. Besides we have to have fires going all night long."

At that time nobody had a wagon. They used to haul wood on horseback or burros, and there I saw a wagon for the first time. I looked it all over and thought, "What a nice thing that is. I wish I had one just like it." Some fellows were on the wagon hauling wood, and so I joined them, just because I liked the wagon. I wanted to ride on it. We were hauling wood all day. That night they had the masks out in the hogan where they were singing, and after everybody'd had all different kinds of food to eat they started singing the Blessing Rite. They sang all night. In the morning I went out where the wagon was. I was wondering how to put the harness on the mules. After a while they brought them over and hitched them to the wagon, and there I learned how to harness a horse or mule. We hauled wood all day again, and my father helped around inside where they were having the singing. That night two fellows put on the masks and gathered together all the boys and girls and grown people who'd never seen the Yeibichai. They undressed themselves, and the two Yeibichai took them inside the hogan and treated all of them. I was in it. I'd never seen the Yeibichai before in my life. We were do-

333

ing the same thing again the next day, hauling wood, and that night there was a still larger crowd, and they all started dancing and danced all night. The next day was the last.

It was a nice, level place where they were holding the chant, and that last day the people wanted to have a race. Everybody went out in the flat, and first they had a long-distance race, and after that they wanted a short one. They said, "Go on, ride out here. Ride your horse out here. Lend us your horse." I looked around, everybody was looking around, and no one knew whom they meant. At last they called me by my mother's name. I said, "This horse isn't a racehorse. I've had this horse hobbled for seven days and nights, and nobody has ridden it for a year. I didn't start riding him until seven days ago." But they said, "Even at that, lend us your horse." Some of the fellows knew the horse. It was a racehorse all right, but it hadn't been used for a year. They kept saying, "Lend us your horse," and at last my father said, "Go ahead. Let them have it. If they want to lose their money and their things let them have it. Let them lose." So I did. The other side had a spotted horse from the top of Black Mountain.

The horse I loaned them started off all right, but as they were coming along it got out of the track and made a circle. So they were beaten. They were mad at the fellow who rode it, but he said, "I can't help it. A fellow isn't able to turn a horse when it's going swiftly. Nobody can turn a horse, or make it go back to the track, when it's going that fast." They said to me, "You ought to have ridden the horse yourself. If you'd got on him we'd have beaten those fellows, because you know how to handle him. You'd have whipped him on the left side; then he'd have run straight. But this fellow whipped the horse on the right side. That's why he got out of the track. If you'd ridden your own horse he'd have come

334

straight on the track, and we'd have beaten those fellows."
They were talking like that among themselves, and I said,
"It's no use talking about it. We got beat. You ought to have
talked about it before. It's no use now."

In the evening, about sundown, three Yei's came to treat
the patient outside, and everybody wanted to see them. After
that they began getting ready for the last night, and that
night some fellows, dressed in the masks, started dancing.
There were six at a time. They kept that up all night, but I
went to sleep, and in the morning the dance was over. Then
I went after the horses and saddled them and tied them there
and went inside the hogan and said to my father, "I have the
horses ready." "Fine," he said, "but we'll wait a while."
Everybody was leaving. They said to us, "Wait until you've
had something to eat. After you eat you can go." They
brought us some food, and we ate, and then we started off.

My father said, "We'll go around where the Oraibi are living, just for fun. We might get something to eat there, and
we might get some peaches." Peaches were good and ripe
then. We went along, and a little after noon we got to the
place I used to go to. They asked us, "Have you any meat?"
My father said, "No, we haven't any with us. We've been at
the chant, and that's where we're coming back from. We're
not from home." They didn't care so much for us then. They
just gave us some scraps that were left over. We were hungry, and so we had to eat them. We never did get a taste of
peaches.

We started from there after we ate, but first we looked all
around. I wasn't thinking of anything, just following my
father. At last he said, "Let's go." So we got on our horses
and rode away. Quite a distance from that place he said,
"We'll go over that hill and stop. From there we'll turn
around tonight and get some peaches. We'll steal some

from them. I know a good place to get them." I was real hungry for peaches, so I said, "All right." The sun was almost down. We went on over the hill and stopped our horses and took off our good clothes, belts and beads and everything, and hid them away and only kept our old clothes on. My father said, "I'm going to sew my double saddle-blanket into a sack." I thought I'd do the same. We gathered some soap-weed stalks and tore them into strips and began sewing up our saddle-blankets.

It was evening then, and we got on our horses and started back. When we got to the place where the peaches were the moon was up, but my father said, "There's nobody around. They're afraid to go out at night, so you don't have to be frightened. Just go ahead and get all you want." It was quite a way from the village. We started picking them off the trees and putting them in our sacks. Some were sweet; some were not. Those that were sweet we picked. They were the great big ones. We were picking peaches a long time, packing them down tight, until both sacks were full. It was just like carrying a log.

When we were satisfied we went back where we'd left our stuff and put our clothes back on and started off. We kept riding all night, until we got too sleepy to go on. At the foot of the mountain, by the place called Big Mountain, we stopped and took the things off the horses and hobbled them. All the peaches were mashed to bits, and our pants and moccasins and saddle-blankets were soaked with the juice. We lay down and went to sleep, and all at once my father shook me. "Wake up," he said. "It's almost daylight. You know we made trouble last night. We've been discovered by now, and they'll sure be after us." We got the horses and started off again. The peaches were just as if you were carrying mud. We went along, trotting our horses all day, and about sundown we got to his children's home; those who belonged to Red From The Waist Down. He took everything off his horse and said, "We want a good fat mutton." Right away they started cooking, and his wife came out and took the peaches inside.

It was dark by the time we got through eating, and I went out then and started off for home. It was quite a way to where I lived. Way late at night I got home, but my mother was still up. She tried to take the peaches in the hogan, but she couldn't. She only moved them around. I said, "Leave it alone. It's too heavy for you." After I'd turned my horse loose I took them in for her. She was glad I'd brought her the peaches.

18.
Two girls accept his challenge . . . He has someone under him again . . . His mother makes a bad bargain . . . He hears of his real mother's death . . . He hides his stuff in a treetop on the mountain, and they move to the cornfield.

IN the morning she put them in the sun to dry. "We'll have dried peaches this winter," she said. While she was doing that she said, "I missed three horses, the tame ones; all the rest are here. They all came and got water, but the day after you left I missed those three. I looked for them every time I went out with my herd, but I didn't see them anywhere. Somebody must have taken them away. If they were around here they'd come for water, but they're not around close by, I think." The horses were just coming to water. I got my rope and bridle and went out and roped one there and rode all around looking for those three, but I didn't find them. From then on I went out every day. Whenever I saw a fellow I'd ask him, but nobody ever saw my horses.

One day as I was riding along I came across some herds. I thought, "I'll go over and ask that herder. Maybe he's seen them around here some place." But there was nobody around. Close by was a little hill with a rocky wall around it. I looked up the hill, and there were three girls sitting on a rock. I went over and asked them if they'd seen my horses, but they said, "We haven't seen any around here." I took the bridle off my horse and let him eat some grass, and I was there, talking with the girls. I was acting and saying funny things to them, and they were laughing. Pretty soon they came up and were all around me, and every time I said some funny thing they'd want me to say it again.

Down at the foot of the wall was a sand drift. I said to the girls, "Come over to the edge of the wall and try to p— across this place. See who'll p— over the sand drift." It was quite a distance down from the top of the wall. They laughed about it, and pretty soon they said, "All right, you go first." I said, "You girls go first. I'll be the last one." But only two of them wanted to do it. Then the oldest went up to the edge of the wall and pulled up her dress and started p—ing. She was leaning over, and her p— was like a rainbow. "Now," she said, "you're next." I took out my c— and thought, "It's easy. I can p— way over that sand drift." I saw where she'd landed, right on top, but I didn't quite reach her. The next one was the youngest. She started to p—, and while she was p—ing she said, "Oh, I got beat." After that they said to me, "You lose. We beat you." But I said, "No, I beat the other girl. So, now, I'm not beaten. We're just even." About then the small girl said, "There's a fellow riding this way." We turned and looked, and, sure enough, someone was riding straight towards us, so they said to me, "We'll let it go." As soon as I saw the fellow I picked up my bridle and ran to my horse and rode away.

I rode over the hill and turned around towards Cottonwood Standing. As I was riding along near that place, north of Lots Of Wool, I saw a boy herding sheep. I asked him, "Are any horses around here?" "No," he said, "there are no horses around here." I told him what kind I was looking for, the colors and what they were like, and he said, "My father saw three fellows riding across the flat toward Black Mountain, and on the way back, he said, they were riding three good horses and chasing the ones they'd been on. That's what my father was telling about the other day, but he didn't mention the color. You might find out from him yourself. That's all I know."

I stayed there, thinking about the horses, wondering if they'd turned them loose. I thought, "If they turned them loose they ought to have been home long ago. Maybe they're still using them. Maybe they've gone some place. Or maybe they've got them somewhere in a pasture. Or maybe they sold them to someone." The boy said, "My father said the three fellows were from the other side of Narrow Canyon. He said, 'I only know one of them. I recognized him. I'm sure it's he. His clan is Many Goats. The two others may have been his sons-in-law, or maybe some of his boys. But,' he said, 'I know this one very well.' "

I asked the boy, "Where are you living?" He said, "I'm living on that hill." I looked at the sun; it was pretty well down. I asked him, "Where's your father?" "My father isn't home. He went over on the other side of Black Mountain about two days ago, and I don't think he'll be back for several days. He went to visit his children. He's got another family over there." I thought, "I'll go over to his place anyway, and besides I know his wife. I'll go and stay overnight." That was Woman Who Flips Her Cards. The boy was her son.

When I got to the hogan two families were living there, two women, the woman I knew and another one. The other one was the wife of Woman Who Flips Her Cards' husband's uncle. That's why they were living together. Her husband was an old man, and she didn't like him, because she was young. I sat there quietly by the doorway for a time; I didn't speak first. Then Woman Who Flips Her Cards said, "Where have you come from? From where did you drop?

We've never seen you around here before." I said, "Oh, I'm just riding around. I've been riding for several days. I missed three of my horses. Maybe somebody's taken them away from me. I was away from home for a few days, and when I came back I missed them. That's what I'm looking for. Whenever I see anyone I ask about them. I ask all the herders, and when I come to a place like this I ask the people, because, I thought, 'Somebody's likely to see them some place.'"

They said, "We don't know anything about horses. Only the men are always going around, doing the same as you are, looking for horses. Maybe some of them saw your horses somewhere." "Where are the men?" I asked them. "What men?" "The men who are on top of you." "We haven't anyone on top of us. You're the only one who has somebody under you." I said, "Sure, I've got somebody under me." I meant her, but it seemed as though she didn't notice what I meant. I was talking with them that way for quite a while, and they were both laughing and saying to me, "You must be crazy."

I asked them again, "Where are the men? I know from his son that he saw my horses." Then she said, "He went away from here two days ago to Spring On Sunny Side. I don't know when he's coming back. When he left he said, 'Maybe I'll be back in five or six days.' So maybe he'll be back in five days or six. And that was right. He said he saw three fellows riding across the flat; I think it was seven days ago." The other woman said, "Yes, it was seven days ago. One horse was white, one blue and the other was a bay." I said, "That's it." "He said he knew them well. It was the man we call White Hair and his sons-in-law. So I guess that's where your horses are." "Thanks very much," I said, "for telling me about it. That's what I want to know. Now I can take my time, because I know now where they are."

I'd been sitting on my heels all this time, but then I sat

down on the ground. I said, "I'm glad I know where they are." Woman Who Flips Her Cards got up and laid a sheep pelt by my side and said, "I've known this man a long time, but I haven't seen him lately." She came up and shook hands with me and was holding my hand as tightly as she could. I knew just what she wanted, and I thought to myself, "I'll stay here tonight."

She started cooking, and I said, "I'd like to stay overnight, because it's about evening now. I've got a long way to go to where my horses are, and it's a long way back home. Tomorrow I can start from here early in the morning. Is there any grass around here?" "Yes, there's plenty on the other side of the hill. We don't turn our herds out that way, because we're using it for the horses." I went out then, and took the saddle off my horse and led him away and hobbled him. Everything was ready when I got back, the boy was in with his herd, and we started eating. The two women were sitting there and laughing all during the meal. After supper they said to me, "Tell us about your trip. You say you've been to the dance. Tell us about that." I said, "Yes, I went with my father, Slim Man." She knew Slim Man. She'd been with him too. I told them all about the trip we'd made over to the dance and back.

When we were through talking they spread out their pelts and went to bed. The boy was already sleeping. I lay down too, but I didn't have a robe with me. After a while I got up and said to them, "I haven't any blankets. I'll lie down between you two." They just laughed, and so I went over and lay down between them. They were lying close beside each other, and it was kind of crowded, but they didn't move at all. They said, "What are you trying to do? You're always wanting to do something funny." "Yes," I said, "because I haven't anybody under me."

I pulled the blankets over me, and we lay there together

talking, and I began to touch them. They both liked it, and Woman Who Flips Her Cards put her arms around my neck and kissed me. The other woman started doing the same, but when she found the other one already had her arms around me she turned her back. I tried to put an arm around her, but she pushed it away. She was jealous, and so I let her go, and after a while she went to sleep. Then this other woman said to me, "We'll go outside." I got up and went out, and she came after me with the sheep pelts and laid them on the ground, and there I had somebody under me again.

I said, "Now I'll go back inside. I'd like to get after the other woman." She said, "No." She held me there, saying, "She must be your wife too, because I noticed she put her arms around you." I said, "No, she's not my wife. I never touched her before. This is the first time I ever got close to her." But she didn't believe me. I said, "I wonder if she'll tell on us." "No," she said, "I don't think so. I know she won't." "How about the boy?" "No, he won't tell either, because he's my boy. He won't say anything. You must be afraid." "Yes, I'm afraid of your husband." "You don't want to be afraid. He won't know. He isn't around, and nobody will tell him anything about it."

We lay there all night talking about different things. She asked me, "Have you got a wife now?" I said, "No, I haven't." "Oh," she said, "I often wish for you. I wish I were with you. I wish about you like that all the time. I try to forget you, but I can't. I'm always thinking about you day and night." Then she said, "I heard you had a wife. Where's she now?" I said, "Yes, I had a woman, but she's left me already, and I just let her go. I didn't like her anyway. I don't care to have a wife. I think it's too much trouble. That's why I'm not thinking of getting one." Those were the things we were talking about, and towards morning we fell asleep.

We slept a little while, and then I got up and put on my moccasins and went after my horse. He was close by. I brought him back and put the saddle and bridle on him, and she already had a fire going in the hogan and was starting to cook. The other woman and the boy were up too. She went out to the herd and caught a great big sheep and called for a rope and a knife and a pan. The boy took the rope out, and after she'd tied it up she came inside and said to the other woman, "Go out and butcher that sheep," and she said to me, "You go and help her."

While the two of us were out there butchering the sheep and cutting up the meat I started teasing her. She said, "Why didn't you tease me last night?" I said, "I was going to, but you turned your back on me." "Yes, I did that, because you had a wife." "I haven't got a wife," I said to her. "Yes, I know you have. That woman inside's your wife. I know." "No, she's not." We kept saying this to each other while we were butchering, and when the meat was cut up we took it inside, and they roasted some on charcoal. We were laughing and talking. Every time I said something they laughed about it. It was just as though I belonged there.

After we'd eaten the other woman and the boy went out to the sheep. While they were out there she came up and put her arms around my neck and kissed me again, and I gave her three dollars. She was very much pleased with it. "Come around any time you want to. Don't forget me, please. I hate to have you leave. I wish you'd stay longer." "Oh," I said, "I'd like to go right now, because I want to find my horses. I'm worrying about them very much, so I've got to go right now. I'll be around some time. I won't forget you. You're always in my mind too. So don't think I'll forget you." "Thanks," she said, and gave me another kiss and let me go.

A long distance from that place I saw some horses way far

ahead of me just going over a hill. When I got on top of that hill, sure enough, there were my horses. They were going to the water. I drove them down to the wash, and they had some water, and so did I, and the horse I was riding. They were looking fine. They'd been used all right, but still they were in good shape. From there I started chasing them straight across the flat for home. By the time the sun was pretty well down we got to Anything Falls In. My home was a little way from there.

My mother was so glad I'd found the horses. She asked me, "Where did you find them?" I said, "Down at Narrow Canyon." "That's a long way from here. I wonder why they went to that place." I told her some fellows had ridden them down there, and she was mad about it. After that she said, "Some people camped here last night. They're trading. They gave me a saddle and two good-sized horses. One's white and the other's blue. They want eighty head of sheep for the two horses and twenty for the saddle. So that's a hundred head of sheep I gave them. But I haven't given it to them yet. They took the blue horse along with them this morning, but they'll be coming back and passing here again tomorrow." I said, "It's too much. We don't want to lose that many sheep, and besides we've got lots of horses. What do you want another two horses for?" "Well, they're both good-sized, and I thought you'd like them. And the saddle's yours. My son also came yesterday." She meant Slim Man. She called him her son. "He was here and said, 'The corn's ripe, and I want you to go and get some for yourself.' I was so thankful. I'm glad we have some corn now for this winter. I want you to go over and see it tomorrow." I was glad too. I went over where she'd hobbled the white horse, and it was kind of poor. I tried to turn her down, but she said, "I like this horse. That's why I'm willing to give forty head of sheep for it."

345

I stayed at home that night, and in the morning I brought the horse in for her. She put her saddle on it and went out with the herd, and I went out to round up the horses and drive them to water. About noon I came home and started a fire and cooked a meal for myself. Quite a while after my mother came in with the sheep, and we cooked some more, and she ate lunch. Then I went with the herd, and she stayed home. In the evening, when I got back, there were those people. They had quite a number of sheep. The man rode up and asked me, "Where's a good place to camp?" I said, "Any place around here." He rode back to the others, and I put my sheep in the corral and went in the hogan. My mother said, "Don't worry about the sheep, my son. We'll have more this spring. So don't worry about it. We'll get the two horses and give them eighty head. Don't be sorry for them. You shouldn't be sorry for the sheep." She told me a lot about sheep that night, but I didn't say a word.

The people came to our place the next morning and told us about their trips. They said, "Everybody wanted this blue horse." The man said to me, "This horse will be yours, and that saddle, and the white one we're giving to your mother. She can use it for herding, because we know she's old; she can't stand herding on foot." My mother said, "Yes, I'm so pleased with that horse, because he's gentle. I rode him all day yesterday, and I liked him so well." She liked the horse all right, but I didn't. I was sorry for the sheep. I thought twenty head would be enough, but she wanted to give forty. She came inside the hogan and asked me again, "What do you think about the horses?" I said, "It's up to you, mother. You like them very well, so you go ahead and pay for them." She said, "I've been using one horse all the time, and I've turned him loose, so I'll use the white one to herd with." I said, "All right."

I got my bridle and put it on the blue horse they gave me. I thought, "I'll try him. See how he is." I rode around and over the hill, and he was lively. There was a good level place out in the flat for about a hundred yards, and I let him run there. As soon as I wanted him to go he gave a quick jump, and he sure did go swiftly and make the dust fly. I was glad to get him, because he was a good-sized horse and quick too, so that I didn't have to use a whip on him. I'd just give a little kick, and he'd start off quickly.

When I came back the man asked me, "Well, how do you like the horse?" I said, "I like him very well, but I don't know exactly what he's like yet, not until I've used him for a while." He said, "That's a good horse. It's a racehorse. I've been using him only when I've wanted to go to the dances. And it's a strong horse. You can ride him all day and all night and the next day, and he'll be just the same. He won't get tired. And it's a young horse too. He's only four years old."

We stayed with them all day, and he asked me, "Have you got a wife?" "My nephew," he called me. "No," I said, "I haven't." "Why, you ought to have one. A man like you without a wife. You ought to have a wife and children by now. There are some fellows who have children even when they're younger than you are. And you ought to have a wife too." I said, "I guess it's all right to have a wife, but, I don't know why, I don't care to get married. I don't like having a wife." "Well, anyway," he said, "you'd better get yourself a woman. You can get one easily, because you've got lots of property and stocks. If you want a woman I can get you one. Lots of girls haven't got a husband. A lot of them at my place aren't married yet. You ought to come over; we've got lots of pretty girls. And you've got brothers and sisters over there too. You ought to come and visit them. Only your mother, your real mother, is dead now. She died a year ago." While

347

he was saying this my mother started crying. "Oh," she said, "I never did get to see my sister. I've been wanting to go and see her lots of times, but I didn't have any way to go, because I can't leave my place alone. That's why I never got to see her again." That's where I heard that my mother had died. That was my real mother.

The next morning we went to the corral and started taking the sheep out one by one, counting them until we had a hundred head. The man was standing there, looking at our sheep, and he had some beads with a strand of turquoise. He said, "I want a hundred head for this." He was starting to untie it, but I asked him, "What are you untying your beads for?" He said, "I'm going to give you these turquoise." "No," I said, "I don't want them. Don't untie it. Keep it for yourself. I don't want to lose any more sheep." "Well," he said, "I thought you'd like to have this strand. You ought to buy these turquoise from me, and give me a hundred more." I said, "No, you keep those beads, because I'm just living on my sheep. I don't live on the beads. So I don't want them." He tied the strand back on his beads, and after that they went away. When they were gone my mother saddled the white horse and took out the herd. I put the saddle they'd given me on the blue horse and said to her, "Now I'm going over to my father's place and look at the corn he let us have." She said, "All right, you'd better go and see about it."

While I was riding along I looked at my shadow every once in a while. I was showing off, and the horse was lively. My father was walking around outside his place when I got there, and he said to me, "Whose horse is that? Who lent you a horse?" I said, "That horse belongs to me." "Well, I thought somebody'd loaned you one, for I don't know that horse or the saddle either." "No, he's mine, and the saddle's mine too." "Where did you get them?" I said, "Some people have been around here trading things for sheep, and while I was away they came to my place and gave two horses and a saddle to my mother, this horse and saddle and a white horse that my mother's using."

He walked around, inspecting the horse and looking it all over, and while he was walking around it he was smiling. He said, "It's a good-sized horse, all right, and it's looking fine. How much did you give for it?" I said, "My mother gave forty head of sheep for each of the horses and twenty for the saddle." He almost fainted. He stood there without saying anything. Then he said, "You must like to lose all your sheep. What did you want these horses for? You've got plenty of good horses. And as for the saddle, you've got a new saddle too. You should have let the people carry those things around. What else did they have?" I said, "There was a long strand of turquoise that they wanted a hundred head of sheep for." "That was the thing for you," he said. "I don't see what you want with horses. You ought to have got the turquoise. You know very well you won't have the horses long, or the saddle either. In ten years that horse will be dead, and the saddle will all be worn. If it was a mare you'd get more horses from her, but out of those two you can't get anything. If you'd bought the turquoise you'd have had something worth while, because turquoise you can't wear out. You'll have it for years and years. And turquoise won't die on you."

He said to me, "Come inside." I went in after him, and he pulled out a sack and got out a bunch of white beads with two good strands of turquoise. He showed them to me and said, "I got these beads and the turquoise a long time ago, when I was a young man, and I still have them today. They're not worn, and they're not dying off on me. Today they're still the same, and I'll have them the rest of my life. So you ought to have bought the beads instead of the horses and saddle."

He put the beads away and got out his tobacco and said, "Let's have a cigarette and smoke." We rolled a cigarette and started smoking, and he repeated everything again. I said, "It's not my fault. It's my mother's, that she'd already paid for these things. I tried to turn her down, but she said she'd already traded with the people. So then I didn't say anything." He said, "A man who's got lots of sheep, horses and cattle, and nothing besides, is not strong. Even though he's got a whole lot of stock, if he doesn't know how to use it, it's good for nothing. If a man knows how to use the stock he can trade his sheep for something that's worth while; then he'll be fixed well. Soon he'll have a lot of things, lots of property. Now you've got lots of stock, you ought to try and get something worth while. Then you'll have something as long as you live. You know your mother's getting old. She doesn't care, she doesn't think any more. She only thinks about something to eat, that's all. She doesn't try to get something worth while. You ought to have given those things back to the people and bought the turquoise."

He made me quite a speech. He repeated everything to me many times. "Now you've got lots of sheep and lots of horses, and you've got some cattle. But you don't know exactly how many cattle you have. Whenever you go up on the mountain you never see them all. It looks as though they didn't belong to you. You ought to have them down here in the flat, then you'd know you had something. If you don't bring them down, pretty soon you won't have any, because everybody who goes up on the mountain will take them and drive them away and sell them. You ought to trade your cattle for beads, turquoise and silverware, things like that that are worth while. You've got a little strand tied on to your beads, but

I don't call that a strand of turquoise. If you'd bought the turquoise those people had you'd have been worth a lot." I was sorry I hadn't bought it, but it was my mother's fault.

We put that off, and then he asked me, "What did you want?" "Oh," I said, "I came to look at the corn. My mother told me you let us have some, and I want to look at it." "Yes, I did. That's what I told your mother the other day when I was down at your place. She said she was hungry for corn, and I told her there was a little patch you could have. And now you can go and see. I tied the corn together and made a line across the field. You can find it easily. From there on it's yours." I said, "That's fine, my father. I'm very glad you let us have some. You're so good to us. You give us something all the time. I'm very glad that now we'll have some corn for winter." I gave him a lot of thanks and then went down to look at it. It was quite a patch. I walked around in the field, and there were some pumpkins and squash along with it. I was so glad and happy. It made me so happy, because he let us have a good-sized field. Then I walked back to my horse and started home.

It was about sundown. My mother was in with the herd and had hobbled her horse. I led mine over where the white horse was and hobbled him, and when I came back to the hogan we started cooking. I built a fire for her and got some water, and we cooked some food. While we were eating I told her about the corn. "We've got a good patch. I know we'll have a lot, and there are some squash and pumpkins too. So we've got lots of food for winter." Then I told her what my father had said. She said, "I wanted to get that turquoise, but you didn't like to lose any more sheep. That's why we let it go. He's right too. What he said to you is all right, because he knows everything about it. But it's too late now. Perhaps later on sometime there'll be other people coming along with beads, and then, the first thing, we'll get some. So just forget about it, and don't be sorry."

I told her about the cornfield again. "We've got lots of corn, and squash and pumpkins with it." She said, "We ought to move over there close by, so we can get some corn, pumpkins and squash whenever we want to eat some. But it's hard to move. We've got a whole lot of things to carry around with us. We ought to put some of them away. You ought to go around the cliffs, maybe you'll find a good place to hide our stuff where nobody could see it." But I said, "I don't think I'll do that, because everybody's moving around, and if we hide our stuff in the cliffs they'll steal it away from us. I'd like to take it all and hide it away on Black Mountain. I don't think anybody will find our things up there. Hardly anybody goes up on the mountain. I'll hide it on the trees. There are some great big trees that have thick leaves on them." "Well," she said, "if you want to do that, hide it away where nobody can see it. And you musn't leave any tracks. If you leave tracks around somebody will surely steal our things away." I said, "No, mother, I don't think anybody will steal them. I know just how I'll take them up there, and how to hide them. I won't leave any tracks, so don't worry so much about it." "All right, you can go ahead and do it," she said.

The next morning I took our stuff out of the bags. There were thirteen buckskins, three double saddle-blankets, all brand new, three buffalo skins and six new robes. I laid aside one buckskin and a saddle-blanket and the smallest buffalo skin. The rest I wrapped in the biggest buckskin of the bunch and put it over my saddle. It was a great, big, heavy bundle. Then I picked up three old robes that'd been used a long time and started off. Nobody saw me crossing the flat. It was hard riding with this big pack, because the trees were so close together. Way up in the middle of the mountain was a little place, and I thought, "I'll leave the horse here, because it's as far as he can go. From here on it's too steep and rough." I had a jug of water with me, and after I'd had a drink I put the bundle on my back and started up the mountain. Halfway to the top I had to sit down and rest. I was all sweat, and the clothes I had on were all wet. I rested and cooled off and then started again. I had a hard time. I almost gave up. When I think of it now I believe I must have been crazy, taking that great big bundle of stuff and hiding it on the mountain.

At last I got to the top, and there I sat down again and rested and cooled myself off. So many rocks were around there a person could hardly see a track, but I thought, "I'll go a little further. Whenever a fellow's looking for horses or cattle he always comes to the edge of the mountain." Quite a way from the edge I got to a bunch of trees that were thick and close together, and right in the middle was a big cedar. I thought, "I'll put my stuff right on top of that tree, and nobody'll see it." So I climbed up and fixed a place, and then I went around and gathered a lot of cedar bark. When that was done I put the three old robes around the bundle and started up the tree. It was so heavy, but at last I got it up and laid it on the bark and put some more on top of it. Then I climbed down and made a circle all around it, but it couldn't be seen from any direction. "My bundle will be safe," I thought. "Nothing can get at it, and there are no tracks around at all." After that I went back to my horse and started down the mountain and got home in the evening. My mother was in with the herd, and after I'd put my horse away we started cooking. While we were eating I told her about my trip. I said, "I hid the stuff where nobody'll see it, and I don't think anything will get at it. It will be safe the whole time." "That's fine," she said. "To-morrow we'll move to the cornfield."

19. *He goes to an Nda and has several proposals . . . And marries the wrong girl.*

I TOOK our things to the cornfield the next morning, and in the afternoon I dragged in some poles and cut off the leaves. The next day I put up a shade. I fixed it up well, and it was nice and cool inside. The rest of the day and part of the evening I dragged in some wood. I had quite a pile by midnight. In the morning my mother said to me, "You herd the sheep today. I'm going to grind up some green corn and make bread." When I came back a little after noon everything was ready. She'd boiled dried peaches and made a lot of corn-bread, and I sure enjoyed my meal. She said, "From here on you herd the sheep. I'll tend the corn. I'm going to make some green corn-bread and want to dry it. When it's dry I'll put it away in sacks. That's good in the wintertime. You can boil it. It's good to eat when it's boiled." I said, "All right, I'll be herding."

I herded a few days, and by then she had a great, big sack full of dry bread. I said, "You've got enough, mother. I think you're satisfied now, and you can herd again. I want to go on Black Mountain and round up my cattle. Some of the calves haven't been ear-marked, and I want to tend to that, and I'd like to drive them down." "You can't drive them down by yourself," she said. "You ought to get one of your brothers to help you." I thought, "I'll do that." "I'd like to go in two days. Tomorrow I want you to make me some lunch to take along." She said, "All right," and I went out with the sheep again.

When I returned with the herd in the afternoon she said, "Your father was here today and said they're having an Nda at Cow's Water. They're going to bring the decorated-stick over this way, to Water Under The Rocks, and give it to Old Man Gentle." Right away I wanted to go. I said, "Mother, I'd like to see all three night's dances." "You always want to go to all the dances. I thought you were going on Black Mountain to round up the cattle. And I want you to do that, too. You must go and round up your cattle. You know you can't get anything out of the dance." But I said, "No, mother, I'd like to go. Please, mother, let me go, and afterwards I'll round up my cattle." "Well, go ahead," she said.

Then I thought, "I'll go over to my father's place and see about it." I rode over, and he said, "Yes, they're going to start it tomorrow. They set a date two days ago, and tomorrow they're going to have the first-night's-dance at Water Under The Rocks. They're having this Nda at Cow's Water." "That's what I heard from my mother. I said to her, 'I'd like to go to all three nights,' but she turned me down. I was going on Black Mountain to round up the cattle, but when I heard this dance was coming up I put it off. That's why she didn't want me to go. She wanted me to round up the cattle instead. She said, 'You can't get anything out of the dance.'" "Oh, she doesn't know what she's talking about. She's getting too old. Let her say those things. Don't bother her. I'm only going to the first-night's-dance. When I come back from there I want to go over Lukachukai Mountain, to Spring Coming Out and way over to Bay In The Mountain. If you're going to all three night's dances you must be careful. Take care of your things, your horse and all you have. Watch yourself closely, because, you can't tell, you might lose something, or you might go to sleep and they'll steal from you." I said, "My moccasin soles are worn. Have you got any?" "Yes, you can have some. Have you the tops?" I said, "Yes, I only need the soles."

I started working on the moccasins the next morning. I did a quick job, and by afternoon I had a brand new pair ready for the dance. But I didn't go that day. In the morning I dressed myself in good clothes, put on my new moccasins and silver belt and beads around my neck, and went to my father's place. "Well, are you going to the second-night's-dance?" he asked me. I said, "Yes." "We're not going. We got enough last night. In two days I'm going over the mountain to visit Blue Eyes. When you come back from the dance will you go and round up my horses for me? If you do that I'll be very glad." I said, "Yes, I will."

Then I went on, taking my time, but nobody caught up with me. It was pretty well toward evening before I got on the hill and saw the dust where they were camping for the second-night's-dance. I rode up in the crowd, and they were glad I'd caught up with them. They said to me, "Why didn't you show up last night? Your girls were looking for you all night long." "Oh," I said, "I was doing all kinds of things at home, so I couldn't come until this morning, when I thought, 'I'll go to the second-night's-dance.' Maybe the girls were looking for me, but they're out of luck." "Well, you'll have to dance tonight, because you didn't last night." "I used to dance," I said, "but I've put the whole thing off. I don't want to dance any more. It's only wasting money." "Nevertheless you dance tonight," they said to me. "If you don't your girls will be mad at you." "Let them be mad," I said.

About then they began beating the drum and singing. I rode a little way out of the crowd and got off my horse and walked up to where Old Man Black was sitting by a fire.

As soon as he saw me he got out a pack of cards and said, "Let's play. We've got nothing to do. All the others are having a good time." He spread a blanket and said, "We'll play for nickels and dimes." He had a lot of them. We started playing, but neither of us won anything. At last he said, "We'll quit. It's no use for us to play, because we can beat each other." So I went away and took the saddle off my horse and hobbled him. A crowd was around another fire, and I took my saddle over there.

Not long after a fellow spoke up and said, "Stop the singing. Something's wrong over here." They stopped, but I didn't go over. After a while I heard the crowd coming towards me. They came up and asked, "Who's been playing cards with that man?" and some of them pointed at me. "That fellow there," they said. An old man in the crowd called Bunch Of Whiskers asked again, "Who was the fellow playing cards with that man?" and they pointed at me again, saying, "That was the fellow playing cards with him." But when Bunch Of Whiskers saw me he said, "Oh, I don't believe it. I don't think he's a witch. The man fainted, that's all. He's been out on the desert all day, riding in hot weather, and just fainted. That fellow isn't a witch. So don't claim he is. Just let him go." When he said this everybody moved away. If he hadn't been there I don't know what they'd have done to me. Bunch Of Whiskers wasn't a headman, but everybody knew him and feared him. He was the richest Navaho on the reservation. They used to say, "He's a witch. That's why he has lots of sheep, horses and cattle, and beads of all kinds, and all kinds of skins." He had everything, and by that everyone knew him and was afraid of him.

After the crowd left they said, "The man's all right," so they started singing again and set fire to the pile of wood and started dancing. They said to me, "Beat the drum." So there I was, beating the drum, when the girl who was carrying the decorated-stick came up and held me. I said, "Go and dance with somebody else. I don't want to." But she kept pulling on me, and soon she got me a little way from the men who were singing. Then a fellow came up and took the drum, and I started dancing. After a while she let me go, and I went back and got the drum again. But then another girl grabbed me. I only danced a short time with her, and when she turned me loose I went back and started beating the drum once more. Not long after that they quit dancing and just sang from there on. I was going to give the drum to another fellow, but they said, "Hold it for us all night." We were singing until morning, and then stopped, while it was still dark, because it was quite a way to the Nda. When everybody was ready we got on our horses, and they said to me, "Here's your drum. Take it along with you." We started while it was still dark and moved on, trotting our horses all the way, and everyone was singing as we rode along. The sun was pretty well up when we got to the place where they were having the Nda. The people on that side met us on their horses, and we began chasing one another four times around the hogan.

They'd built a shade for us, and there we camped. A lot of hogans were around and lots of herds. They had a lot of meat. Even though there was a big crowd we all had enough. We sang for a while, and then they fed us, and after that they wanted us to go to the hogan and sing over there. We went over and started singing, and all the people on that side went in, taking calico and other stuff. After they threw the things out to us some fellows came and gave their friends presents. At last I got a big bundle of calico. Some tobacco was tied onto it, and a vest with silver buttons was with it too. When we returned to our camp I gave the drum to Old Man Gentle and laid the calico on top of my saddle right beside him in the shade. Then I stepped back and got some water, and while I was drinking the girl with the decorated-stick got up and took my calico. The crowd laughed and said, "The beaver dragged a pole away." I didn't say a word.

I was so sleepy, and so I lay over against my saddle and went to sleep until a little after noon. They'd finished treating the patient by then, and everybody was coming back into the shade. Late in the afternoon they started the circle-dance until the sun was down, and then we took the horses to water. When we came back they started singing. It was evening then. Pretty soon a crowd went over to the hogan where the patient was and started shooting and chasing one another around, and after that they sang for a long time.

I thought, "I'll start home tonight, while it's cool, so that tomorrow I won't be riding in the hot weather." I had my saddle outside, and my horse was close by. I went out, but there was no saddle. I looked around and asked for it, and then from inside the shade they said, "The saddle's here. They've got two saddles in here and are taking care of them." I went in and said, "Where?" and there was my saddle, and the girl who had the decorated-stick was lying against it, and she had my buffalo skin spread out and was sitting on it. I wondered if she'd taken those things away from me too. I thought, "I hope not." I went away and thought about it, but I said to myself, "I'll see tomorrow. If they take my things away from me I won't let them, because I can't ride my horse bareback. It's a long way to go."

While we were eating our lunch they started the dance, and the girl with the decorated-stick went out, and the rest of the girls went after her. I just lay over and went to sleep. All at once a girl grabbed me. I didn't notice anything until she was dragging me by the fire. When we got out of the shade I asked for her clan. She was Red Clay, and so I went ahead and danced with her. When she let me go I went back to sleep again. But then another girl grabbed me. This time I noticed her as soon as she took hold of me, and I asked about her clan and her father's clan. She said, "My father's clan is Bitter Water, and my clan is Salt." While she was holding me a fellow said, "She's your granddaughter, because her mother's father belongs to your clan." So she let me go, and I went back inside the shade and lay down again.

I was about to go to sleep when the same girl grabbed me. I said, "You're my granddaughter." But she kept pulling on me, and so I went and danced with her. I tried to get away, but she held me as tight as she could and started dragging and pulling me out of the dance to where her mother and the others were sitting. Her mother shook hands with me, and I said, "What's the matter with this girl? She's my grand-daughter. I told her to let me loose, but she doesn't want to." Her mother laughed and said, "Well, she must like you, and if she does, go with her, because she's always wanted to marry a man of my father's clan. So you can take her right now."

I tried to take the girl's hand away, but she was hanging onto me as tight as she could. Her mother said, "Well, my father, we'll go home tonight. As soon as they quit dancing I want you to go back to our home with us. You can have my daughter, because she likes you." I said, "I don't think I'll go tonight, because I'm too tired, and I've got my saddle inside the shade. It's way under a pile of stuff. I don't like to tear up other people's things. I'll wait until tomorrow morning." But she said, "We can get it out for you, if you want to. We don't care if we tear up the other people's things. They won't do anything to us. So we'll get your

saddle, because we want you to come back with us tonight."
I said, "I can't say I'll go home with you right now. If
you want me very badly you'll have to wait, or, if you
don't want to wait, you can go to my place. It's up to my
father and mother. If I give myself to you right now, without letting them know, maybe they won't like it, and then
it'll be too much work for you. So, if you want to be quick
about it, you'll have to do that; go and see my father, Slim
Man, and go and see my mother. See what they'll say." But
they didn't believe they'd say, "All right." "If it's up to them,
why is it they don't try to get you a wife? We don't want
to go and see them. We want to go home with you right
now." I said, "Wait until morning." "Well, we're going to
start right now, and we'll stop on the way. Tonight we'll
camp at Cow's Water, and there we'll wait for you." I said,
"All right, I'll do that. I'll be there tomorrow morning."

But the girl kept holding me. She sat down and pulled
me on the ground beside her, and there I sat among the
women. Her mother said, "It's my father who wants you.
He said to us, 'If you see him at the dance be sure and get
him, and when you get him don't let him go. Hold him and
bring him back with you. I know he'll come. I know he
hasn't got a wife, and I know he's got lots of properties and
stocks, and he's all alone, just with his mother. He has nobody to help them. When you get him, if you bring him
home, then, from there on, you can help him, and he'll help
you too.'" I sat there beside them and said, "I'll go home
with you tomorrow."

Still the girl just kept hanging onto me. I tried to get
away, but she held me tight. I said, "It'll be all right with
me, but I don't know what they'll say, if I go home with
you now, without letting anybody know about it. But anyway I'll go with you tomorrow." I wanted to get away

from the girl and tried to take her hands away, but she held me tighter every time. At last I took off my bracelet and gave it to her and said, "Let me go, and I'll be with you from tomorrow on." After a long time she let me loose, and I walked away from there back to the shade.

Just about then they stopped dancing. The girls were in already, and there was a crowd inside the shade. I stood by the fire with the crowd, and the girls who'd been dancing were all sleeping. There was a place close by the girl who'd carried around the decorated-stick, and I went there and lay down and tried to go to sleep, but I couldn't. I began thinking about that girl and her home. She was living over at Navaho Mountain, and I was living far away from there, at Anything Falls In. I was thinking about the distance between the two places. It's about a day's ride across the flat and over the mountain. I was thinking about all those things and about my sheep and horses and cattle. I had all kinds of thoughts. And I thought about the girl with the decorated-stick, so I just couldn't sleep. I was awake all night.

While it was still dark I got up and took my rope and bridle and went after my horse. As I got out of the crowd they stopped singing, and the whole thing was over. There were lots of horses, lots of white ones, but none of them were mine. I looked all over and had gone pretty far when I heard someone say, "Here's your white horse. We've got him with us over here." That was the crowd bringing in the horses. I turned around and started back, and when I got to the camp my horse was standing there. It was almost daylight. I went inside the shade and got my saddle and saddled my horse and was ready to go. Some of Old Man Gentle's outfit had already left. He said to me, "I had a horse yesterday morning. A fellow gave me one for a present, but it got away, so I sent a man after it. He went with my horse, so I've got to wait for him. You two can go ahead after the others." He meant me and the girl who had the stick. I turned my horse around and started off, and the girl was right behind me. The whole crowd was looking at us. I wanted to catch up with those people, but they'd already gone. Then I thought, "I'll go slowly and wait for the others." I looked back every now and then, but nobody was catching up with us. It was a long, level stretch, but we couldn't see anyone moving anywhere out in that flat. We only saw the smoke way down where they'd had the dance.

There were two ways to go. One trail branched off by a spring, and the other was a short cut. I asked her, "Are you thirsty?" She said, "No." "Well, then, we'll cut right straight across." From there on we both got very sleepy. Every time I turned around she almost dropped the stick. We went a long way, and then I said, "We'll get out of the trail and rest a while." Quite a way from the trail we took the saddles and bridles off our horses and hobbled them. There was lots of green grass. We went in the shade under the trees and talked a while, and then we fell asleep.

We slept almost the whole day. When we awoke we were lying in the sun and were wet with sweat and thirsty. It was still a long way to our home. Way towards the north, at the foot of a blue mesa, was a spring. I asked her, "How about it? Shall we go around where that spring is?" She said, "All right." It was a long way, but we went fast, and it didn't take us long to get there. We watered our horses and had some water ourselves and then went on again. The people had gone back long ago, but we didn't care. We took our time from there on. I asked her about the saddle. "Who took my saddle inside the shade?" She said, "My mother and father told me to bring it in. They said to me,

'Tomorrow we want you to go back with him.' That's why I brought it in. And now we're going home, and you'll be with me all the time. That's what my father and mother said to me. So you're going home with me."

After we'd gone a long distance we came to a place where a trail branched off. One went to my home; the other went to hers. "Well, there's your trail, and here's mine." That's what I said and turned my horse towards home. "I'm going to take this trail, and you take that one, because that trail goes to your place. We've had a fine ride all day, and so now you take that trail, and I'll take this one." I started off, trotting my horse, and looked back; she was riding along slowly. I looked back twice, but she was still going slowly on the trail to her home. That was the last I saw of her.

I got home in the evening and told my mother all that had happened. I said, "At the second-night's-dance they claimed I was a witch." She almost died when she heard that. But I said, "That was all about that. And at the last-night's-dance, that day when we arrived there, I had a bundle of calico given to me, and the girl who had the decorated-stick took it away from me." "Who is that girl?" she asked. I said, "She belongs to the Salt Clan." "Oh, well, then you're my father-in-law." She joshed me about that. "You're my father-in-law, because she's my father's sister." Then I told her about the other girl. I said, "I was dancing with that girl, and she kept holding me. I told her to turn me loose, but she kept pulling me and took me over where her mother was sitting. There her mother said to me, 'You can have my daughter. We want you to go home with us.' I promised them I'd go, but I didn't." My mother said, "Maybe it's your grandfather who wanted to get you. You ought to have gone with that girl. I want you to go over there." I said,

"No, mother, I don't want to go, because it's too far. I don't want to ride back and forth all the time, because it's a long way. About this other girl that I came back with, she said to me, 'My mother and father want me to marry you.' But I said, 'It's up to my father and mother.' So it's up to you two. But I've got to wait until my father returns, and then I'll tell him about it and see what he says." "Well, then, we'll wait until he comes back. We'll see after that, my son. I know lots of them are trying to get you. I know there are lots of places where they want you very badly."

The next morning I said to my mother, "When I started from here to go to the second-night's-dance, on my way I stopped at my father's place, and he said to me, 'I'm going over the mountain for a visit. While I'm gone you round up my horses for me every once in a while until I return. I'll be gone six or seven days.' It's about four days ago that he told me that. So this morning I want to go and see about his horses." I went out and got two horses, one for her and one for me. While she was turning out the herd I got on my horse, but she said, "Wait a minute. How about the corn? We ought to get the corn in, because it's good and ripe. You ought to work on the corn first, so we'll have it out in the sun to dry." I said, "It's not all ripe, mother. We'll wait a few days. We'll get it in, all right, so don't hurry about it, mother. I'll tend to it when all of it is ripe." "All right," she said, and then I went out towards the flat where my father's horses were. He used to have a great many. I rode all over the flat, far away from my home, but every one of his horses was looking fine. None of them had been used lately. Some of them were scattered out towards Lots Of Wool, and late in the afternoon I thought, "I'll go among those before it gets too dark." I rode up there and went all around, but they were looking fine.

Over the hill was a hogan, and I was wondering if some people were living there. It was almost sundown, and my home was a long way off. So I turned my horse and rode around the hill, and there was the hogan. I went inside, and a man whom I knew was living there. He used to live at Narrow Canyon, but he'd moved to this place for water. His clan was Many Goats, and I called him my father. His wife's clan was Bitahni. She belonged to my clan, but I'd never met her before. She was a nice woman, kind of short and stout. I called her my niece. The man asked me, "Where are you from?" I said, "From my old place, at Anything Falls In. I'm looking for Slim Man's horses. I'm only looking for the ones that have been broken. I saw some today, and a lot of wild horses of his, too." He said, "I was out all day, but I didn't see any. But I know they're scattered around all over here. Turn your horse loose. There's plenty of grass here." So I did, and when I returned the woman was cooking some food for me. He said, "Go ahead and eat. We've had our lunch, so you just go ahead. Eat plenty, because you've been riding all day, and I know you're hungry."

When I'd finished eating we started talking, and I told him all about the trips I'd made, but I didn't tell him about the girls. I didn't mention any woman to him. We'd been talking for a long time, and then he said, "We'll go to bed now. I'm tired, and you're tired too, so we'd better go to sleep." I went out and took a leak, and when I came back a place was fixed for me, and I went right to sleep. I never did wake up till morning. As soon as I woke up I went out and looked for my horse. He hadn't gone very far. I got him ready and tied him up and then went back inside. Everybody was up, and they were just starting to cook.

After breakfast my father said to me, "Where do you think you're going this morning? Are you going down be-

366

low?" "No," I said, "I'm not looking for wild horses, so I guess I'll start back from here. I'd like to go to Narrow Canyon sometime, but I can't make up my mind." He said, "G-String is there now." "That's the man I'd like to visit," I said. "Well, you ought to go and visit him while you're close to that place. And there the peaches are ripe. You ought to go from here." I thought, "I'll do that." I started for that place, but then I changed my mind and turned around to look for the rest of the horses.

Two days after that my father came back. I'd been herding that day, and in the afternoon when I came home with the herd my mother said, "Your father's back. I guess he's home now. He didn't stop here. He just passed by and went on to his home. I was going over to his place, but I thought I'd wait until you got back with the herd. Now, I guess, I won't go. You can go and see him and tell him about his horses." When I got to his place he said, "I was away from my home for eight days," and then he asked me about his horses. I said, "I went around a couple of days, looking for them, and they were all looking fine." "That's good. I'm glad to hear that. I went over the mountain and got to a place called Red Willows Coming Out. My mother's sister, who raised me when I was a child, was living there. She was very glad to see me again. I stayed two days. She wanted me to stay longer, but I said, 'I'd better go and visit my relatives. I'm thinking of making a quick trip.' She said, 'We're thinking of going over where you live. We want to move back over there with you, because we don't like this place.' I said, 'That'll be nice. Then we'll live right together.' So I went on to Bay In The Mountain; other relatives of mine were living there. The woman's name is Red Woman. She's my sister. She had a little boy, and she said, 'My husband is treating me badly, so I want to leave him. I can't stand it any more, because he's cruel. We'd like to move to your place.' I said, 'It's all right with me.' Everybody wanted to come and move over here."

While he was still telling me about his trip he said to his son, "My son, you go over to the sweat-house and heat it up." But then he said, "We'll all go over together, and while we're in the sweat-house I'll tell you more about my trip." We went over and gathered some rocks and built a fire on them, and when they were good and hot we put them inside. After that he said to his son, "You'd better go back and take out the sheep again." While we were in the sweat-house he told me more about his trips, and then I started telling about mine. I told him all that had happened, and I told him about the two girls. I said, "Their mothers and fathers wanted me. There are two ways for me, so I don't know which way to go. One is way over on the other side of Navaho Mountain, at Spring On Sunny Side. That's just too far for me. I don't want to ride back and forth that distance. I don't care to be away from my home and leave my mother all alone with the work. They wanted me very badly, and I promised I'd go with them, but I changed my mind. And in the morning the man who got the decorated-stick and his wife told me to go back with their daughter. So I came home with that girl. My mother said, when I told her about this, 'You ought to have gone with the people who live at Navaho Mountain, because that's where your grandfather is. You ought to go and stay with him. He wanted you, so you should have gone with those people.'"

My father said, "Your mother may be thinking that way about you, but she doesn't know what she's talking about. She doesn't remember about herself. She forgot herself. She thinks she's got lots of help, but she's all alone. If you'd gone over there she'd be looking for you right now. And I, myself, don't want you to go there. We'll wait a while. I don't want you to leave this place. We'll see. Maybe we'll get a woman around here close by. Then you'll be right at home and can tend to your work. I'm thinking of one. That's the younger sister of the girl you talked about. I don't like the girl you came back with, because she's too tall and has long legs, and she's not good looking. Her sister is short and stout. But we'll see later on. When you get home don't say anything about it. Just keep it to yourself, until I let you know." I said, "It's all right with me. If you want to get me a girl I'll be glad, because now I'm thinking about a wife. I've been without one all this time. So, if you want me to get one, it will be all right with me."

That's what we were talking about all afternoon while we were at the sweat-house. Then we went back to his place, and everything was ready. All we had to do was sit down and start eating. He said to his wife, "I was so awfully tired, but now, I believe, I'm rested up, because I've been at the sweat-house, and here we're going to have nice food to eat. That's what I like. I appreciate seeing all this good food already prepared. All we have to do is start and eat." When we were through I said, "I'm going home now." He said, "Tomorrow morning you go and get some horses and have them ready, and I'll be over. I told you at first to keep everything to yourself, but now, when you get home, you can tell your mother about it. I'll be there tomorrow morning, and we'll talk it over with your mother."

I went home and told her everything. She said, "That's what I thought he'd say. I wanted you to go down where that grandfather of yours is, but now your father doesn't want you to. Well, it's up to him." I said, "He's coming tomorrow morning. He told me to get the horses and said when he got here he'd talk to you. That's what he said when I left

his place. I don't know what he'll say when he comes here."
In the morning I went out looking for the horses, but I
didn't find them until the sun was pretty well up. Then I
brought them back and drove them in the corral, and there
he was. He'd already come. He said, "I got here early this
morning, and we've been talking about what we said yesterday. Your mother here says she'd rather have the older girl,
because she's old enough to know and do anything. But I
told her I wanted the young one. She's prettier, and she
knows everything about the sheep, too, and how to take
care of things. So I'm going over and see about it." "It's up
to you, my father. Just go ahead and tend to it." He asked
me, "How about the horses? Which one shall I ride?" I
pointed to one, and he went over and roped it. My mother
was ready to go out with her herd. The way she looked
at me it seemed as though she didn't like it. She saddled her
horse without saying anything, but I didn't bother her.
Then she must have changed her mind. She said, "You go
out with the herd this morning, and I'll tend to the corn.
It's all dry now, and I want to get it in."

When I came back with the sheep a little after noon she
was home for lunch, and a woman was there with her. My
mother said, "I was glad she came and helped me. We were
in the field all morning, working on the corn." The woman
was of the Red Clay Clan. She was the niece of Lost His
Moccasins. She had a husband, he was an Along The Water,
but she had no children. My mother said, "Your father just
got home. You'd better go over and bring back the horse."
After lunch I went over on horseback. He was just starting
to eat, and he said to me, "Eat again. I was over at that girl's
place, but I didn't have to say much. As soon as I said, 'I
want my son to marry your daughter,' they said, 'We do
too. We want our daughter to marry your son.' I stayed

370

there, and we talked about things, and I told them you had lots of work to do at home. 'You know he's all alone, just with his mother, and they both need help. So now we'll all help each other. You help us, and we'll all help you.' After that I said, 'My son and I will give you twelve horses. We'll bring the horses and our son with us.' That's what I said when I left the place. But just as I was leaving the girl's mother said, 'I'd like your son to marry my oldest daughter, because the other, I think, is still too young.' But I said, 'I want the young one. That's what I came for, and we've already promised each other.' She didn't say any more about it. I said, 'Set a date for me, either tomorrow or the day after.' But the woman said, 'I don't want to make a date too soon, because I'd like to let my two brothers know about it. One brother of mine is way over near Flagstaff. The other's at Many Streams Flowing All Around. I want to let them know. I want them to be here when we have the wedding. So it will be about ten days.' We talked it over again, and at last we all decided we'd have it then."

He always spoke to me every once in a while about living, about life and about women. He said, "When you get that woman, when you're married, you must take good care of her, so you can live long together. Even though you're old enough to know everything, still you don't know how to live with a woman." He said a lot of things to me, what I should do and what I shouldn't do. "You'll find out for yourself later on. You'll learn it all by doing right. You'll soon know how to live with a woman. And when you get children, from there on, you'll have more lessons. You'll know more about living, more about taking care of things."

After that I went home and got out my herd, and my mother went to the cornfield with that woman again. About evening I came back and started hauling the corn off the field in a blanket, until it was dark, and then I went out for wood. The woman went home that night. In the morning my mother said she'd work on the corn again, and so I went out with the sheep. I was herding all morning, and at noon when I returned the woman was there once more. She'd come that morning and helped on the corn. My mother was preparing some food, and after we ate she said, "There's still some corn to work on." I said, "You go out with the herd now, and I'll tend to it." So she did, and I went to the field and put all the corn in one pile and then started packing it off in a bag. By sundown I'd brought it all in, and the woman who was helping us went home. When my mother came back with the herd she asked me, "Has that woman gone?" "Yes," I said, "she went quite a while ago." She said, "I told her about the wedding. I said, 'We'll have a wedding in about nine days,' but she said, 'I don't think you'll have that wedding. I guess you'll have it, all right, but not in the right way.' That's what she said when I told her about it, and I was wondering why. How did she happen to say that? Is that woman your wife?" "No, mother, she's not. She may be wishing for me, but I don't like her. I never think about her. So I don't know why she said it."

I said to my mother the next morning, "I'll go out with the herd again, and I'll be gone all day." At noon I drove the sheep under some shade and left them while I went to look for the horses. I rounded them up, and when I brought them back where the herd was the sheep were just starting to go out again for feed. I turned them towards home and drove the horses after them. When I got back I took the horses to the lake and watered them and let them go from there and came back home. There was the woman again with my mother. It was evening. She said to me, "Will you please take me back? I'm barefooted. I left my moccasins at home, and it's quite a distance. I don't like to go bare-footed all the way." Right away I thought, "I'll do that. I'll help her."

There was only one horse, and I said to her, "Come and sit behind me." She climbed up, and we started for her home. We crossed the wash and went around behind the hill where her hogan was, and I said, "This is as far as I'm taking you. You can go home from here." She got off the horse, but as soon as she got down she held the bridle. I said, "Let the bridle go. I want to go home." "No," she said, "I want you to go with me." I said, "No," and told her again to let the bridle go. But she kept holding it, saying, "I won't let you go. I want you to stay with me." She kept saying that to me, and it was getting late, and I was tired sitting on the horse, so I got down. As soon as I got down she held me again. So there I stayed with her all night.

Early in the morning I said, "You've got a husband, and I'm afraid of him. If he finds us he'll kill me." "He won't find it out. I won't tell him anything. And he's got a wife, so I won't tell him anything at all." Then I left and went to where the horses were and rounded them up and drove them to the lake, where they all had water, and then I let them go. The date was seven days off. I took the bridle off my horse, and while I was watering him the horses all looked towards the west. I turned my head and looked in the direction the horses were gazing, and there was a boy coming towards me. He was about ten years of age. I asked him, "Where are you going?" He said, "I'm coming here to you." "Why?" "My sister wants you to come over and have breakfast." I said, "All right, you go back, and I'll be there." The boy left, and after a while I caught up with him about half way to his place. When I got to her home she was cook-ing, making some thin corn-bread, and she had meat boiling on the fire. She had a place for me back against the wall of the hogan, and I sat down there on a sheep pelt. It was a great, big one and black, with lots of wool on it. And there she fed me. She said, "I heard you were going to marry. When I heard that I went to your place; I went because I want you. I don't want you to marry that girl. I want you to marry me, and now we have, we're married. So you're mine."

When I was through eating I left. I wanted to go home, but I changed my mind and turned around and went from there to where the horses were. I got me another and put the saddle on him and then went home. My mother was still there. She'd turned out the herd and let it go by itself. I never got her a horse that morning. I was bashful and ashamed of myself for treating my mother that way, for not getting her a horse and letting her do all the work. It made me feel ashamed, and I was sorry, but I didn't say anything. She asked me, "Where did you stay last night?" I said, "I stayed out all night." "I know exactly what you did. I know you've been with that woman. I didn't like your taking her home last evening, but you went and did it." That was all she said to me. I said, "I'll go after the herd." "Eat something first, before you go." I said, "I don't want anything." I was herding all morning, and when I came back in the afternoon there was that woman, sitting there again. She'd brought a lot of corn-bread to my mother. I was bashful when I saw her at my home.

That day her husband arrived at her place. He must have lain around the hogan all morning and afternoon, and the woman's grandfather, Mexican Blanket, saw him there, all alone, and asked about his granddaughter. They said, "She always goes down to Abaa's place and stays all day." Right away he got mad. "A woman like her doing those things!

She knows she has a husband. I know what she's going down there for. She's after that man. It's not right for her to do that, because she's got a husband, and her husband is home. He's in the hogan all alone. I'll go after her and chase her back."

A man was coming towards us on horseback, coming as fast as he could. The woman said, "That's my grandfather, Mexican Blanket." He rode up, and he was as mad as he could be, coming right straight for her, kicking and whipping his horse. When he was right close to her she got scared and jumped up. He almost ran over her, and then he whipped her. He whipped her twice, and she was crying, and he was telling her to go home, right quick. She was running around, and he was going around after her. Then my mother got up and ran to the old man and grabbed the bridle, and she grabbed his wrist. She almost threw him off the horse. She gave him a good scolding, saying, "What are you trying to do? What's the matter with you, are you crazy? You old evil spirit, you. Mexican serape, coyote, coyote, evil spirit, evil spirit!" Then he quieted down, and I came up to him and said, "Well, old man, whip me. It's I who's doing these things. Why are you whipping your granddaughter? I don't call that a man. You're a man, and your granddaughter's a woman. If you want trouble, or if you want to fight with someone, get down and fight me." He didn't say anything. He hung his head and was leaning over the saddle. After a while he said, "I'm sorry, because I thought she was coming over here for nothing, but I've found out now that she's helping you." My mother said to him, "Yes, she's helping me, and she's mine, too, now. She's not yours. She doesn't belong to you any more, so don't bother her again, because she belongs to me." He said, "I'm sorry. I didn't know any-

375

thing about it, but now I've found out she belongs to you." Then he went back to his home.

While this was going on Slim Man's family saw us from the other hogan, and after the man left he came over. He said he wanted to know what had happened. "It looked like years ago to me, like what the different tribes of Indians used to do to us. Who was that fellow riding around here so swiftly? I thought we were going to have a war." My mother said, "Oh, it's that old man, Mexican Blanket. He came to whip his granddaughter. He was crazy, that's all." "I thought something was going on. That's why I came." Then he spoke to the woman. "Do you belong to us now?" She said, "Yes." Then he questioned us both. "Do you like each other? How long since you made up?" I said, "We started last night. I wasn't thinking about her. She's been staying around here with my mother, helping her on the corn, and last evening she wanted me to take her home. I didn't want to at first, but then I thought, 'I'll help her.' But we didn't get to her place. We stayed this side of it all night. So it was last night that we started this. And so it's not my fault, my father."

Then he gave us a little speech. "That's the way with you young people. When a man tells you something you won't listen to him. Like myself now, I told you a lot of things about three or four days ago. I told you you mustn't do this and you mustn't say that, and here, today, you've done wrong. You both did wrong. And I'm so ashamed of myself for the people with whom I made a promise. We promised to have a wedding, and you both have spoiled the whole thing. That's what makes me so ashamed. I don't know what the people will say to me about it." He said to me, "You ought to have known better. You shouldn't have gone with her. You ought to have lent her a horse and told her to turn it loose when she got home. I feel very badly about it."

376

He said to my mother, "You'd better look at her, where she was struck by the whip. She looks as though she's got an awful pain." My mother went up to the woman, and over her shoulder and on her right hip the skin was almost torn off. My father was sure angry, but he said, "It's your own fault. I feel badly about it, but it's your own fault. If you'd let my boy go, if you'd left him alone, you wouldn't be suffering as you are now. What do you think? Do you think you're suffering because of your own fault?" She said, "Yes, it's my own fault. It's two years ago that I started thinking about him, and from last year on I thought about him more. I was that way all summer, and now I'm with him, because I like him so much. So he's mine now, and I'm his." My father said to her, "How about your husband?" "I haven't got a husband. A man comes once every three or four months, or once in summer and in winter. I don't call that a husband. So I want to let that fellow go, and I'd like to stay with him."

"That's the way with all you women. Even though you have a husband, if you see another man you like, you always want to leave your husband. That's the way with you now. You've got a husband, and when you saw this fellow you wished for him, and at last you got him, because you like him better than your husband. Now it's up to you. You're in wrong, and you're in trouble, and I don't think you'll live long, either, because you can't tell anything about your husband. When he finds out about this he'll sure get mad. And I know him very well. I know just how he is. When he gets mad he'll kill you both. You won't live long. That's the way I'm thinking about you two. But I can't say anything, because you like each other. I can't separate you, so you both can stay in trouble."

He started back for his home, but after he'd gone a little

way he turned and came up to us again and said, "You two go right ahead. I'll be sorry for you, because I know very well you won't live long. I know that man will come sometime with a rifle or a revolver and kill you both. If he doesn't, if he lets you go, then it will be fine. From there on, if I want to say something to you again, about life, I will. Now I won't say anything." My father didn't say any more. He went home, and the woman stayed with us there that night and never did go back.